THAT'S LIFE

Many Mini-Memoirs

of

Carol Petersen Purroy

Acknowledgements

To my editors/critiquers: Mary Lee Fulkerson, Vonda Novelly, Celeste León, Betty Johnson, Karin DeRocco, Helen Stevens, Joy Phillips, Sandee Giolli, Mary Hallock, Anne Urquhart, Dr. Neal Clement, Ron Allen, Hannah Purroy, and Tony Masia.
You were all enormously helpful and I appreciate you.

A - Z Publishing
1840 Radcliffe Drive
Reno, NV 89502

www.a-zpublishing.com

Book Design by Carol P. Purroy
Cover Design by Carol P. Purroy
Cover Photo by Ronald V. Allen

ISBN: 978-0-9764400-5-5

Printed in the United States of America

Life is for living and forgiving, for enjoying and laughing and dancing and singing and learning and growing and adventuring and loving. Especially loving.

CONTENTS

Appendix   341

*To all who helped make my life what it has been,
and all who will help make it what it will be.*

Preface

My mother used to say, "Carol can do anything she wants to. She just doesn't want to do very much."

Little did she know. The truth is, I want to do it all. I want to do everything, go everywhere, learn everything, experience everything, be everything. Everything that interests me, that is. And a lot of things interest me.

Part of what my mom saw when I was a kid was that while I had above-average capabilities and intelligence, I was an underachiever in school. Or rather, I was an erratic achiever. I did just fine in subjects that interested me and couldn't care less about those I didn't. This, of course, frustrated the heck out of my mother and my teachers.

Except for its social aspects, school always seemed like a colossal waste of time. Most of my real learning took place outside of school. I read voraciously, had good friends of all ages and descriptions, was a keen observer and a good listener, acquired new skills, wandered as far as my legs, and later on, my bike, would carry me, earned money in various creative ways.

As kids, though, we're judged by our school achievements (i.e., grades) rather than those in the greater world. Because I indulged in what I wanted to do rather than in what they expected of me they thought I didn't want to do much.

The living of my life has proved them wrong. I have earned academic degrees and professional certifications and awards, and had a number of careers. And I will probably acquire and practice a few more before I quit this planet.

I love learning and become proficient at new skills. Then, once I've mastered and practiced them awhile, I want to learn and do something new.

I've been extremely fortunate to have traveled to a great many places in this world and hope to travel to a lot more. I'm fascinated with people and cultures.

I seem to need change, newness, variety. And I need challenges. I've often tackled a thing just to see if I could do it. I need the feeling of accomplishment when I've met the challenge. Of course, that means I've taken risks and known failure. But that doesn't keep me from continuing to seek out and take on new challenges.

People often remark, "Carol, you really are something!"

My response is to laugh and say, "Yeah, but nobody's ever been able to figure out what." I say it in jest, but it's true. As soon as they think they've got me pigeonholed I do a "180" and become something else.

It's also a fact that I usually do several things at once. I'm usually juggling at least six projects at a time. And there are always more things on the drawing board.

Not long ago, a friend of mine, a Thai mystic, asked to see my hand. She examined my palm -- a myriad of lines going ever-which-a-way, constantly intersecting and interrupting each other. She nodded and said, "You don't have any choice about all the changes in your life. It's your destiny."

Well, maybe that explains it. Perhaps it's as much a part of my DNA as the color of my eyes or the shape of my toenails. And perhaps it's why I've always been drawn to the new and the different. It's my destiny.

And because of it I've had a wonderful life. Not every part of it was wonderful, but overall it's been amazing. I've written this book to share it with others. I hope you'll enjoy it.

Carol Petersen Purroy

Part I

Childhood & Teen Years

I Was Named, by God

Almost two weeks old, I still didn't have a name. Mom and Dad couldn't agree on one. They had a boy's name ready, but not a girl's. It had been decided that they were having only two children, and they already had a girl. So this time around they were sure they'd have a boy.

Their son was to have been named after his paternal grandfather, Jens Petersen, and "carry on the family name". Art and Pat (Arthur and Zelpha) Petersen were so intent on having a son that the alternative hadn't occurred to them.

This baby -- me -- was supposed to arrive on its mother's 27th birthday, October 25, 1935, but showed up four days late, fat and healthy, with a terrific set of lungs but no male parts.

My birthplace was the same as that of my father and his three siblings, as well as my own older sibling -- a farmhouse on Fig Avenue, south of Fresno, California.

My sister, 2 years 2 months and 2 days older than I, got their favorite girl's name, Patricia Ann. Mom loved it so much she used "Pat" as her own nickname. They didn't seem to have a second-favorite.

While Mom lay in bed, as was customary after giving birth in the '30s, and Daddy worked in the fields and barn, both thought and thought about what to name this superfluous girl child. At night they told each other the names they'd picked. And every night, they vetoed each other's choice.

One night, lo and behold, both came up with the same name: Carol Frances. So that's what it was. That's who I am.

Several years later, when I was 8 or 9, I heard that story for the first time.

I recalled a similar tale I'd heard in Sunday School. In the Bible there's this couple who had a baby. Both its parents independently picked the same name, so it was said that *that* baby was named by God.

I simply borrowed that biblical story and made it my own. I chose to believe that I, too, was named by God. I felt very special.

I was never treated like the disappointment I must have been. I guess they fell in love with me, as I did with them, and decided I was okay after all.

But, since Mom and Dad had only daughters, the Petersen lineage did end with my dad, Arthur W. Petersen. After him, there was no one to pass the family name down to future generations. It must have been a high priority for my parents and grandparents, because I heard that phrase time and time again.

The Barnyard Terrorist

T he thing that terrified me most was not the bogeyman or imaginary monsters under my bed. What scared me silly was very real, and it lurked just outside our back door.

We had lots of animals on the farm. It was a dairy farm, so, of course, we had cows. They spent their nights in the barn and, after the morning milking, made their way single file out to pasture. At day's end, they returned for the evening milking. Mom used to say you could set your watch by those cows. They had a rhythm all their own that was soothing to watch, their massive bodies swaying as they sauntered across the fields and made their way into the barn, each into her own stall.

Milking machines were new and expensive, therefore not in common usage, so Dad and Grandpa milked the old-fashioned way morning and evening. Grandpa maintained that a barn was no place for a lady, so Mom and Grandma stayed out of it. But his rule didn't apply to me, and I loved to watch Daddy milk the cows. Perched on a squat three-legged stool, he was surrounded by a semi-circle of eager cats keeping an eye on his every move. Every once in a while he aimed a squirt of milk at one. It opened its mouth wide and lapped it up. Daddy made sure each got its share.

We had barn cats and house cats -- mousers, all. Cats, of course, reproduce every chance they get, so we often had a litter of kittens. We'd let Mama cat keep one, ". . . so she won't go berserk". Daddy put the rest of them in a gunny-sack and took 'em down to the irrigation ditch. That was "animal population control" in those days.

In the kitchen was an apple-green and cream electric range up on legs. In the winter months, Mama cat and her kitten were warm and cozy in a cardboard box beneath it. Other times we often had a box full of just-hatched chicks under the stove. My sister and I loved having babies in the kitchen to play with.

The kitchen was the heart of the house. In the winter, it was the only room that was heated, unless company was coming or somebody was really sick. When that happened, a fire in the black pot-bellied stove in the living/dining room warmed that part of the house too.

One time I was very ill and my seafoam-green cast-iron crib was hauled out to the living room to be close to the coal stove. I was treated with hot mustard plasters on my chest. Mama gave me a powdered aspirin dissolved in orange juice. I was 3. Sometimes our medicine was a potion of whiskey, honey and lemon juice.

The kitchen is where we took our Saturday night baths. Daddy brought in a large galvanized tub and set it on the linoleum floor. Mom heated the water in large pots on the stove. One at a time we bathed: me first, followed by Pat, then Grandma, Mom, then Grandpa, and Daddy: littlest to biggest, or maybe cleanest to dirtiest.

Both Mom and Grandma were great cooks who created wonderful meals out of next-to-nothing, which is mostly what we had, it being the Depression and all. There was usually a soup or stew simmering on the stove or something baking in the oven. The kitchen was the place to be, with its warmth and delicious aromas and goodies. *Gemütlichkeit*, as the Germans say.

Our telephone was attached to the kitchen wall. It was black, with the earpiece connected by a cord, and a protruding mouthpiece. It was a party-line; our signal was two short rings. Everybody on the line listened in on everyone else's conversations.

Next to it was the radio, a round-topped wooden affair, on a shelf near the window so a copper wire antenna could be strung outside. Through the radio came music, "Elmer's Tune", "When They Begin the Beguine", "Jeepers Creepers", "Pensylvannia 6-5-O-O-O". And *Ma Perkins, The Whiz Kids, The Breakfast Club*. Once a week, the adults gathered around to listen to President Roosevelt's *Fireside Chat*.

Our wooden kitchen table was covered with oilcloth, worn in spots. Next to the back door was a sideboard with large metal bins for flour and sugar; over in the corner, next to the pantry, sat a porcelain sink with a cold water faucet (our only plumbing) and a drainboard. Grandpa and Grandma had put in electricity and were ready to install plumbing when the Depression hit. That had to be put on hold until the economy turned around.

Above the sink was an open cupboard for everyday dishes. We also had a pantry where 'most everything else was kept. On the back porch sat an icebox, along with two stone crocks -- one for curing green olives and one for black. How I loved reaching down into the cool liquid in those crocks to sample one of Grandma's olives.

Raucous roosters crowed to raise the sun every morning, and hens produced the eggs we gathered twice a day.

We sometimes raised a hog for bacon, ham and pork. An old saying goes, "The only part of a pig that doesn't get used is its squeal." That was true on our farm.

Buster, a black and white Boston bull terrier, sat by the kitchen table at mealtime hoping for a handout, which he usually got.

Sometimes there was a visiting bull, snorting and pawing in the pasture, eager to meet and greet our cows. We kids were sternly warned to stay out of the field and were not tempted to disobey.

My grandparents, Jens Christian and Elsa Marie Seewaldsen Petersen (photos on page 344), were founding members of Fresno's Danish Brotherhood, as well as the Danish Creamery, a cooperative of dairy farmers. There was a fair-sized Danish community in and around Fresno, and Danes are oriented toward cooperative endeavors. When they got to California's Central Valley and started dairy farms they banded together for mutual success. They jointly owned and shared a bull, a horse or two, a tractor, and other farm equipment. The Danish Creamery is still prosperous.

In the barnyard were outbuildings of weathered wood: a barn, a garage for Grandpa's 1915 Dodge Touring Car, chicken coops, and, a good distance from the house, the outhouse. Enormous eucalyptus trees that Grandpa planted long ago shaded the barnyard. Occasionally, Grandma placed a hapless chicken on a eucalyptus stump and lopped off its head with a hatchet. We were fascinated by that headless creature hopping around the yard.

Behind the house was the lawn, bordered by a picket fence and petunias in the summer. Before her first baby was born, Mama defied her mother-in-law by digging up plugs of Bermuda grass from the fields, planting and tending them into a lawn. Grandma's thickly accented response: "Hmmmph! Damn foolishness! My children got along *yoost* fine without a lawn and yours can too." Mama disagreed and by the following summer, when Patty was old enough to crawl and toddle around, there was a play yard of cool, clean grass.

And there was the barnyard terrorist -- a goose named Peter. Where my grandfather was concerned, Peter was a "pussycat". He walked alongside Grandpa like a dog at heel. But everyone else had better watch out.

I was just a little girl and my tiny heine was just the right height for ol' Peter. When he was nearby, I spent most of my time twisting and twirling, trying to keep my tush turned away from his hard, sharp beak. He was persistent, though, and quick as lightning, so he usually managed to get in a peck or two. His nipping, hissing and flapping scared me silly. And I wasn't the only one.

One day my lanky teenage cousin, Bill O'Malley, was visiting. As I stood on the back porch watching, he was on his way to the barn when ol' Peter came up behind and grabbed ahold of Bill's rear end with his beak. He held on for dear life while Bill ran across the barnyard as fast as his long legs would carry him, hollering, his arms windmilling behind him as he tried to swat Ol' Peter off. And Peter's huge wings were stretched full-out, flapping as if in flight, all the way into the barn.

And then there was the privy, the little house with the half-moon cutout in the door. Whenever anyone went into the outhouse, Peter ran over and parked himself in front of the door, trapping whoever was inside. When that person finally got out, Peter went on the attack. Ours was a two-holer, so he sometimes had two people trapped inside. We learned to carry a big stick when going out to the outhouse.

Another cousin, Muriel, who lived all her life in San Francisco, was 13 or 14 years older than I. When she was a child, she and her two brothers came to the valley to spend their summers on the farm.

Muriel said, "As soon as I was old enough to say No and make it stick, I refused to go to the farm. Remember that goose? Remember how, every time you'd go to the outhouse, he'd run over and stand there so you couldn't get out?

"Well," she continued, laughing, "I'd put off *going* until I couldn't wait any longer. Whenever I was at the farm, I was **constipated** the whole time!"

That explains my lack of childhood memories of Muriel at the farm.

I'd like to think that when we left the farm, Peter got his just desserts. I want to believe he was somebody's Christmas dinner or got stomped to death by an angry bull.

But I imagine Peter the Barnyard Terrorist simply died of old age.

Miss Monkey Penny

A trip to town was exciting.

I was 4 or 5 years old and we were on our regular Saturday trip to town. As always, we'd dressed in our best. Daddy wore his good suit and a fedora, his shoes polished to a high shine; Mama completed her outfit with hat and gloves, high heel pumps and nylons.

In from the farm, Daddy had things to do, so he dropped us off and we went shopping at Sears Roebuck, The National Dollar Store, J.C. Penney's, or the Fresno Drygoods Store. Or maybe we just window-shopped up and down Fulton Street. On rare occasions, for a very special saved-up-for treat, we went to the lunch counter at Woolworth's. With Mama's help I'd climb up on one of the chrome stools and order a Bacon & Tomato Sandwich, triple decker, toasted. I liked to watch the bread go around on Woolworth's big Ferris wheel of a toaster.

When the waitress took my order she placed three slices of bread on this contraption. They went all the way around and dropped off, toasted golden, at the starting point. Her hands flying, she spread them with mayonnaise and lay crisp strips of bacon on one piece, crunchy iceberg lettuce on another, and tomato slices on the third. She stacked them into a sandwich and slapped it on a plate, then swung around and placed it on the counter in front of me, all in one smooth motion. "There ya are, honey." It was so thick I could barely get it into my mouth.

After lunch we'd go to the library on Broadway, up its broad marble steps -- 20 or 30 -- the stairway to heaven. Patty and I would go into the children's section to browse and choose our books while Mom went into the grown-ups' library.

That library was my favorite place on earth. I loved everything about it: its hushed quiet, the musty smell of old books, its child-sized tables and chairs, the nice ladies who smiled and stamped each book I'd take home. I felt important having a library card with my name, `Carol F. Petersen`, on it in real typewriter letters. But what I really loved was the books. It was there that I learned about their magic. I don't think we owned any books, so those that we could take home for two weeks at a time were pure gold. And it didn't cost a thing. Gold -- for free.

After awhile, Daddy would pick us up in his Model-T Ford. We'd go to the Safeway on Ventura Avenue for the week's groceries, and hurry home for the afternoon milking.

This particular day, on our way from Woolworth's to the library, we walked up Broadway. There on the sidewalk ahead a crowd had gathered. As we got closer we heard music -- happy, lively music. *Funiculi, Funicula, Funiculi, Funiculaaaaaaa, la di da di da, Funiculi, Funicula.*

The group expanded to make room for us. In its center was a man -- an organ grinder --wearing a black felt bowler. He had a long black mustache that curled up at the ends so he looked like he was smiling even if he wasn't. He turned the crank on a box that hung by leather straps from his shoulders. Attached to his wrist by a long slender chain was a cute little monkey in a red bolero jacket, bright blue satin pants with a slit in the back for his long tail, and a tiny black felt hat, like the man's. The monkey's tail moved in time to the music as he tipped his hat to one person and then another.

I'd never seen a monkey outside the zoo. Or one wearing pants and a hat. I was so excited I couldn't stand still.

Children around the circle held out coins to him. He took their coin, tipped his hat, and crossed over to the organ grinder, who dropped it into the pocket of his baggy black pants, then moved on to the next person while the man jingled the coins in his pocket.

I desperately wanted to give the monkey a coin, so I begged Mama for one. She dug in her purse and took out a penny. Even a penny was more than we could afford. It was 1939. Like most people, we had no money to spare, and certainly none for monkey business.

Bubbling with excitement, I held out my penny. It seemed as if the monkey visited every other child first, taking his or her coin, tipping his hat, giving the coin to the organ grinder, taking his time and flirting with each child. This ritual played itself out all around the circle and seemed to take forever. While I waited I fidgeted.

Finally, it was my turn. The monkey came over and stood right in front of me. Ever-so-timidly I extended my hand, palm up, with the penny in it. His bony little fingers scratched the palm of my hand as he took it. I shivered and giggled, pulling my hand back.

The monkey did not tip his hat to me. He did not flirt with me as he had with the other children. He did not take my coin to the organ grinder. And he did not move on to the next person. Not yet. He just looked at my penny, turning it over in his tiny brown hand, examining both sides as if he could not believe his eyes. Then, with what seemed like great disdain, he gave it back to me and walked away.

My cheeks grew hot. I knew they were as red as the monkey's jacket. My heart pounded. My whole body quivered in embarrassment.

Mama grasped my fist with the penny clutched in it and we left the circle, continuing on up Broadway to the library. As we climbed its marble stairs and entered the magnificent cathedral of books, I began to feel calmed. The children's librarian smiled in welcome, further comforting me. The library's hushed atmosphere and musty aroma were soothing too.

I selected a book and sat down at one of the low tables to read. Instantly, I was transported to a world that didn't have a single monkey or organ grinder in it, a world in which a penny bought anything I wanted. The book was a magic carpet that carried me far far away on a flight of fantasy and delight.

Many, many times since, I have flown that same magic carpet to places unimaginable, transported to worlds only dreamt of.

Grandma's Stereopticon

T he only stereo system we knew about was not something you listened to, it was something you looked through. It was a wondrous contraption, and all the entertainment my sister and I could have hoped for on a sizzling summer afternoon.

The coolest place in our San Joaquin Valley farmhouse was my grandmother's bedroom on the north side of the house, shaded by the umbrella trees that were planted when she was a bride, straight from Denmark. If there was any breeze at all, it came through her open windows, fluttering the lace curtains and riffling the bouquet of roses on the washstand.

Beneath her bed was a small box, a treasure trove, which she brought out infrequently. It was special, and to us it had a magical mystique.

One scorching day the summer I was almost five and Patsy turned seven, Grandma invited us into her room where the combined scents of fresh roses, lavender sachet, and furniture polish greeted us. She had a surprise. With loving, smiling eyes, my tiny Danish grandmother, herself smelling of Rosewater & Glycerin, knelt beside the bed, her joints stiff and her movements awkward. Lifting the crocheted bedspread, she pulled the box out from under, lifted the lid and exposed its contents as if revealing Aladdin's treasure.

Excitement tickled through our small bodies.

In the box was a unique apparatus -- a stereopticon -- along with a stack of thick postcard-sized photographs. The stereopticon had a metal eyepiece --a little hood -- similar in shape to a modern snorkeling mask. Attached underneath was a wooden handle and, extending out front, a wooden slider.

Atop that was a wire picture holder you could adjust, nearer or farther, for perfect focus.

The photographs were peculiar: identical side-by-side sepia-toned photographs, some of which were painted in vibrant colors. There were photos of vacationers on the boardwalk at Atlantic City; Native Americans in their tribal villages; exotic Hawaiian Islanders in grass skirts and flower leis; skyscrapers in San Francisco, New York, Chicago; corseted women in high-necked puffed-sleeve dresses and magnificent hats, with men in driving coats, caps and goggles, driving early-day automobiles; nature scenes: Niagara Falls, Rocky Mountain bighorn sheep, Yosemite's Half-Dome. Each image was more wonderful than the one before.

The amazing thing about the stereopticon and its stereo-images was that when you put the pictures in the holder and gazed through the hooded eyepiece they sprang to life, becoming three-dimensional. They were so real you felt as if you could walk into the scene and become part of it, and I'm sure we did in our childish fantasies. I still don't understand how or why those flat photos came to life through this strange-looking device. All I know is that they did. It was amazing and miraculous, and we were thrilled.

That day, after Grandma opened the box and removed its contents, she left the room, leaving us to enjoy its wonders unattended. We knew we were being entrusted with something precious. We treated it with virtual reverence, knowing that if Grandma let us use it unsupervised we must be pretty grown-up and deserving.

We sat on the hardwood floor of Grandma's room, our bare legs grateful for its smooth coolness, and spent the afternoon engrossed in the enthralling images, sharing the scenes with one another, having forgotten the heat.

It was magical -- awe-inspiring. You know, I feel a little sorry for today's kids. If anything, they're so over-entertained, overstimulated, and even over-informed, that nothing seems to thrill them, nothing excites them, nothing entertains them. It seems as if there's not much awe about anything.

Part of me wishes my granddaughter could visit my childhood for an afternoon. We'd sit together on the cool floor of my grandma's bedroom and, filled with delicious anticipation, pull the box of magic out from under her bed to share an afternoon of enchantment.

But realistically, she'd probably be bored. Its only moving parts are the ones you move yourself. It doesn't talk or rap or shriek or play ear-damaging music. It doesn't leap about or flash colored lights or vibrate. It just sits there quietly. And when you look through it, something flat and lifeless is transformed into something three-dimensional and vibrant.

That's probably not exciting enough for today's kids.

As for me, I'm grateful I was a child in an era when we could be filled with wonder and awe and appreciate life's simple pleasures; when parents and grandparents held some things back, keeping them special, giving them a mystique -- and perhaps even more important -- making a child feel so very special when they were brought out.

Backstory

My mom and dad probably met at a dance.

"We were always going to dances," said Uncle Roy when I asked him about it much much later. My mom and dad were terrific dancers. They could have hit it off while tripping the light fantastic in that first dance, and nature took its course.

Uncle Roy (Hartley) was my dad's best friend since first grade at Orange Central Grammar School. And he married my mom's sister, Billie.[1] After Mom and Dad and Aunt Bill were dead and Uncle Roy was in his late 80s, I asked him, "How did my parents meet?" He couldn't say for sure, but guessed it was at a dance.

Mom and Dad's wedding at the Fresno County Courthouse on June 25, 1932 was a simple affair. The Great Depression was felt by everyone, especially farmers. Probably the marriage license and Mom's plain gold band were all they could afford.

Daddy took Mama straightaway to his parents' home on their dairy farm. The young couple would take care of the old folks and Dad's ailing sister, Signe, and run the farm, which they would inherit upon the death of his parents, as was the Danish custom.

Some adjustments were necessary, but by and large it worked well. Mom and Grandma and Signe learned to love one another while sharing a kitchen and home -- and sometimes the two-holer. Grandma and Grandpa were delighted that their only son, nearly thirty, had finally married. They hoped he would now

---

1. Mom's other sister, Margaret, was married to Roy Hartley's brother, Walter.

produce offspring for them to spoil -- offspring to carry on the family name.

Times were hard. The stock market had crashed and taken the country down with it. Although we had chickens and ducks on the farm, and sometimes a pig raised for slaughter, most meals were vegetarian -- a lot of eggs, homemade breads and cheeses, and many varieties of vegetable soups, stews and casseroles. Meat was for Sunday dinner and special occasions.

I recall watching Mama rip up her own dresses to make clothes for Pat and me. Nobody had money for patterns, so neighbors and the farm women's sewing circles traced patterns on newspapers, cut them out, and passed them around. We had few toys, and those we did have were homemade. Our paper dolls were the fashionable ladies and gentlemen that Mama cut out of the Sears Roebuck or "Monkey Ward" catalog.

According to my older cousin Kitty, Mom and Dad worked like slaves on the farm, but were wildly in love and happy as could be.

They never got a salary, or even any spending money that Daddy didn't have to ask for. Grandpa maintained that since their basic needs were taken care of, they didn't need money. Daddy had to go to his father for 50¢ for a haircut, 35¢ for a pouch of Bull Durham tobacco and rolling papers, or a buck-and-a-half for the movies and a libation at Feretta's Beer Garden on the way home.

So they had no savings. And Dad had no life insurance. The farm was his "insurance".

His parents were old. Dad was considerably younger than his two sisters, Caroline and Signe. (Signe died when I was a baby.) The house and outbuildings, plus 40 acres, farm equipment and livestock would belong to Art and his wife someday.

My childhood on the farm was idyllic. There was much love and little tension in our home. I was a secure little girl in a warm and loving environment, surrounded by her parents, sister and grandparents. Among my early childhood memories are these: broadcasting chickenfeed to the chickens; gathering eggs from under clucking hens in my apron or the front of my skirt; walking barefoot from the barn to the house watching my long late-afternoon shadow; wearing sunbonnets Grandma made to protect our "delicate Danish skin" from the blistering Fresno sun; swinging in a tire-swing hung from the gnarled fig tree in the front yard; 3 o'clock coffee-time with Grandma's Danish pastries; lots of company -- Grandma and Grandpa were very social; going places in the car was exciting, but the leather seats burned my bare legs and bottom in the summer and froze them in the winter; playing in the backyard on hot summer evenings, watching hundreds of yellow butterflies flutter around lavender petunias; then having to go to bed inside the hot, hot house that reeked of fly spray.

My father plowed the fields behind a horse, and sowed seed from a gunny-sack slung over his shoulder. My mom sometimes sent me out on a hot after-noon with a jug of iced tea to share with him.

A couple of times a year, a salesman drove up our driveway. His Model T Ford had stuff hanging all over it -- pots and pans, sewing notions, canning needs -- a little bit of everything a farm wife might need. He repaired pots and sharpened knives. Before leaving he gave each of us kids a stick of Wrigley Spearmint gum.

At Christmas, Grandma's holiday decorations came out. The tree was decorated with strings of large colored lights, thin blown glass ornaments, and strings of little Danish flags. On our last Christmas Eve at the farm, we had a visit from Santa. Costumed in a pillow-stuffed red suit edged with cotton bat-ting, and a white cotton beard, he climbed through the parlor window (in lieu of a fireplace), pushing his sack of presents through and settling it on the floor next to the Christmas tree before stepping through himself. I don't remember any of the presents, but I do remember Santa.

As we did every year, we went into town one night to drive slowly, slowly through Fresno's Christmas Tree Lane. Not only were the sky-piercing Giant Sequoia trees decorated with thousands of colored lights, many of the mansions' lawns along North Van Ness Boulevard had Christmas scenes, some with music played over a loudspeaker, even.

This was pure magic, a Christmas fairyland, one we looked forward to every holiday season. Along with the Fourth of July fireworks, it was the highlight of our year.

We spent Christmas day with my mom's family. We were a large family and everyone had to pinch pennies, so we drew names for the gift exchange. That year, my cousin Leta, who was already grown up and married, picked mine. Her gift to me was a booklet of *Gone With the Wind* paper dolls. I loved Scarlett's full hoop skirts and picture hats. From all my childhood Christmases, that's the only gift I remember, so it must have thrilled me to pieces.

Our Father,
Who Art in Heaven

The sky wept as the coffin settled into its permanent home. Between the mourners and a bevy of flower wreaths on tripods, the open grave yawned. Rain dripped from our hair, our aqua Easter dresses hung limp, our white Sunday School shoes squished.

The mortuary's black limousine had carried us out to Mountain View Cemetery on West Belmont Avenue. To make room for the grown-ups, Pat and I perched, facing backward, on little shelves that folded down from the back of the front seat. To keep costs down, all the Petersen clan rode in one limo. In solemn procession, it followed the hearse, its windshield wipers snapping back and forth. Behind the limousine, in a long line of cars with headlights on, came the other mourners.

This was my first funeral. Pat and I hadn't gone to Grandma Petersen's three months earlier. We were just little kids and Mom and Dad decided it wasn't necessary. Pat was 7 and I had just turned 5.

But, despite our tender age, we had to be at this one. That coffin held our father. It was late March, 1941.

Our Father, who Art in Heaven . . . .

For a long time after that day, whenever the Lord's Prayer was recited I thought it was about our father, Pat's and mine. "Our father, who Art in heaven, hallowed be thy name." Daddy's name was Art and he was in heaven.

Arthur Waldmir Petersen, 38, died due to a misdiagnosis and lack of care. Dr. Jorgensen told him, "It's just the stomach flu. Go home and go to bed. You'll be fine in a few days."

But it wasn't just the stomach flu. It was appendicitis. Daddy's appendix burst and peritonitis set in. He wasn't fine in a few days. In a few days his body lay in a gold-satin-lined casket.

The smell of the flowers -- especially the stocks -- made my nose twitch. And the scratchy thread-things inside my starched dotted swiss dress made me fidgety.

Why do they call this place a funeral home or a parlor? I wondered. *It doesn't look like any home or parlor I've ever seen. It's more like a theater. Why don't they call it a funeral theater?*

I'd never seen grown men cry before, to say nothing of my mother. *Everyone is crying except me. I feel bad that I'm not. It seems like I'm supposed to. I'm sad, but I don't feel like crying.* I was too interested in the unusual goings-on.

After some dreary organ music a man sang a hymn, then our minister talked on and on about my daddy and how he was in heaven with God. From the small "family room" off to one side of the funeral home, I watched as everyone we knew -- relatives, friends, neighbors -- and a lot of people I didn't know, walked one-by-one past the flower-topped casket, peering in, shaking their heads. Many wiped eyes, blew noses, leaned on one another. Then they left.

The enormous hall had emptied. Just Mama, Pat, and I remained. Mom took Patty and me by the hand, one on each side, and led us down to look in the casket.

The night before, Mama had said, "Go get in the car, girls. We're going to the funeral home to see Daddy."

My reply was, "What do I want to do that for? He's dead."

She hadn't insisted. So this -- after the funeral service -- was my first "viewing" of a dead person. From the first glance it was obvious my daddy wasn't in that fancy box. Half its lid was propped open to show the body from head to waist. The figure lying there looked like Daddy. Sort of. And it wore his suit and favorite tie. But it wasn't him. My daddy was lively; laughing and hugging and telling stories. He was not there in that stiff, empty body.

So when Mama leaned over and kissed "him" on the lips, I cringed, hoping no one had seen. Silently, in my head, I said, "What do you want to do that for? He's dead."

If Only........

My idyllic childhood came to an end, first with my father's death, and then when we left the farm the summer I was 5. Now I'll tell the part of the story that I didn't know about until after I was married, after my mother was dead. My mom's sister Billie spilled the beans. She didn't imagine that Mom had never told us, but she hadn't. Mom never breathed a word of it.

Caroline, my father's sister, came to Fresno for Daddy's funeral. As set out in Grandpa's Last Will & Testament, Mom and Dad were to inherit the farm, while Aunt Caroline was to get her parents' stock portfolio. Granted, it was the Depression and the stock wasn't worth much, but the farm's value had plummeted too.

Aunt Caroline set to work to get her brother and his wife's share of her parents' estate. With her 86-year-old father hovering at death's door, she flew to the attorney's office to get a new will drawn up naming her the sole beneficiary.

Zelpha (Mom) had been specifically named as a beneficiary in the existing will. Since Daddy's death, however, Caroline was the only surviving child of Elsa Marie and Jens Christian Petersen. To her way of thinking, everything they owned was rightfully hers, which it would have been had Mom not been in the will.

Besides that, the conventional wisdom of the day was that a woman without a man to look out for her wasn't capable of handling money and should not be entrusted with it. So Caroline set out to make sure her brother's widow didn't get any. Since the farm could be transformed into money, Zelpha must not be allowed to inherit it or any part of it.

Caroline was safe from that old conventional wisdom trap. Her husband was alive and well.

No matter that Mom and Dad had been workhorses, literally slaving 24/7 without pay all those years. No matter that they were assured Daddy didn't need life insurance to protect his wife and children in the event of his death. "You'll have the farm." No matter that Mom had lovingly cared for her husband's sister and mother, and was still caring for his frail father.

During my parents' marriage, Caroline was in San Francisco living a far easier life. Her family was not rich, but Caroline was a homemaker in a city apartment while her husband was the breadwinner. She sent her children to the farm every summer. So my mother cooked and cleaned for them, too. (The boys worked on the farm those summers, though, so they pulled their own weight.)

No matter. Caroline should be the inheritor of her parents' estate. The *sole* inheritor.

She shoved the new will, fresh from the typewriter in the attorney's office, in front of Grandpa. Guiding his hand, she got his "signature". It was a done deal. Then she went after control of Pat and me. She insisted on being named executor of our "estate". I can't imagine what our "estate" could have been. The $18 a month we each received from Social Security's survivor benefits?!

Back to the attorney she went.

He stopped her in her tracks. "You've already stolen everything else from that poor woman," he said. "If you insist on this, I'll see to it that you don't get anything!"

She backed off.[2]

Twelve days after Daddy died his father followed him in death. What a huge difference those twelve days made.

If only Daddy had lived twelve more days, Caroline wouldn't have had a leg to stand on, nor the means of impacting the lives of her brother's widow and his children.

If only Dr. Jorgensen had correctly diagnosed and treated my father's appendicitis . . . how different our lives would have been. That's my favorite *if*

---

2. My mother's sister, Billie Hartley, who worked at the Fresno County Courthouse was acquainted with Fresno's attorneys. This story came from her.

only. I've often wondered about that one. Would I be the same person today? In what myriad ways would my life have been different?

If only . . . .

According to Aunt Bill, my mom said, "It wasn't the money. Caroline could have had that. It was the way she went about it."

But I will point out, it *was* the money. If we'd had a little, Mom's life would have been very different. She might have made very different life-altering decisions. As, no doubt, would Pat and I.

The impact of Caroline's avarice was far-reaching.

First Night In Town

That was the first night any of us ever spent in a town. Cars, motorcycles, and trucks whizzed up and down Palm Avenue, horns honked, sirens screeched, train whistles moaned, strangers walked by within a few feet of us, talking, coughing, and guffawing as if they were all alone in the world.

We were accustomed to the night sounds of nature: frogs croaking, crickets chirping, breezes blowing, cows lowing, an occasional dog barking, and silence. Lots of silence. Our farmhouse was set back from the country road, which got little traffic even in the daytime, and was far removed from other houses.

My cousin Virginia, about 14, stayed with us while Mom was at work that night. As we lay in bed in the strange house, she wondered aloud, "What if somebody knocks on the door? I'd be too scared to answer it. You kids' would have to go." She was joking, I think. Thankfully, we didn't have to find out.

We three slept on mattresses on the floor in the front bedroom. Our furniture and the dozens of boxes got moved in, but were far from settled. Little had been put away before Mom had to go to work. The house next door was about 10' feet from ours. Its windows were open this August night, as were ours, in the hope of a cooling breeze. In the middle of the night, our neighbor, whom we'd yet to meet, sneezed a window-rattling sneeze, *Aaaaaaaaah-Chooooooooo!,* scaring the beejeezus out of us. We jumped and screamed. Then, embarrassed at being such rubes, we laughed.

Such was our first night in town.

Aunt Caroline had let us stay on the farm through the summer. At the end of August, just before the start of school, we moved to a rented house in town. I would go to first grade, Pat, third grade, at John Muir Elementary School.

Mom had a job at the 24-hour diner on Broadway (where Highway 99 swung west before turning north again at Roeding Park). The "Help Wanted" ad in the Fresno Bee said, "Experienced Only". She had no waitress experience *per se,* but had spent her whole life waiting on people. How hard could it be? So she lied and got the job. The customers liked her and she learned quickly. The owner let her keep the job she so desperately needed.

The car, a Ford Model T, was registered in Daddy's name, so we got to keep that. It enabled Mom to get to her job in town . . . after she learned to drive it.

There was no one to teach her, though. With Pat beside her in the front seat and me in the back, she bucked and jerked along the country roads, figuring it out as she went. She always said, "I never would've learned to drive without Patty." Concentrating on how to shift gears, and where and when to place her feet, she was oblivious to everything else. Pat alerted her when we approached a stop sign or when another car came toward us. She finally learned, got a driver's license, and drove to work and back daily.

One day, the old Model T wouldn't start. It had a hand-crank below the radiator that you had to turn hard several times to get the engine started. She cranked and cranked, but it wouldn't turn over no matter what she did. It was getting late. She had to get to work. Giving up on the car, she hiked up the road to the nearest house. Our neighbor, Johnny Ventura, had a brand-spanking-new car. Mom asked if he'd drive her to town. She had to get to work.

He simply held out his car keys. She nearly fainted. She refused them, begging him to drive her. But he wouldn't take no for an answer and Mom didn't have time to argue. She was probably going to be late as it was. He sent her off to town in his gleaming black 1941 *Cadillac.*

Trembling all the way to town and all the way back, novice driver that she was, she collapsed with relief as she pulled into the Venturas' driveway that night.

That day, somebody -- probably Uncle Roy -- came over to fix whatever was wrong with the car. While he was at it, he installed an ignition button on the dashboard so she didn't have to crank it anymore.

Mom was forever grateful to Johnny Ventura, not only for the loan of his new car, but for his confidence in her.

She rented the house on Palm Avenue. It was on "the right side of the tracks", but only just barely. With two little girls to raise, and her gone at work a lot, that was important. Unlike the farmhouse on Fig Avenue, it had hot water right out of the faucet, a real bathtub that stayed put in the house, and an indoor flush toilet, all of which I thought was wonderful. Especially the bathtub.

Best of all, though, no goose.

Whatever Aunt Caroline couldn't use or didn't want in our old house was ours to take. It was all we had (except the piano, which had been at Aunt Bill's since Mom and Dad's marriage). So we had what we needed, furniture-wise -- a kitchen table and chairs, the brown mohair couch and 2 matching chairs, and beds and dressers.

Grandma had lovely things: Limoges and Haviland china, sterling silver flatware and serving dishes, a Tiffany-style hanging gas lamp over the dining table, etc. Mom especially loved a few things of Grandma's, e.g: a milk pitcher with raised ducks marching around its bottom. Grandma had promised them to her, telling Daddy, "Now Arthur, you make sure, when Papa and I are gone, that Zelpha gets this." But, of course, he wasn't there to make sure, and I'm positive Mama never mentioned Grandma's promises to her husband's sister.

Caroline, being magnanimous, offered, "Pick out one thing you'd like from the house. You can have one thing."

After much consideration, Mom chose a large framed painting from the set of two that hung in the living room.

When moving day came, all the furniture was loaded onto a neighboring farmer's flatbed hay truck, while Mom's special treasures went into the car. That painting was foremost among them.

It stood on the floor between the front and back seats, where it filled almost the entire space, floor to ceiling. We were all packed up, ready to go, with just one or two more things to be loaded. I carried something out, with instructions to pack it in the car so we could get going.

As I was putting it in the backseat, I knelt on the running board. I couldn't get it in just right, so I maneuvered this way and that, oblivious to the painting. Before I knew it, my bony knees had walked right through it.

When Mama saw the ripped painting she slumped over, like all the air had gone out of her. Resting her forehead on her arm on the roof of the Model T in the driveway, she sobbed, huge gut-wrenching, body-quaking sobs.

I've never felt so terrible in my life. That was the only time I'd ever seen my mother cry, except at Daddy's funeral, when everyone was crying, so that didn't count. It broke my heart to know I had caused her pain. I now know it wasn't the painting she was crying about -- though she felt bad about it. That was "the straw that broke the camel's back". After being so strong and holding up through everything, it took something relatively small to break her.

Of course, I blamed myself. It's my most vivid childhood memory. After awhile, Mama recovered and we got on with the move.

I still haven't gotten over it.

Aunt Caroline and her family returned to San Francisco. Through a local realtor the farm sold for $7,000. In 1941 it was a lot of money.

We all moved on, our lives forever changed.

First Grade

Kitty took me to register for school the week before Labor Day Weekend. I was the only child there with someone other than her mother. Mom couldn't take off work for anything short of dire circumstance. I was I was proud of my pretty young cousin, but keenly felt my mother's absence. For the first time I became aware of feeling different, and wanting to be like the other kids.

Before the first day of school, Mom told Pat, "Now you make sure Carol gets up and is dressed on time, her dress is on straight and her hair is combed. And make sure she brushes her teeth and takes her lunch." At eight, in addition to being big sister, Pat became my surrogate mother. I was her responsibility, and she took it very seriously.

The day after Labor Day, Pat and I walked the two blocks down Palm Avenue to school. Pat dropped me off at my classroom. My teacher, Mrs. Britton, asked my name.

"Carol Frances Petersen." I stated, flouncing a bit.

Clasping her hands under her chin and smiling a sappy smile, she crooned to a second lady, "Oh, isn't she *cute!*"

One Friday early-on, my first grade classmate, Thelma, and I exchanged shoes. She squeezed her normal-sized feet into my ultra-narrow brown leather oxfords, and my feet "swam" in her larger, wider ones. Our plan was to trade back at the end of the day, but we forgot and wore each other's shoes home. I'm sure my shoes pinched her feet every step of the way, and I had to curl my toes to keep hers from falling off.

My mother was furious. But there was nothing that could be done about it. I didn't know where Thelma lived …… didn't even know her last name. We were stuck with each other's only shoes until Monday morning when we got back to school.

Shoes have been a problem most of my life. I was 60 years old before I could walk into a shoe store and buy a pair of shoes off the rack. My very tiny, very narrow feet were nearly impossible to fit. When the time came to buy new shoes my poor mother dragged me from shoe store to shoe store -- every store in town that sold shoes -- in the hope they'd have a pair, just one pair, that fit.

Shoe stores had X-Ray machines. We stood on the platform and stuck our feet in, wearing our prospective new shoes, to see if they fit properly. We kids loved seeing our skeleton-feet inside the outline of the shoes. When I finally found a pair that fit – if I were so lucky – we bought them, style be damned. What they looked like didn't matter. Ugly? Different from the other kids'? So what? They fit. Wear them.

Twice a year my sister and I got new shoes: brown leather oxfords in the fall for school, and in the spring, white leather go-to-meetin' shoes for Easter and summer. That was a big deal. Shoes were expensive.

So when I came home wearing someone else's ill-fitting shoes, with my own new shoes getting stretched out on somebody else's feet -- Mom went through the ceiling.

All summer, like most valley kids, I went barefoot. Shoes were for school and Sunday School. By the end of summer, my soles were tough as rhinoceros hide. I walked without flinching on hot asphalt, gravel and twigs, across littered vacant lots.

Grown-ups kept telling me that going barefoot would spread my feet and end my shoe fitting problem. It didn't. I still go barefoot in warm weather unless I absolutely have to wear shoes. And I still have ridiculously small feet.

Mama worked long hours. The nights she was home, though, when the house was quiet and she was sure everyone was asleep, muffled sobs emanated from her bedroom.

Pat and I were the only girls at school who wore slacks. Mom was ahead of her time. Like Katherine Hepburn, she often wore slacks to work and elsewhere. And in cold weather, we wore them to school. "They're warmer than dresses," Mom said. If we got sick she couldn't take off work, so she did everything in her power to keep us healthy.

I was ahead of my time, too. While all hell was breaking loose back at the farm, Pat and I had most of the childhood diseases. Busy running both farm and the farmhouse, and taking care of Grandpa, Mom sat me down with Pat, a second grader. "You listen to Patty read and do her arithmetic. You can help her with her lessons."

So by the time I started first grade (our country school didn't have Kindergarten) I already knew everything that was taught through the end of second grade. I was a good reader and I could write, and add and subtract, *et cetera*. The teachers didn't know what to do with me. I finished my work in a fraction of the time it took the other kids. There were no accelerated or "gifted" classes. To keep me occupied, the teacher let me draw or color while the other kids did their lessons, or sent me on errands with notes to the other teachers.

What should have been a great advantage turned out to be a great disadvantage. I quickly concluded that school was boring and became disinterested, which didn't change all through my public school years.

It's been said that the first child gets to be who she is, and the second child gets to be whatever's left. At the beginning of each school year my new teacher sing-songed, "Oh, you're Patty Petersen's little sister. Well, we expect great things of you."

I didn't want to just be Patty Petersen's little sister, I wanted to be me. So I took what was left. Although I was every bit as smart as she, Pat always made the Honor Roll; I never did. She was the pretty, popular one; I was the geek. She was the neatnik, I was the slob. She was the dutiful, responsible older sister: I was the devil-may-care, irresponsible little sister.

December 7, 1941

Three weeks before Christmas, Japanese planes bombed Pearl Harbor and we went to war.

At about the same time, with Christmas coming, Pat's third grade friends informed her there was no Santa Claus. She couldn't wait to run home and tell me the news, which was at least as devastating to this 6-year-old as a world war. Maybe more so.

The demography of Fresno quickly changed.

Fresno became a military town. Fresno County Fairgrounds was hurriedly turned into an Army base, which meant there would be no county fairs or Fourth of July fireworks[3] displays "for the duration" -- a phrase that was to become part of our vocabulary. Another Army base – Pinedale – was built at the north end of Palm Avenue, and Hammer Field, an Army Air Corps base (where Fresno International Airport is now), opened. Fresno was loaded with soldiers.

In February, 1942, "Japantown" emptied, and the beautiful, serene Japanese Tea Garden in the west end of Roeding Park disappeared.

Every neighborhood had a volunteer Air Raid Warden with a helmet and armband. During air raid drills he marched around the neighborhood checking to see that no light escaped from any door or window in his jurisdiction.

At school, during air raid drills, we crouched beneath our desks, waiting for German or Japanese bombs to crash through the roof.

---

3. No Christmas Tree Lane either.

Moving Again

Our next house -- right next door to the last one -- was both my most favorite and least favorite of all the houses I've ever lived in. I loved that house because it had a floor furnace. Standing over it, with my feet on its outer rims and my clothes billowing out from the rising hot air, was like being in a glorious heated tent. In addition, the marbled blue linoleum floor in the large living room/dining room was perfect for dancing.

But I also hated it because it had only a shower. No tub. As anyone who knows me well can tell you, I love my bath.

Rent was frozen for the duration, so ours stayed at $35 a month. Virtually all my memories of the war years revolve around that house.

My cousin Virginia, 15, came to live with us to escape her abusive stepfather, and help Mom with us kids. She finished high school in town. Another cousin, Kitty, 18 or 19, moved in too. She helped Mom with us, and with the family budget. She recently told me, "Not only did I have to take care of you kids, I had to pay for the privilege."

Teenaged girls in the house added considerable laughter, liveliness and love. We were a happy, loving family.

The country was solidly behind the war effort. Rationing went into effect. Shortages abounded. Lines began appearing down the sidewalk in front of stores for whatever was in short supply. When a shipment came in, word spread quickly and a line formed. Nylon stockings were the Number One hot item. Virtually impossible to get, women smeared on tan leg make-up instead, drawing lines up the backs of their legs with eyebrow pencils to simulate seams.

Schoolkids contributed weekly to War Bonds -- 10¢ a week for a stamp, which we pasted in our books. At maturity, a full stamp book yielded $25.00. These books were precious and we looked after them carefully.

Also, once or twice a year, the March of Dimes had a fund-raising drive. For this, we kids all lined up to toss our dimes into a big container outside the principal's office. This was for research to find a cure for Infantile Paralysis (Polio), which confined our president, Franklin Delano Roosevelt, to a wheelchair. It mostly affected children, though, so our parents were terrified of us catching it. We weren't allowed to go to public swimming pools because they were thought to be breeding grounds for the crippling and sometimes fatal virus.

My second grade class put on a program for the PTA at John Muir Elementary School. My teacher, Mrs. Overholser, taught us a song and dance. On the night of our performance, before going to the auditorium we gathered in our schoolroom, all of us in our best clothes. Mine was a maroon taffeta dress. Mrs. Overholser blackened our faces with burnt cork. We were to perform in blackface. It was a minstrel show!

Up on stage we performed a cute little dance while singing,

> Put on the skillet, put on the lead,
> Mammy's gonna to make a little short'nin' bread;
> And that ain't all she's gonna to do,
> Mammy's gonna to make a little coffee, too.
>
> Mammy's little baby loves short'nin', short'nin',
> Mammy's little baby loves short'nin' bread.
>
> Three little chillun, lying in bed,
> Two was sick an' the other 'most dead;
> She sent for the doctor, the doctor said,
> "Feed those chillun on short'nin' bread."
>
> Mammy's little baby loves short'nin', short'nin',
> Mammy's little baby loves short'nin' bread.

Nobody thought anything about it. No one was scandalized. I don't know that the word "racist" was in usage yet, but this is as racist as anything I can imagine.

Mom started dating Dean Livergood, a hitherto confirmed bachelor she'd met at the diner. He worked for Hills Bros. Coffee Co. in Fresno. We teased him, calling him "Liverbad" and "Liverwurst". Sweet man that he was, he laughed along with us.

I believe he truly loved Mom and us kids.

I think she loved him, too. But he was 20 years older than she, and that scared her. Surely he'd die long before she would. So, when he proposed marriage, she turned him down.

I overheard her tearfully telling her sister Billie, "I've been widowed once. I can't go through that again." [4]

Heartbroken, Dean arranged for a transfer to Hill Bros. Coffee Co. in San Francisco.

He was a dear, dear man -- sweet, kind, generous, loving -- probably the man she should have married.

---

4. Kitty recently told me, "You were a funny little kid. You were always hanging around listening while the adults were talking."
I replied, "Well, of course. How're you gonna learn anything if you don't listen?"
I learned a lot.

Family Gatherings

From *Carol's Cookbook*

Nowadays when the extended family gets together it's usually catered, or we get cold cuts and salads from the deli, frozen lasagna, and over-sized pies from COSTCO " … so no one will have to work too hard, and we can enjoy ourselves."

The food seems incidental. Oh, the get-together is still wonderful and we have an outrageously good time, but it's not like it used to be. (We no longer all live in the same town, either, which affects the event's preparations.)

In our growing-up years the food was all-important. The women spent a couple of days preparing for the get-together. For our summertime gatherings it went something like this:

The preparations for cooking a big pot of beans started the night before. One of us girl-kids was given the task of sorting the beans. This involved taking each handful of dried beans and letting them fall through our fingers into a colander, while searching for small dirt-clods, rocks, or bugs. Then they were rinsed and set to soak overnight. The next morning the water was drained off and replaced with fresh cold water. They were slow-cooked for several hours with a ham hock, onions, bell peppers, and seasonings.

Potatoes and eggs were boiled for the potato salad. My mom made the best potato salad, so that job was hers. Her potato salad celebrated all the senses: fresh celery and red onions for texture and crunch; black olives, red pimiento and yellow mustard for color; vinegar, mustard, salt and pepper for flavor. Its aroma made your mouth water.

Aunt Margaret brought her delicious sour milk chocolate cake, made from scratch with eggs still warm from being under the hens. Some of the other women brought cakes or fresh fruit pies, as well.

The day of the event, we kids were sent out to the garden to pick beefsteak tomatoes, bell peppers, cucumbers, and sweet onions for the salads, and green beans to be cooked up with bacon bits. And there was just-picked corn-on-the-cob. And chowchow and relishes and pickles and olives -- all homemade.

Aunt Bill's fried chicken was the world's best. My mom's was close, but no cigar. And none of our generation can even come close. Oh, our kids all think their moms make great fried chicken, but that's because they never tasted Aunt Bill's or don't remember it. Hers was deliciously golden, crispy on the outside, tender and juicy on the inside. And flavorful? Our family used the term "finger-lickin' good" long before it was popularized by "The Colonel". She had two or three big cast iron skillets going at once, at just the right temperature, the chicken sizzling away filling the house with delicious scents. It was fried right at the last and served piping hot.

The women spent the day of the gathering in the kitchen. Aunt Bill always said that she and my mom, her baby sister, worked together like a well-oiled machine. Discussion was unnecessary. It was pure harmony and efficiency; it was like one person with two sets of hands. The rest of us worked around them to get the dinner together so everything was ready at the same time.

While all this was going on in the kitchen, the guys were out back engaging in man-talk and getting the homemade ice cream ready.

That morning, someone went to the icehouse for a big block of ice and carried it out to their vehicle with heavy-duty ice tongs. With an ice pick they separated off big chunks and put them in a gunnysack, then crushed them with a sledgehammer. The ice was layered with rock salt in a wooden freezer pail, around the metal cylinder that held the mixture of cream and sugar and fruit and/or flavorings that would be ice cream.

The men and boys took turns turning the crank, the task becoming more difficult as the cream froze. They started slowly, then, as it became colder and thicker, picked up the pace to produce a rich, creamy consistency. This gave the guys a chance to show off their muscles and joke about each other's manliness.

More crushed ice and rock salt were added throughout the process. When the product was declared ice cream, the ice and salt were scraped away from the top, the lid came off and the paddle pulled out, ready for a finger-swipe and a lick. As it was pronounced "Mm-mmm good", the lid was put back on the cylinder and more ice packed all around. Then the whole thing was covered with the gunnysack until it was time for dessert.

Our favorite homemade ice cream was fresh peach. We usually had a get-together toward the end of summer, just before school started, when peaches were ripe -- probably over Labor Day weekend. The peaches would be mashed so as to mix in smoothly, with little chunks, too.

By dessert time we were all stuffed, but no matter. When the ice cream came out of the freezer, it was, "Get outa my way. Ice cream!" We could always make room for homemade cake, pie and ice cream.

Everyone congratulated everyone else on a job well done. "The best ever."

As I look back, I think that for our parents and grandparents, and us kids, as well, a large part of the enjoyment of the family gathering was the food preparation: the camaraderie, the doing what each excelled at, and the love that went into it. No one felt overworked or thought (they) were missing out on the fun, because (they) were in the midst of it. Food and its preparation were integral to the gathering. Even cleaning up afterward was fun -- if not without complaints -- because it was shared. That's how we kids bonded with our cousins, while the adults enjoyed a well-earned rest in an assortment of lawn chairs under a big shade tree, drinking iced tea and fanning themselves with cardboard fans from a local funeral parlor.

Isn't it ironic? Now that cooking is comfortable and easy, with air-conditioned kitchens, and ranges that don't heat up the house, and all kinds of labor-saving devices and fancy-schmancy gourmet gadgets, we have our gatherings catered or get prepared food from the store. Now that we have appliances and conveniences undreamt of by our parents and grandparents, we deny ourselves the pleasure and camaraderie of creating a wonderful meal -- because we might be overworked and miss out on enjoying the party.

Maybe we're missing the point. I think maybe our parents and grandparents had it right. The fun of it is in the doing. Together.

Barbara

When Barbara moved into our house, an electric refrigerator and a phonograph came with her. Since we were still using an icebox and a wind-up Victrola, I was thrilled.

Her father, Ted, was the divorced custodial father of two: an older boy, and Barbara, who was between Pat and me in age. I'll guess I was 7, Barbara 8, and Pat 9. Ted had been a school friend of my dad's, and he and his wife had been part of my parents' social group.

The country was in high gear in support of the war effort. When Ted went off to work in Oakland's shipyards, his son went with him. But he couldn't imagine what he'd do with a little girl up there, so she came to live with our family. I always thought it was just a convenient arrangement and Barbara was sort of like our foster child.

My sister tells me in no uncertain terms that Barbara's father, Ted, was Mom's boyfriend. It was a trial situation. If it worked out and Barbara fit into our family, he and Mom would get married.

Mom treated the three of us exactly alike, sewing beautiful dresses for us all. There's an Easter Sunday picture of Pat, Barbara and me, in the pretty dresses Mom made for us. (Page 353.) Whatever one of us got, all of us got, including her love and attention.

Barbara and I convinced everyone at school we were the real sisters and Pat was the interloper. Barbara was tall and skinny and I was short and skinny, and we looked more alike than either of us looked like Pat. As much as Pat protested, the kids believed us instead of her, which tickled us and ticked her off.

Barbara and I had great times. We really clicked. And we loved playing tricks on Pat. Nothing bad, just funny -- to Barbara and me, anyway. But it emphasized our connection, and might have made Pat feel even more like the outsider.

Bottom-line: Pat didn't want Barbara there. Barbara's presence in our home and in the midst of our family represented more change than we'd already suffered. If we three girls got along, our mom would marry her dad. I think Pat was afraid someone -- anyone -- would replace our adored daddy. And nobody was going to take his place if she could help it.

It's also possible that she resented a third "daughter" taking Mom's time and attention.

I doubt this was conscious or deliberate. But subconsciously, she must have known that if she and Barbara got along, we'd have a stepfather. So she made sure they didn't. She let it be known, in many ways, that Barbara was not part of our family and never would be. Obviously miserable, she sulked and moped.

Mom's greatest desire was for her daughters' happiness, and Pat was not happy. So Barbara -- along with the electric refrigerator and phonograph -- went back to her father.

Another of Mom's boyfriends was sent packing.

Who Was That Man?

Before Betty Friedan and *The Feminine Mystique,* before the Women's Movement, before women in large numbers demanded "Equal Pay for Equal Work", life was a sisyphus-like struggle for a single woman. A woman was expected to have a husband to support her, and she was expected to be a homemaker. Period.

Society punished women who would not or could not fit that role. Women who worked outside the home were paid a pittance; not nearly enough to live on, much less support a family. The disparity between men's and women's wages and opportunities was significant.

Although Mom often worked two or three shifts, she could not adequately provide for us. For that she needed a husband.

~~~~~~

The first time I remember meeting Tracey was the day he became my stepfather.

It was an early September Saturday in 1943 or '44. I was 8 or 9; Pat was 10 or 11. Pat and I had gone to a movie matinée -- a full afternoon's entertainment with cartoons, a cliffhanger serial, the full-length movie, and a shared bag of popcorn.

After the movie we took the city bus home, blissfully unaware that our lives were about to change. Forever. Again. On the front porch stood my mother in her good suit. Beside her was a man -- a stranger -- in an Army sergeant's uniform.

As we advanced up the front walk, Mom said, "Hello girls. This is Tracey. We got married this afternoon."

Stunned, we wondered, *How could she?! How could she marry a man we don't even know?! How could she get married without us? How could she just let us go off to the movies like it was any old Saturday, knowing she would be married by the time we got back?* She'd never said a word, never hinted, never let on.

While we were munching popcorn and watching Bugs Bunny and Roy Rogers, she and this man, this stranger who would impact our lives in myriad unforeseen ways, were vowing, " . . . 'til death us do part."

When Mom dropped her bombshell, Pat slumped on the porch steps and wept. From that moment on, she was resentful and disagreeable at home and around the family (though still sparkly and pleasant elsewhere). I was happy for Mom. I knew how lonely she had been.

So, who was this man Mom had married? Her husband; our stepfather. Tracey, Scottish/Irish, was from upstate New York, a different culture. He was about the same age as Mom -- mid-to-late thirties -- and healthy.

During WWII, anyone wearing a military uniform was a hero. A sergeant in the Army, he qualified. She hadn't known him long and didn't know him well. But it was wartime, a time of many a marriage-in-haste.

Shortly after their wedding he was deployed to Jackson, Mississippi, where he was stationed for the duration. So nothing much changed for awhile, except I imagine our finances weren't so strained.

A Kid in Wartime

Virtually everyone was involved in the "war effort". World War II may have been our country's finest hour. We Americans all pulled together and did whatever we could to help win the war.

We kids collected any metal we could, including tinfoil gum wrappers. We removed tin cans' lids and bottoms and stomped them flat before recycling. Nothing went to waste. We believed our scrap metal went into battleships and bombers, but it probably made new tin cans leaving other metal for war machines.

We sold rubber tires to the service station on the corner of Palm and Belmont. That was a rare occurrence. When we got our hands on a tire, it was a real coup.

Rationing was in effect. We got our ration books at the schoolhouse -- one for each person in the household. "Red stamp rationing" covered meats, butter, fat, oils, and cheese. "Blue Stamps" were for canned, bottled, and frozen fruits and vegetables, plus juices and dried beans and processed foods, such as soups, baby food, and catsup. Gas was strictly rationed, so most people, including my mom, let their cars sit idle and rode the bus or streetcar. By war's end Daddy's Model T Ford had disappeared. I guess she sold it.

Our First Lady, Eleanor Roosevelt, encouraged Americans to plant a "Victory Garden," to free up farm workers for the military or industries supporting the war. She planted a vegetable garden on the White House grounds. Since Fresno is the most fertile area in the world, 'most everyone had a garden anyway, but now growing one was patriotic.

Mom got an office job in the Motor Pool at The Fairgrounds Army Base. It was far easier than waitressing, and maybe the pay was better. Anyway, she was happy to get the job and do her part for the war effort.

Since Pinedale Army Base was at the end of Palm Avenue, convoys of army trucks with young soldiers hanging out of them went by right in front of our house. We kids loved that. The G.I.s waved and hollered to us, and we waved and hollered back. Sometimes they threw us candy or sticks of gum. Great fun.

Mom got to know some of the young soldiers stationed at The Fairgrounds, kids away from home for the first time, on their way to fight and perhaps die in a war. She, like many others in towns with military bases, invited some to our house for wholesome family time. Of course, she was at work a lot, but Pat and Virginia and I -- and our friends, entertained them: popping popcorn, grilling cheese sandwiches or making fudge and Kool-Aid; they jitterbugged with Virginia and her girlfriends, and played the piano. And they played cards or board games with Pat and me. In other words, they hung out.

Years later, Virginia told me, "Not one of those boys ever tried to get fresh. They were all perfect gentlemen." No doubt Mom screened them very carefully. And I'm certain they respected her enough to be respectful in her home, whether or not she was present.

A few years older than Virginia, Kitty had quit college and taken a job at The Fairgrounds Army Base too. She fell head over heels in love with a soldier I'll call Tim. Well, Tim was stationed at the Fairgrounds, waiting to get shipped out to the Pacific theater. Here's her story:

Tim told her, "I'm going off to war. I might get killed. If you won't have sex with me we have to break up. I don't want to die without having had sex." (Nice girls didn't have sex before marriage.)

Kitty was devastated; brokenhearted. But he was right, she wouldn't. He tried. She refused. However, Tim had noticed our neighbor, Mary, a cute little thing, and rightly assumed she would. He struck up a "friendship" with her right under Kitty's nose. (Kitty later learned that he'd lied. He was a married man. Scumbag!)

On holidays, we hosted as many soldiers as would fit around the table. We extended the dining table as far as its leaves allowed, adding the kitchen table and a card table or two. If we had to borrow chairs or piano benches, we did. On Christmas, Mom had some small gift -- a carton of cigarettes or a box of hand-kerchiefs -- for each soldier, " . . . something for them to open when the rest of us are opening presents."

Downtown, on Broadway, were the USO and Service Centers sponsored by the various denominations. Although both Mom and Aunt Bill had daytime jobs, they sometimes helped out at the Lutheran Service Center on Broadway in the evening, serving coffee and do-nuts, homemade cookies and cakes, etc. When they did, Pat and I went along. Although the guys undoubtedly would have preferred girls closer to their own age, they seemed happy to have kids around too. They played ping-pong with us, Checkers, Parchesi, Rummy, whatever. To us kids it was fun.

Two months after the attack on Pearl Harbor, all the Japanese on the west coast were rounded up and imprisoned in "internment camps" or "relocation centers" for the duration. The excuse was that they might spy for Japan. It has since been revealed that the real reason was racism. It was the law of the land that Japanese people -- even those born here -- could not purchase property in the U.S. But some had purchased farms and homes before that law took effect. If they didn't pay their property tax the government could confiscate their property. Their "relocation" to internment camps made sure they couldn't, so, with few exceptions,[5] the government ended up with their homes, businesses, and farms.

My teenage boy cousins Junior (Francis Carl O'Malley, Jr.) and Bill were in the service, Junior in the Navy and Bill in the Marines. Oh my, how handsome they were in their uniforms! Fairly early-on in the war, Junior's Navy plane went down in the Pacific.

His grieving mother, my Aunt Bill, enlisted in the Navy herself ". . . to take Junior's place." She was forty. No matter. In 1943 she enlisted in the WAVES (**W**omen **A**ccepted for **V**olunteer **E**mergency **S**ervice).

However, as she was about to leave for the Navy, the car in which she was a passenger went over a cliff in the Sierras, causing multiple injuries. Her career in the Navy was over before it began. She told her daughter, Kitty, "You have to go in my place."

Kitty says, "It never occurred to me to say No. Back then, girls simply did as

5. In some cases, Japanese families' neighbors paid their property taxes for them, thereby saving their farms or homes.

they were told." So, she enlisted in the WAVES and, after a few months, went off to boot camp on the east coast.

After several weeks in traction at the hospital, Aunt Bill came to our house. A rented hospital bed was set up in the dining room. We kids took care of her while Mom was at work. It was summertime and we were out of school.

The war was foremost in everyone's mind. So it's not surprising that the favorite occupation of all us children was playing *War*. We spent a lot of time building forts and digging tunnels on the vacant lot on the corner of Palm and Belmont. One summer, we had a whole underground network of tunnels -- way better than trenches. After Christmas, we collected Christmas trees around the neighborhood, dragged them home, and built forts. We had entire battlefields of Christmas trees and whatever junk we found.

For ammunition we used ingenuity. Almost anything was okay, but the best nature provided was seed pods from the huge magnolia tree across Palm Avenue. They made terrific hand grenades. We manufactured rifles and pistols out of whatever sticks or boards we could lay our hands on. Bombs and other explosives were created from our active imaginations and self-produced sound effects.

Winter or summer, we could always get a gang of kids to play *War*.

We played softball too. We never had enough players for two teams, so we played "work-ups". No parents were around to supervise or umpire. Sometimes adults joined in the game, but they weren't in charge -- no one was. We just played -- boys and girls, men and women -- anybody who wanted to -- and everyone was equal. If we had a problem, we solved it without ourselves.

We listened to the radio a lot. Saturday morning was the best. "Let's Pretend," on which fairytales were dramatized, with marvelous sound effects -- where the magical place was "East of the sun and West of the moon."

Also on Saturday mornings were "Grand Central Station", "The Billie Burke Show", and "Baby Snooks". On Sunday nights, "Inner Sanctum" with its squeaky door opening, scared the heck out of us, "The Shadow", with a man's voice intoning demonically, "Who knows what evil lurks in the hearts of men? The Shadow knows." "The Green Hornet", "First Nighter", which the announcer opened with, "Two on the aisle", as if we were right there in the theater, taking our seats. "Lux Theater" dramatized and condensed movies from past and present, and sold Lux beauty soap. "The Jack Benny Show" and "Fibber Magee & Molly", kept us laughing. "One Man's Family" and "Molly Goldberg", were heartwarming family sagas set on opposite sides of the country and opposite ends of the socio-economic scale.

And, not to be forgotten, the after-school radio shows, such as "Jack Armstrong, The All-American Boy!" and "Terry and the Pirates".

"Send in six box tops from Quaker Puffed Rice -- Kapow! shot from guns! -- and four box tops from Quaker Puffed Wheat -- Kapow, shot from guns! and get your secret code ring, so you can send secret coded messages to your friends." Or "Six box tops from Kellogg's Rice Krispies -- Snap, Crackle, Pop! -- and 10¢ will get you a beanie button. C'mon kids, be the one in your neighborhood with the most buttons on your beanie!'"

We had a lot of topless boxes of uneaten cereal in our cupboard . . . until Mom put a stop to it. She didn't mind buying them if we'd eat them. But, despite our promises and good intentions, we didn't.

Which brings to mind funnybooks. Nowadays they're called comics or comic books, but in the '40s they were funnybooks. And the comic pages in the newspaper were "the funny papers". A common way to say goodbye was, "See ya in the funny papers!" We kids had stacks of 10¢-funnybooks and traded them back and forth. We hid them when our mothers cleaned house, because they'd have gone in the trash. We loved "Superman", "Batman", "Archie and Veronica", "Lil Audrey", "Tubby", "Little Iodine", "Wonder Woman".

That makes me think of drugstores. When we had no money, which was most of the time, we stood over the drugstore's magazine racks looking at funnybooks until the owner chased us out.

And soda fountains. In the '40s, drugstores had a soda fountain, with a teen-aged kid behind the counter. We spent a lot of time and most of our money in the drugstore, either at the funnybook rack or the soda fountain.

One day when I was 9 or 10, I found a dollar bill on the sidewalk. A fortune! I didn't tell my mother because she'd make me give it back. To whom, I didn't know. I quickly gathered up the neighborhood kids and took them to the soda fountain at Imperial Ice Cream Company, at the southern end of Palm Avenue, just half-a-block from our house, for humongous double-decker ice cream cones at 10¢ apiece.

Money was in short supply for us kids -- as it was for our parents -- and we were always involved in money-making schemes, most of which only kept us busy and never netted us much, if any, monetary gains.

Once, all the neighborhood kids put on a circus in our backyard. I was the fat lady. I wore one of Mama's dresses, stuffed with pillows fore and aft.

From time to time we put on a play or talent show, which, of course, everyone would want to see, and even buy tickets for. No doubt we were influenced by the Judy Garland, Mickey Rooney movies in which a bunch of kids decides, "Let's put on a show!" So they do, after weeks of rehearsals and professional set construction, costume design and creation. They put on a professional-level show, which people come from miles around to see, and they make a lot of money. And there's a talent scout in the audience who gives them all movie contracts.

If it happened to them, why not us? Our set construction consisted of a shower curtain or two dividing our front porch -- one half for the stage, the other for the audience. But we made costumes, and we rehearsed. More than once I wrote (or adapted) a play for our productions.

One time I was a tomato in a play, the setting of which was the produce aisle of a grocery store. I wore a red crepe paper costume with green crepe paper leaves bobby-pinned to my head. Other cast members were a potato, a banana, a bell pepper, a head of broccoli, *et cetera,* all in crinkly crepe paper costumes over our underwear. The only line I remember is, "Peel your eyes, Potato," which my kids tell me I said when I wanted them to pay attention. Another time, I was Bing Crosby, singing "Moonlight Becomes You".

The main challenge was in enticing an audience to come to our shows, even for free. But, no matter. All this kept us occupied during long summer days. And it forced us to be creative. We spent a lot of time thinking up new productions, figuring out how to do them, and executing our plans.

Of course, Mom was at work during the day while the other kids' moms were home. So our house was the neighborhood Activity Center. Pat and I were Activity Directors -- the ones who thought up stuff to do and got the other kids to do it with us. We were all good kids and never did anything bad, but we didn't tell our parents everything, either.

Every year at Christmas, Pat and I organized the neighborhood kids to go caroling. We didn't demand anything from carolees, such as figgy pudding, nor did anyone offer. We just bundled up and caroled around the neighborhood for the fun of it. And it *was* fun.

Even now, at Christmas, I yearn to gather people to go caroling.

April 12, 1945:

A girl came into my 4th Grade classroom and handed the teacher, Mrs. Shirley Ludecke, a note. Our teacher signed it and handed it back to the girl, who left. Mrs. Ludecke said not a word, but sat weeping at her desk. We wondered, but she said nothing. Her students looked at each other with question marks in our eyes, and shrugged in answer. It wasn't until after school when I stopped at the corner store for a 1¢-Tootsie Roll that I learned our president, Franklin Delano Roosevelt, was dead.

FDR was the only president I'd ever known. He'd been president since before I was born. And, to everyone we knew, he was a god.

What was the country going to do now, with two wars going on? No one thought FDR's invisible vice-president, Harry Truman, could handle the job. A great deal of hand-wringing went on. What was to become of us?

Within a few weeks, the war in Europe was brought to conclusion, and then, three months later, Japan surrendered. With the help of the atom bomb, which took many years to develop and test, "Give 'em Hell Harry" had what it took, after all.

On VE Day (Victory in Europe) -- May 8, 1945, and especially VJ Day (Victory over Japan) -- August 15 -- the country exploded with joy and celebration.

One night shortly after the war, Mom and Tracey and I went to the movies at the Warner Bros. Theater in downtown Fresno. A feature-length newsreel showed the grisly discoveries our soldiers made at concentration camps in Europe: Dachau, Auschwitz, Buchenwald, *et cetera*. I was ten, not nearly old enough for that. I got sick to my stomach and had to leave. Sitting in the lobby, loneliness overtook me. I wanted to go back in and sit with Mom but couldn't force myself to.

If we ever doubted the correctness of the U.S. going to war in Europe, those newsreels dispelled our doubts.

Rude, Crude & Lewd

A t the war's end Tracey came to live with us. We soon found out that our stepfather had ideas very different from ours about virtually everything. He was the man of the house now. His word was law.

For the past few years, Mom had had to be strong and independent and make all the family's decisions. Now, it seemed to us that she had no say about anything. He dictated her personal behavior, her manner of dress, and her habits and vices -- minor though they were. She had to do this; she couldn't do that. She was now a wife, not a person.

This did not set well with Pat and me. To our way of thinking, we got along without him before we met him, we could get along without him now. Our household had been relaxed and happy before Tracey. We all had our chores, which got done in good time.

Tracey had a different approach: "When I say 'jump', you jump. You don't ask, 'How high?' or 'Why?' Just jump!"

Ridiculous! What difference does it make if we do it right this second or 15 minutes from now? It'll get done.

When he told us to do something we had to stop what we were doing -- no matter what it was, no matter how important -- and do as he said. Right now. If we didn't he'd "fly off the handle". He'd rant and rave. He'd shout and call us names, insulting us and our ancestors. This was new to us.

Before Tracey, voices had never been raised in anger, nor had insults been heard in our home. Ever.

My sister -- the Honor Roll student -- was smart enough to stay gone most of the time. She was usually off with her friends. But I was just there.

In our household proper manners were important. We knew how to hold a fork, which fork to use. We knew to wait until everyone was seated to begin eating. We knew not to slurp our soup or talk with mouths full. We knew to finish something on our plate before taking more of it. We knew to take small enough bites not to offend while chewing.

It was important to Mom. She made sure our manners were such that we'd be comfortable and acceptable in polite society.

Tracey knew none of that. Or, if he did, he chose to ignore it. He was as likely to pick up a whole pork chop and gnaw it caveman-style as not. He talked and laughed with his mouth full, spewing food over other diners.

Our genteel upbringing dictated that we not call attention to one's bad manners. But we wanted to scream at him. We wanted to kill him! We'd catch Mom's eye and silently plead with her to *do* something. She'd signal us to put up with it. We did, but we rarely invited friends over, which was not at all what Mom wanted for us.

To Tracey, everything was a dirty joke. He was lewd and lecherous in look, manner and speech. He seemed to think this normal and acceptable. I'm sure there were many times when his crudeness made Mom squirm. He was so opposite her in every way.

His behavior toward me was often inappropriate. Later, when I was married and my husband came up behind me unexpectedly and caressed me as Tracey had, my reflexes kicked in. Without thinking, I smacked his hand away, as I had my stepfather's. This hurt and angered John. Even when I explained, he couldn't understand.

"It shouldn't be that way," he'd say.

No, it shouldn't. But it was.

When I was about 15, I had a "Come As You Are" party for my girlfriends. Mom agreed that she and Tracey would stay in the rumpus room at the back of the house, leaving the kitchen, living room and dining room free for my party. The girls came as they were dressed when receiving their invitations, in a variety of costumes, which was the whole idea: pajamas, nighties, a bath towel, or odd combinations -- whatever they were wearing when I called or they opened their invitation. We were having a great time.

Then I spied Lascivious Tracey in the doorway, leering. He thought we should be flattered. I felt violated. I raced to the rumpus room and demanded that Mom get him out of there. I was mortified. She was furious.

Tracey loved to "get someone's goat". He goaded people until they blew up, then laughed and declared, "It didn't take me long to get his goat!" I guess it made him feel powerful or clever.

To his mind, causing pain or trauma was funny. One time Pat came home from a day at the pool with a painful lobster-red sunburn. He came up behind her and scraped the backs of her legs hard with hands as rough as cheese graters. He thought that was hilarious. And Pat was ". . . a crybaby who can't take a joke".

Then there was his all-time favorite knee-slapper. I was his victim. On summer evenings in central California, huge, hard-shelled, hissing Junebugs buzzed around outdoor lights. He loved to grab a handful and put them down my shirt. Then he laughed and laughed, throwing back his head and slapping his thigh as I screamed in terror and squirmed in revulsion.

When at 13 I had my first period I told my mom, innocently believing this intimate confidence would not be broken. Imagine my shock and shame when that evening Tracey announced to a backyard full of guests, "Carol's all growed up now. She became a woman today." I ran to my room, slammed the door and hid out.

I've forgiven my mother. As an adult, I understand that this is information she would share with her husband, but I still cannot understand his taking pleasure in embarrassing an intensely shy, sensitive young girl. It *was* typical Tracey behavior, though.

Before Tracey, our household was peaceful. My mom and dad never argued. She maintained that there was never a cross word between them, and I believe her. I cannot even imagine them fighting.

After Daddy died and we were a household of females, Mom, Pat, Kitty, Virginia, and me -- and Barbara, briefly -- everything was harmony and co-operation.

But all that ended with Tracey. He brought disharmony with him. He and I fought. He could easily "get my goat". One time when I was 10 or 11, in the heat of an argument, I threw a cooking pot at the back of his head. I missed, but it clattered off the wall and bounced on the floor, making a very satisfying racket. And I slammed a lot of doors. He once said, "Me and Carol, we get along fine. She blows up and then she's over it. But Pat, I can't get through to her at all." Pat maintained her aloof, distant stance. She stayed out of his way, but seethed.

Tracey and Mom fought -- mostly about us kids and their opposing expectations and treatment of us. She went from being a naturally happy person to a miserable one. We wondered why she put up with his rude, crude and lewd behavior -- his insensitivity, crassness, and downright cruelty.

We desperately wanted to be free of him. Why didn't she leave him?

Mom's New Appliances

Mom's new refrigerator, the newest innovation, had shelves right in the door. It was a Crosley Shelvador. She couldn't have been more proud if she'd designed it herself.

With Tracey's separation pay, they put a down payment on a house several blocks away from our rental home on Palm Avenue. Our post-war house wasn't much different from the wartime one -- about the same size, about the same era, about the same layout: the bedrooms and a bathroom on one side, living room, dining room and kitchen on the other. And it had a front porch the width of the house, like the old one. It was on a quieter street, though.

With the war behind us, industry returned to production of consumer products. New cars and trucks started rolling off the assembly lines and began to appear on the nation's streets and highways. All manner of household items became available as well: washing machines, stoves, mix masters, toasters, refrigerators, furniture, lawn mowers, and farm equipment. Also, nylons and other clothing could readily be purchased. Production of all such things for ordinary citizens had slammed to a halt when we entered the war and industry switched to war machines and military goods.

So Mom got her new refrigerator. Its edges were rounded, and it was a lovely off-white enamel. In addition to shelves in the door, it had a freezer in the top-center, with room for two ice cube trays and a pound of hamburger. Whenever company came over she ushered them out to the laundry room where her new refrigerator stood, swung the door wide and proudly exclaimed, "Look! It has shelves right in the door." Everyone was suitably impressed with this new kind of refrigerator.

At some point she also got a new washing machine. A Speed Queen. It was transitional from the wringer washer to the automatic, which wouldn't be available for several years. Automatic dryers were much farther off. It had the same old-style round tub as our old one, but it also had a smaller cylinder attached to one side. Once after washing, and again after rinsing, we took the wet clothes from the washer and put them in the small container, which spun the water out. It was a lot easier and quicker than running each piece through the wringer. Then we hung them outside on the clothesline.

I don't recall that she showed off this piece of equipment as she did her new refrigerator, but she was happy to have it. As was her habit, she did a load of wash nearly every morning. By the time she left for work it was on the line, drying in the air. The Speed Queen's spin-dry feature was a real labor-saver.

Elsewhere in the country, television sets were available. They being purchased in huge numbers. California's Central Valley, however, didn't get its big TV antenna until 1953, so if we wanted to see television we had to travel some distance, e.g; to San Francisco or Los Angeles. TV remained exotic and unattainable to us valley folk. Our home entertainment continued to be the radio, a book, or each other.

But no matter. Our home had a Crosley Shelvador and a Speed Queen. What more could anyone want?

A Bizarre Ritual

D espite the warmth of the summer evening an icy shiver shot through me. I crouched behind the weathered tombstone, making myself as small as I could. A ghostly moan wafted over the graveyard, raising goosepimples on my bare arms. I gave no thought to my formal gown or the fragrant gardenia pinned to it.

Pressing against the rough granite grave marker, I held my breath. The earth beneath me vibrated with heavy footfalls as the teenaged boy came nearer, nearer, ever nearer.

He was so close I could have reached out and touched him, but he didn't see me. When he passed my hiding place I started breathing again.

A voice called out from the portico of the mausoleum across West Belmont. "Carol, you're next!"

My heart thumping, my hands cold and clammy, I stood up on trembling legs, smoothed my skirt, and left my hiding place, secure in the knowledge that the call gave me immunity.

But at the mausoleum across the road a far greater terror lay in store. I wanted to turn and run but didn't dare. I hurried past the headstones, stumbling over the uneven burial plots in the old cemetery. The filmy material of my full skirt caught on something. I yanked it and sped on, unwilling to make them wait. That would only make it worse.

Pulling open the heavy doors to the great room, I tiptoed in and sank into a chair at the rear of the hall. Up front were two black-lacquered grand pianos, their lids up-tilted, flanked by tall wicker baskets of violet gladiolas, maybe left from a funeral. A blond girl about my age (10-11), dressed in yellow organza and black patent leather Mary Janes, sat at one of the pianos, playing her recital piece. She lost her place and had to start over, a chilling reminder of my own worst nightmare.

I tried to calm myself as I waited my turn, taking deep breaths and exhaling slowly, my hands pressed against my thighs to quell my quivering fingers. The girl finished and, with a *Thank God, it's over!* roll of her eyes, stood, curtsied as we'd been taught, and bolted for the door.

The person responsible for this bizarre ritual, Bessie Anderson - Piano Teacher, stood elegant and formidable in floor-length black crepe, reading from the program. "Carol Petersen will play *Barcarolle* by Jacques Offenbach."

Making my way up the center aisle with all the enthusiasm of the condemned approaching the guillotine, I reached the piano and sat on the bench. Positioning my trembling fingers on the keys while my foot stretched for the pedal, I started to perform the piece I'd practiced and practiced.

Mrs. Anderson served as organist for many of Fresno's funerals, which enabled her to hold her annual student recital in the funeral parlor of her choice. She always chose this mission-style mausoleum, which her young students were dying to explore.

Off the foyer, to the right, were heavy glass doors through which a long corridor was visible. Inside the marble walls were crypts filled with dead people. Then, to the left, through another thick glass door, down another long corridor, was the crematorium where, we were told, huge ovens turned dead bodies into "gritty little piles of ashes".

The adolescents among us regaled us younger kids with visions of ghosts and ghouls. They chanted, "The worms crawl in, the worms crawl out, The worms play tiddly-winks on your snout . . . ", accompanying each other with ghastly, ghostly sound effects.

Across the road was Mountain View Cemetery where, between our musical tortures, we played Hide-and-Go-Seek among the tombstones. It was great spooky fun.

Sign My Book?

It's a dead art form. For those of us who grew up in the U.S. before the 1960s, the autograph book was the medium for remembrances in the 6th, 7th, and 8th grades, before the more polished yearbooks of the more worldly high school kids we would become. This book was the way we left our marks on each other's lives, or at least, in each other's books. It covered those years of awkwardness and self-consciousness, the years between childhood and the teens.

We tried to be witty, 'though I suspect most of the clever little ditties we scribbled in each others' books were passed down from older siblings or previous generations. And I'm sure we stole shamelessly from each other. Although most of them are pretty awful, their innocent charm is not lost on me.

Rummaging through boxes that hadn't been unpacked in the last couple of moves, I found my little autograph book. I had forgotten about it and giggled as I read from its faded pages. I remember most of the kids, although some have slipped my aging mind. My book, bound in cordovan *faux*-leather, with *Autographs,* in *faux*-gold letters across the front, is filled with pastel pages. Its entries are from 1947 to 1949.

We went all-out to get everyone's signature. Those last few days of school, we carried our little books everywhere, shoving them in classmates' and teachers' faces, saying, "Sign my book?" No one refused, but we had to ask.

We girls would gather our courage to ask the boy on whom we had a crush, and after the signing, scurry off to be encircled by a gaggle of giggling girlfriends, flipping through the pages to find out what he'd written. Most often it was disappointing. Boys generally avoided much self-expression.

The inscriptions fall into categories. First, the jingles which had to do with weddings or marriage:

At your wedding, which will not be soon,
Don't be hasty and swallow the spoon.

❄

When you get married and live in a tree
Send me a coconut C.O.D.

❄

When you get married and have twins
Don't come to me for safety pins!

❄

Remember me when far away
Though only half-awake.
Remember me on your wedding day
And save me a piece of cake.

❄

and some that are just plain idiotic:

When you were a wee wee tot
Your mother put you on a wee wee pot
Whether you had to wee wee or not.

❄

I wish I were a little fish
swimming under the ice,
And when the girls go skating by
wouldn't that be nice?

❄

I had a little pig and I tied him to the heater,
And every time he turned around he burned his little seater.

❄

I saw you in the cellar
I saw you at the sea
I saw you in the bathtub
Oh! Excuse me!

Then there were the insults:

Roses are red, Pine is green
You have the shape of a submarine!

❄

Don't worry if your job is small
And your rewards are few.
Remember that the mighty oak
Was once a nut like you!

❄

Roses are green, Violets are pink.
Dopes like you belong in the clink!

❋

I write on pink because you stink
And leave the yellow for your fellow.

❋

I love you little, I love you big,
I love you like a great big pig.

❋

A few were neutral or even nice:

In your golden chain of friendship
Please consider me a link.

❋

Smile at the world, and when you do
See the world smile back at you.

❋

When far away and friends are few
Think of those who think of you.

❋

Can't think,
Brain's dumb.
Inspiration won't come.
Can't write,
Bum pen.
Best wishes,
Amen.

❋

I write on white to be polite
And save the yellow for your fellow.

(There was a lot of concern about my fellow!)

❋

No more pencils, no more books,
No more teacher's dirty looks.

❋

There were clever entries using only letters and numbers to spell out or add up the signator's sentiments. (This was more than half-century before texting and Twitter):

U.R.A.Q.T. I.N.V.U.

❋

2 Ys U R
2 Ys U B

ICUR
2 Ys 4 ME
✼
2 nutty
2 cute
2 be
<u>4 got-</u>
10
✼

Those were generally added, like a postscript, after something else, as were these expressions of affection:

Yours till Goat Island has kids.

✼

Yours 'til the ocean wears rubber pants to keep its bottom dry!

✼

Yours till Russia gets Hungary and fries Turkey in Greece.

✼

Yours 'til George Burns Gracie Allen.

✼

Some had drawings incorporated in the jingle, such as this bit of 7th grade wisdom:

Life is like a deck of cards:
When you're in love it's ♥s
When you're engaged it's ♦s
When you're married it's ♣s
When you're buried it's ♠s

✼

My 6th-grade heartthrob signed,

(His name). Best wishes.

(And "my fellow" did sign on yellow. Coincidence, no doubt.)

✼

And there were signatures and bits of advice or appreciation from teachers, Girl Scout leaders, and one from the principal.

The most precious entry is this:

Dearest Carol,
May all the things I have wished for you come true.
Love, Mother

It brought a tear to my eye to unexpectedly come across that little message in her own beautiful and well-remembered hand, in the turquoise ink she always used in her Parker fountain pen.

At the very end of the book, on the inside back cover, is this determined kid's autograph:

By hook or by crook
I'll be the last to sign in your book.

✳

I'm glad I've kept my little autograph book -- for laughs, and its archival value. I've no idea what I wrote in other kids' books. And if you ever find out, please keep it to yourself.

(I omitted names as an act of mercy.)

Mom's Piano

The night was thick with the tule fog that is the central valley's winter curse. A truck pulled up out front. Its doors slammed hard, the sound of steel striking steel reached our ears. Two pairs of heavy footsteps approached our front door.

"Do we have to sell it, Mom?" asked Pat in a last-ditch effort.

"Please don't sell it!" I begged. "It just won't be the same around here without it."

Mom gave us that look that meant her mind was made up, her lips pursed. "We need the money. For doctor bills," she stated matter-of-factly, then shrugged. "Nobody ever plays it anymore anyway."

The doorbell rang.

"We'll play it, Mom. Honest, we will!"

Mom pressed her lips tighter. "Answer the door, Carol," she instructed from the platform rocker where, in her weakened condition, she now spent her days. "They're here for the piano."

My feet matched my heart -- heavy as lead -- as I hauled myself to the front door.

When, just out of high school, Mom got her first paycheck, she bought a piano, the one thing she'd yearned for. She wanted to play for the joy it would give herself and others. And she absolutely wanted it so her someday-children would have advantages she'd not had. She was taking no chances. She *would* have a piano. And her children *would* know how to play it.

Mom loved happy times and laughter and song and dance. She loved people, and it was mutual. In those days, when people entertained at home, a piano and the ability to play it were virtual necessities.

The last installment was paid. She had her piano. She took a few lessons and learned some of the popular tunes of the day.

> Nothin' could be finer
> than to be in Carolina
> in the mo-o-orning.

Some years later, she and my dad met, fell in love, and married. Dad moved her into his parents' farmhouse south of town.

Grandma's pump organ sat proudly in the parlor, so Mom's piano had no place there.

Mom hated organ music. "It always sounds like a funeral. Someday we'll have our piano. Then we'll have lively music in this house. You girls will have lessons and learn to play." She made it sound like a wonderful thing.

Of course, that would not happen so long as Grandma lived. Then my dad's sister would undoubtedly want the organ, and Mom's piano would have a home.

As fate would have it, that house never did have our piano in it.

Nine days before Christmas in 1940, Grandma died. She wasn't sick. She just didn't wake up one morning. Soon after, Grandpa had a stroke and needed constant care, along with the farm requiring my parents' backbreaking work. Household changes were put off 'til things eased up. No one was in a hurry to make major changes just then anyway. "All in good time," said Mom.

In the next few months, however, there were more changes than anyone could have imagined. Mom had to listen to an inordinate amount of organ music that year.

Our life as we knew it was gone. First Grandma, then Dad, then Grandpa. Then the farm -- all gone.

When we moved to town, Mom's piano was brought from Aunt Bill's house. That was probably the only good thing to happen that year.

No matter how grave the struggle for survival, when each of us kids turned eight we took piano lessons. That was top priority. Whatever else we did without, Mom made sure we had piano lessons. Her major goal was a good life for her daughters, which was symbolized by the piano and our ability to play it.

Although our lives were upside down, the piano gave Mom hope that all would still be all right, that her children would still have a good life.

The men stepped into our living room.

"The piano's in the rumpus room, out back. Come on out." Mom rose slowly and, leaning on me, led them through the dining room, the kitchen, and down the steps into the room at the back of the house where we were greeted by the warmth and aroma of oak logs burning in the fireplace.

"I'd like to play it. To try it out," said one of the men. Mom nodded. He sat on the bench and, adjusting it for his long legs, placed his right foot on the pedal, his fingers on the keys. He brought that piano to life, playing it for nearly a half-hour. Every kind of music. It had always had the most wonderful tone, as good as any Steinway, but tonight it sounded especially rich and full as the music bounced off the knotty-pine walls.

Pat, the eldest child -- the dutiful daughter -- practiced diligently and played well. When we had company she played for our guests while Mom beamed.

I continued taking lessons and was supposed to practice after school, but Mom was at work. She assumed both of her daughters would take full advantage of this opportunity. I'm ashamed that I didn't. As a result, I cannot play the piano and deeply regret it.

My love was song and dance. To my sister's great annoyance, I was always dancing -- tap, ballet, ballroom -- to the radio, singing along at the top of my lungs with Frank Sinatra, Jo Stafford, Al Jolson, Doris Day, whoever was on. When I was about ten, I convinced Mom to let me drop piano and take dance lessons. Tap & Adagio was what was available. I didn't care. I was dancing.

During most of World War II, our cousins, Kitty and Virginia, lived with us. They and their friends enlivened our household and gave the piano a good workout.

Mom's young soldier friends from The Fairgrounds came to our house. Many played the piano: boogie woogie, classical, jazz, rinky-tink, big band ballads, plus a lot of "Chopsticks" and "Heart and Soul". They enjoyed our modest home -- and our piano.

When Junior's plane went into the sea, Kitty found great solace in the piano.

It got her through that terrible time. She played by the hour, its sweet music lifting her despair.

As the man played Mom's piano, a confusion of emotions played on her face. She was ecstatic at the music coming from it. "It's nice to hear it the way it should be played."

That her dreams had let her down was also apparent. A stranger, rather than her own children, was playing her piano.

Sadness at hearing her most treasured possession for the last time showed too.

What a gift that man gave us, even as he prepared to take it away. He could have just played the scales, but no, he gave us its last performance, the best ever. Maybe he sensed how important it was that it not just be loaded onto a truck and carted away.

On Christmas Eve, friends and relatives always gathered at our house. Pat played the piano while I led the caroling. This we did willingly and our guests suffered it graciously.

As Pat entered her teens, her busy social life increasingly kept her away from the piano. And, by that time, I played it rarely. Kitty and Virginia had moved on into their adult lives. The piano gathered dust.

We always made sure the piano was situated on an inside wall -- to protect it from the cold. Mom insisted on that. Whenever we moved, the first thing we looked for in the new house was an inside wall for the piano.

In 1950, Mom's surgery and therapies cost more money than we ever thought of having. Before long it became apparent that her cancer had returned and spread. She had to quit her job at City Hall. Debts mounted. Her piano was the only thing we could sell. Nobody played it anymore anyway.

Mom's ad in The Fresno Bee was answered by a man from the Presbyterian church on Olive Avenue, across from Tower Theater.

"Yes," said the man. "It has a very good tone. We'll take it."

The other man reached into his pocket, counted $75 into Mom's hand. They shook on the deal.

Pat and I wiped our wet cheeks with the backs of our hands as the piano left the house, and watched from the front porch as the truck carrying it vanished into the fog.

"I wonder if they'll know to put it on an inside wall," I croaked, my throat tight with trying to hold back tears.

Mom's most cherished possession was gone.

A Cup of Tea

I bolted through the door, slammed it as hard as I could, raced across the street and around the corner to Cathie's house. My stepfather's latest dastardly deed had infuriated me and I was in a rush to talk to her. I could always count on Cathie to listen and care.

Her mother opened her kitchen door. "Carol dear, come in, come in. Catherine's not in just now," she stated in a crisp British accent, her voice high-pitched and lyrical. "She'll be back soon. I'll put the kettle on. We'll have a cup of tea." By the time the words were spoken the kettle was on the stove with blue flames licking at its base. I felt comforted just seeing Mrs. Bailey and being welcomed into her cozy kitchen. If she noticed my frantic state she didn't let on.

Initially disappointed that Cathie wasn't home, I was soothed by her mother's familiar greeting and apparent pleasure at my unexpected visit. Under a cheery cover-all apron she wore a dark housedress. Her shoes were unstylishly clunky, and she wore nylon stockings. Her dark hair, threaded with silver, was twisted into a knot at the back of her head, with soft tendrils framing her kind face.

She took a brown teapot from the cupboard. When the kettle's whistle reached the right pitch she poured boiling water in the pot, swirled it and let it rest a bit, then emptied it into the sink. "To make a proper pot of tea one must use a brown porcelain teapot," she declared, "and preheat it, of course." From the shelf she took a colorful tin, pried off its lid and scooped three teaspoonfuls of Ceylon tea into the pot, added boiling water, then stirred vigorously with a fork. She covered it with a puffy tea cosy and set it on a brass trivet on the cherrywood buffet in the dining room.

While the tea steeped she instructed me to lay the table, adding, "We've lovely scones, fresh-made this morning." From the buffet, I carefully lifted fine china cups, saucers, and dessert plates, then silver spoons, and soft linen napkins. The table was covered with an embroidered linen cloth; at its center sat a small bouquet of fragrant yellow roses.

As we sat down to tea Cathie arrived. Mrs. Bailey lifted the cosy off and poured milk into their two cups -- I take my tea black -- then poured the strong tea. Mine first, then Cathie's, then her own. Holding the delicate cup in my hands and breathing in the aromatic steam, I felt soothed and nurtured. This was just what I needed. Our conversation was lively and, blessedly, not centered on me and my troubles. The calm ordinariness of it took the edge off my taut emotions.

By the time we'd had our tea and scones and tidied up I felt less agitated. Still, Cathie and I went off to her room where I unburdened myself. She was understanding and supportive as I knew she would be. Now I could go home and make it through another day.

Many times, over my teenage years, this ritual was repeated. I wasn't upset every time I visited the Bailey household, of course. Most often, Cathie and I just revealed our hopes and dreams, our fears and fantasies, and current teenage issues, which always included boys. Sometimes we played the piano or phonograph and sang along. We especially loved the music from the current Broadway hit shows, "South Pacific" and "Showboat". And sometimes we read to each other, or individually, silently. In other words, we just hung out, as best friends do.

But there was also the angst. We both had some, being teenage girls, but my life seemed to provide more than hers. For one, there was my sadistic stepfather, who constantly made me wish he'd been drowned at birth.

Her own father was wonderfully unexciting. A neurosurgeon from Canada, he was reserved and stuffy, but a good soul. She wished he weren't so straight-laced. But the more she learned about my stepfather the more grateful she was for her dad.

And there was the fighting. My mom and stepfather had frequent, loud fights, which made for a lot of stomachaches and distress.

I can't imagine raised voices in the Bailey home.

Then there was my sister, who regularly ticked me off -- she was snippy, snotty, surly, sarcastic -- a big sister's job description, in the teen years anyway.

Cathie's only sibling was away at college. Four years older than she, Robert was barely on her radar screen and didn't bug her at all.

Money was always tight at our house. My mom had to have a job, in an era when most mothers were stay-at-homes. And I always had odd jobs -- baby-sitting, lawn mowing, haircutting and home-perming, sewing and altering -- whatever I could convince someone to pay me for.

Cathie never had to give a thought to where money came from.

Then there was the terrible business of my mother's cancer. As she got sicker and sicker, thinner and thinner, weaker and weaker, I was more and more distraught.

All through my teenage years I needed a peaceful haven.

I doubt I realized then that it might have been Cathie's mother -- Ivy Bailey -- as much as it was Cathie to whom I ran. It was for her invariable cheery welcome -- "Carol, dear", and "We'll have a cup of tea" -- and the constancy of her tea ceremony, as much as it was for solace from her daughter, my best friend, Cathie Bailey. (Photo on page 353.)

A Pact With the Devil

To this day I wish I hadn't overheard this conversation. But I did, and it explained a lot.

Tracey shouted, "You promised that if I helped support your girls you'd have my baby."

Mom screamed back, "You know the doctor said I can't have another baby. He said it would kill me."

"But you promised! I've kept my part of the bargain. You haven't kept yours!"

In that terrible moment it became clear. A deal had been struck. Tracey would contribute financially, making it possible for us to live in a decent house, for Pat and me to have nice clothes and spending money, for me to have braces on my teeth. In return, she was to have his baby. And he would hold her to their bargain . . . even if it cost her life.

Oh my god! What had she done! She'd made a pact with the devil, one it turned out she couldn't keep, but which kept her trapped and imprisoned nonetheless. She'd sold herself -- her happiness -- to buy ours. But it had backfired.

The one thing she wanted most in life -- her daughters' happiness -- was the very thing she had traded away. Didn't she know we'd rather be poor than have Tracey in our lives?!

And in the end, I believe Mom's deal with Tracey did cost her life. Stress, i.e., anger and depression, diminishes the immune system, allowing cancer to get a foothold. I believe her marriage to Tracey killed her.

The Summer of '52

I t was the summer of '52 and my mother was dying, but I didn't want to know it. I didn't want to believe it. It was simply too terrifying. Just 16, with my senior year of high school ahead, I had no idea who or what I wanted to be when I grew up. What would I do without her?

I ignored the more and more undeniable truth. So did she. She never talked about it. Back then people didn't talk about impending death.

She had discussed it with Dr. Ginsberg and her sister, Billie, though. When she died I discovered it had been pre-arranged for Aunt Bill to be my legal guardian. But she hadn't talked about it with Pat and me.

The summer started with Pat's wedding. I'm sure Mom was relieved that Pat would "have a good man to take care of her" before her departure. I was her headstrong, independent, resourceful -- if capricious -- daughter. I believe she knew I'd be okay.

On June 7 Pat married Stan Manchester. Aunt Bill made Pat's wedding dress and Mom's Mother-of-the-Bride suit -- champagne lace over matching satin -- in addition to my yellow taffeta and net Maid of Honor dress, and one for herself. We all decorated the church and cooked and fancied up our backyard for the reception. That's how our family did weddings.

Mom never looked more beautiful. She was slender for the first time in her life. Her hair had grown back after radiation and was silky soft. She was weak, however, sitting when possible and accepting assistance when required to stand or walk.

Relatives and friends who hadn't seen her for awhile asked in shock and dismay, some in tears, "Why didn't you tell us sooner?"

Her physical deterioration had been gradual and we who saw her every day didn't realize how much ground she'd lost. But I still refused to know she was dying.

Mom and I had a lot of time alone now, but we'd always spent as much time together as possible. We were always close -- the kind of closeness where words are unnecessary. The time came when she needed watchful care, so I stopped going to school. She wanted me to have a normal teenage life, though, and encouraged me to go out with my friends in the evenings. Where we usually went, a couple of times a week, was to City League softball games.

The team we cheered on was that of the First Presbyterian Church, where my friends and their families were members. After the game we went to someone's house for cake and ice cream or ice cold watermelon, or stopped at Stan's Drive-In. To me, the ball game was irrelevant. It was a social event. It was being part of a group. It was an opportunity to be a kid and forget, for a few hours, the ominous adult issues that crowded my consciousness. Mom was glad I was having a bit of a social life and didn't want her dying to get in the way of it.

When I got home I recapped the evening's highlights, often having her in tears she laughed so hard. That summer I mentally recorded everything with which to entertain her, giving it a comic twist, if possible.

Although I'd had a passing interest in boys for awhile, they'd shown no interest in me. I was shy, skinny and, from 6th grade until the day before Pat's wedding (6 long years), I had braces. But then, in the summer of '52, my braces came off, I began to flesh out a little, and I finally began to overcome my shyness. Boys began to notice me. I still didn't date but was getting a few glances here and there.

There were some interesting boys on the team -- college boys from Fresno State. One in particular caught my eye. John Purroy. He had gorgeous brown eyes rimmed by the longest, darkest lashes I'd ever seen, perfct teeth and a smile that could melt granite. He was athletic. But he was shy and stayed in the center of a gang of guys, so I never had a chance to talk to him.

I placed all my adolescent hopes and fantasies on him, dreaming of the day he might look at me with those lovely dark eyes, of the day when he might call me, of the time we might go out on our first date -- my first date with anyone.

Mom's condition worsened, requiring hospitalization. (Home Hospice didn't exist.) I spent my days at her side at St. Agnes Hospital, and Aunt Bill spent her nights there after working all day at the county courthouse. Mom was grateful for our presence. I sat holding her hand most of the day.

We still never talked about it. By then there was nothing to say.

Pat came in after work for a brief few minutes' visit. She always cried. I'd shoot her a look that said, "Knock it off." One day I took her outside and told her, "Do your crying somewhere else. Mom doesn't need to see it."

One day a nurse in a white uniform and cap, who came in to check on Mom, called me out into the hall. She put her hand on my shoulder and, looking me in the eye, said, "Are you aware that your mother is critical?"

I nodded. I'd never heard "critical" in that context, but figured out it meant Mom wouldn't last long.

"It makes me so damn mad!" She slammed her fist into her hand. "It's not fair . . . Someone so young. Only 44 years old! With kids still at home! I hate so much to see this . . . " she couldn't finish. Tears welled in her eyes; her chin quivered and puckered. Then she hugged me, something that wasn't done, especially by strangers, in 1952, even in California.

Several things in that exchange astonished me:

• Someone was finally talking to me about the fact that my mother was dying. The taboo was broken and I felt relieved.

• She'd called my mother young. I thought 44 was old.

• And most astonishing, someone who didn't even know my mom cared enough to cry about her.

I spent an eternity that summer on the third floor of St. Agnes Hospital watching my mother die.

Much later, Aunt Bill, then in her mid-80's, felt it was time to tell me some things she'd neglected. Among them was that during that summer, Mom's doctor told her, "You've got to get Carol out of there. She's just a kid. Her mother could die any minute and she wouldn't be able to handle it."

My aunt told him in no uncertain terms, "No, Carol stays. She's the only one in the whole family who could handle it."

So I stayed.

As it turned out, Mom didn't die on my watch. The call came in the middle of the night. Knowing the end was near, Pat and Stan were at our house. Stan got up to answer the phone. Aunt Bill said, "She slipped away peacefully in her sleep."

Stan came out to the rumpus room at the back of the house where I was sleeping to tell me. I told him, "Go to Pat. She needs you." I didn't need anybody. And I didn't need to cry.

My first reaction was, "Thank God it's over." My second was to feel guilty I hadn't been a perfect daughter, but that didn't last long. Mom always said, "I don't want my kids to be perfect. I just want you to be normal."

The next few days were filled with picking out a coffin (that fell to me), making decisions about the funeral, the burial, and so forth. Pat and I talked about flowers for the funeral. We'd rather not have the funeral home filled with flowers, reasoning that the only one to benefit would be the florist. We'd rather have the money go for something useful, like cancer research. But we figured the rest of the family would prefer the traditional flower-filled funeral home. We didn't find out for at least 20 years that they'd had the same discussion and reached the same conclusion, but didn't mention it to us since we were just kids and would probably want the traditional display of flowers.

The day of Mom's funeral arrived. She was laid out in the champagne lace suit she'd worn at Pat's wedding, just four weeks earlier. Pat cried all through the funeral and burial. I didn't. Partly because I was relieved Mom was out of her misery, and partly because I refused to. I hadn't cried at Daddy's funeral 11 years earlier and I was damned if I was going to cry at Mom's.

In the weeks that followed, we adjusted to life without her. I stayed on in the house where I'd lived since 6th grade. Since Aunt Bill lived on the other side of Easton, on a farm way out in the country, I stayed in town to finish high school with my friends and in familiar surroundings. I didn't have to make those adjustments, too.

Mom's death had a sobering effect on us. Tracey and I were simply two adults living under one roof. He didn't try to be the boss of me and his lecherous behavior had ceased. I was a mature and responsible 16-year-old.

I kept going to softball games, and I kept dreaming about that Purroy boy.

During those last few weeks of summer I developed a condition that needed medical attention. The insides of my eyelids were as gritty as sandpaper, and my eyes were extremely light-sensitive, requiring dark glasses, even in movies, even at night. Any light reaching my eyes burned and made them stream like leaky faucets.

During that time the phone rang one evening. It was one of the boys from the First Pres. team. Not the one I dreamed about, though. It was the team geek -- the one above all others I could've said no to. Except that he just said, "Would you like to go out with me?"

I didn't know how to say no without hurting his feelings. God forbid I should hurt someone's feelings! At a loss, I gulped and said, "I guess so."

He had tickets to a Fresno Cardinals game. A night game. We got there, me in my dark glasses with "King Geek" from the school across town. The bright lights in the stadium made my eyes water, so I dabbed at them with a hanky. Through the blur I saw that all the really neat guys from school were there . . . the jocks . . . the honor students . . . the cute, popular boys -- all the guys who had never noticed me, whose notice I longed for.

At some point during the game they discovered me, in dark glasses, with "K.G.", and began taunting me. They called to each other, "Hey look, there's Carol Petersen." "Why is she wearing dark glasses? It's a night game!" They even started, one by one, walking up and down the bleachers to get a better look, calling things like, "Carol Petersen, Carol Petersen, who's Carol Petersen with?" "Does she think she's a movie star?" *Et cetera.*

My 15 minutes of fame.

I never went out with that guy again, no matter how he asked. And those boys? Back at school, they never paid me any notice again.

But it didn't matter because before long I was going out with that Purroy boy.

Within a week or so of that game, I entered the office of an optometrist, randomly selected as I walked down Fulton Street. I walked in and asked for an eye exam.

After the exam, this kindly man who knew nothing about me or my situation said, "You don't need glasses, dear. Your problem is emotional. When you've cried enough tears you'll be fine."

How he knew, I've no idea. And he never billed me. Eventually, I guess I cried enough tears.

I've never stopped missing my mom. I'm sorry she never got to know any of her grandchildren. My greatest regret, however, is that they never got to know her. They'll never know what they missed.

You Wouldn't Want Your Sister to Marry One

Fresno had its share of prejudice, bigotry and racism. When I was growing up, the city was divided by the railroad tracks. Two sets of them: Union Pacific and Sante Fe, with the downtown in between. On the east side lived only white people. On the west side lived "coloreds" -- Mexicans, African Americans, Asians, Polynesians, Native Americans, and other non-Europeans. Some whites lived on "the wrong side of the tracks" (whites could live anywhere), but no "coloreds" lived on the "right side". No one would sell or rent to them, which was perfectly legal.

Fresno wasn't Alabama. There were no "Whites Only" restrooms, drinking fountains, or lunch counters that I recall. But it was customary, and legal, to discriminate in real estate transactions, club membership, team sports, *et cetera*. It's just the way it was. It wasn't questioned, at least, not by most white folks, who enjoyed a privileged status.

Other than downtown or at the county fair, segregation was the rule. The path of "whites" never crossed that of "coloreds", except in very wealthy neighborhoods where one might see colored servants and laborers.

According to my 12th grade Civics teacher, not too terribly long ago, Fresnans considered Armenians colored (he used the word "niggers"). So they couldn't live on the "right" side of town. In my growing-up years, Armenians were called "Fresno Indians". It wasn't a compliment.

Fresno is home to the largest Armenian population outside Armenia. Their names are colorful and lyrical, ending in -yan or -ian: Mardikian, Obanian, Agajinian, Bagdassarian, Sarkisian, Saroyan.

Most of Fresno's teachers didn't bother to learn how to pronounce

Armenian names, though. On the first day of school, reading the class roster, they butchered them.

I once asked my mother, "Why do people dislike Armenians so much?"

Her reply was, "Maybe they're jealous. Armenians are very good business-men, so a lot of them are rich." I couldn't figure out why that was reason to dislike them.

In time, Armenians lost their "nigger" status and lived on the right side of the tracks, so we were in school together. But there was still a "color barrier". Non-Armenian girls didn't date Armenian boys. "You wouldn't want your sister to marry one."

The summer I started dating John, one of his softball teammates pulled me aside at a game and, jerking his head toward John, demanded, "Are you sure you want to go out with him?"

"Huh?"

"His *real* name is Purroyan. His father changed it when he came to this country." (Translation: He's an Armenian.)

He could have been. He had the dark hair and eyes, the dashing good looks of an Armenian. And *Purroy* does lend itself to a -yan on the end -- rhymes with Saroyan.

In addition, John hung out with Armenians. His two closest friends were Bob Mardikian and Pete Parnegian. The three were Lambda Chi's. Lambda Chi Alpha was the only FSC fraternity that accepted Armenians.

Some of Fresno's Armenians *had* dropped the -yan or -ian from their names.

So his team member's assumption was not unreasonable.

I was forced to give the matter some thought. It didn't take me long to decide it didn't make any difference and I continued dating John.

Come to find out, he *wasn't* Armenian after all.

Class of '53 Graduation

P omp and Circumstance provided the cadence for the processional. The path to the stage was lined by the Daisy Chain – Junior girls in full-skirted pastel formals, holding thick ropes of fresh Shasta daisies. Passing between them in alphabetical order, we climbed the stairs to take our seats on the platform. As I listened to speakers' platitudes and admonitions, I looked out over the crowd of parents, intensely aware that mine were not among them.

My emotions were a-jumble. I was as excited as anyone, and filled with optimism and anticipation. I was eager to move on and discover my life.

And I was scared. *What's next? I'm supposed to be an adult -- independent and self-sufficient. I'm not ready. The decisions I make from now on will affect my whole life.*

I was 17, a high school graduate. I wanted to be an adult and, most of the time, felt like one. But not that night. I felt like a little kid who wants and needs a safety-net.

And I felt sad. Looking out over the sea of parents' proud, smiling faces, I struggled to smile. I pushed back the sleeve of my graduation gown. I wore Mom's wristwatch -- a round gold Bulova. It comforted me. I'd worn it since she died.

After walking across the stage and receiving our diplomas in one hand while shifting our tassels from one side of our caps to the other, we stepped out onto the lawn to receive congratulations from our families.

Aunt Bill said, "We would have given you a watch for graduation, like everyone else. But you already have one. So we're giving you this instead." She handed me a card and a gift-wrapped box. "You're always taking pictures with that old Brownie camera of yours."

My graduation present was a modern Kodak camera, with a flash attachment and flashbulbs. But I guess no one thought to put film in it because there are no pictures of the occasion.

"Your mother would've been proud," said Aunt Bill. My chin quivered. Wordlessly, I nodded.

I handed Pat the camera in its box. "Take this home for me. I have to go turn in my cap and gown. I'll meet you all back at home."

And to John, "I'll be right back."

Wearing my diamond-shaped cap, its tassel swaying as I walked, and a powder blue organdy dress, I carried my gown over one arm as I entered the building.

Upon my return 15-20 minutes later, John's face was concrete, his demeanor icy. His eyes burned with hurt and rage. In my brief absence, something -- everything -- had changed.

Mystified, I asked, "What's wrong?"

"Go get in the car," he said through tight lips, starting off across the lawn like a locomotive with a full head of steam. I ran after him, wobbling in high heels.

"What's the matter?" I called after him.

After placing me in the passenger seat he slammed the door, then went around to the driver's side and got in, slamming his door, too.

He put the key in the ignition but didn't turn it. He just sat there fuming.

"What's got into you?" I pleaded.

Finally, after a few deep breaths, his lips tight, he demanded, looking straight ahead through the windshield, "Did you enjoy kissing all those boys? Are they good kissers?"

"What are you talking about?!"

"Bill (a fraternity brother) saw you. He said you kissed every boy in sight!"

Dumfounded, my stomach clutching, my body trembling, I shook my head, wordlessly protesting my innocence. Nothing could be further from the truth. I didn't know any boys to *talk* to, much less *kiss*. Incapable of speaking, I emphatically mouthed, "No."

He didn't believe me. He had an eye witness.

I was in shock. The one person I thought I could count on -- needed to count on -- had turned on me. My trembling body felt like it belonged to someone else. My brain shut down. The rest is a blur.

Days later, Bill admitted it might not have been me he saw that night. See, there was this girl in a blue dress, wearing a graduation cap, who kissed some boys.

No matter. The damage was done. I was guilty until proved innocent.

. . . .

That should have been a red flag, but what did I know? *Maybe this is how relationships work. It's how Tracey would have acted.*

I'd had neither training nor role models to teach me to demand respect from a man.

In 1953, a girl was considered lucky to have a boyfriend.

John was a "BMOC" -- Big Man On Campus. He'd just been named Editor of Fresno State College's student newspaper, *The Collegian*, for the coming year – his senior year. Obviously, he was going places.

I was so alone. I needed to feel as if I belonged to someone. (Pat and I weren't close. Tracey and I were antagonists. I rarely saw Aunt Bill. So I was on my own.)

I needed to believe someone loved me, even if that love was expressed through jealousy, mistrust and anger.

What if no one else ever wants me? I better hang onto him.

At 17, I had a lot to learn. And I took a very long time to learn it.

We got past that incident and our courtship continued.

In My Boyfriend's 1941 Ford

When I hear a particular Nat King Cole recording I'm transported back in time. Once again, I'm in the passenger seat of John's white 1941 Ford coupe: we were parked at the curb in front of my house after a City League softball game in which he played shortstop. On the way home, we, along with the rest of the team and its cheering section, went to Stan's Drive-In for a Coke.

I was reluctant to say good night and go inside. He was in no great hurry either.

The radio was on. It was a hot summer night so the windows were open. The scent of the sycamores arching over the street mingled with his Old Spice and shortstop sweat. I was in heaven. I was 17 and he was 20; we were each other's first love.

At his urging, I scootched across the seat 'til we touched. His arm came 'round my shoulders as he took off his horn-rimmed glasses and placed them on the dashboard. I removed my retainer, wrapped it in a hankie and set it in my lap. These preparations complete, we turned to each other. As our lips touched I tingled all over.

From the radio the satiny voice of Nat King Cole crooned,

> They tried to tell us we're too young,
> Too young to really be in love,
> They say that love's a word
> A word we've only heard
> But can't begin to know the meaning of
> And yet we're not too young to know

This love will last though years may go
And then, someday they may recall,
We were not too young at all.[6]

Although we'd gone steady for almost a year we were still completely innocent, due in part to the caring efforts of my across-the-street neighbor, "Mrs. H." Mostly, though, it was the times. Most girls remained chaste until marriage. And now that Mom was dead I was fully responsible. I was stricter with myself than she ever was.

However, since her death a little more than a year earlier, Mrs H. had appointed herself a sort-of guardian. Whenever we pulled up out front after a date, whatever the hour, she gave us about ten minutes. Then all her outside lights came on and out she stepped onto her front porch. Watering can in hand, she tended to her geraniums. If she ran out of water before we were ready to call it a night, she nonchalantly picked off dead leaves and blossoms until we were.)

That summer night she wore only a nightgown, a long chartreuse nylon jersey gown. The porch light behind her displayed her ample silhouette through the filmy nightie. As she bent over the flower boxes, her plentiful bosom all but overflowed.

By this time John and I were laughing so hard our romantic mood was broken. Illuminating his gold Bulova watch with his Zippo lighter, he sighed, shrugged, put on his glasses, and came around to open my door. I took his hand and stepped out. There was a crunch underfoot.

I'd stepped on my retainer. Again. "Damn!"

At my front door he kissed me good night. Mrs. H. had turned away, but her presence was still felt. I stepped inside the dimly lit living room and closed the door behind me, singing softly, "And then, someday, they may recall, we were not too young at all."

---

6. Composers: Sylvia Dee and Sidney Lippman

Part II

Married

The Wedding of my Dreams

Sometimes our dreams betray us. Insisting on having "the wedding of my dreams" turned out to be a bad idea.

Like most little girls I dreamed of the far-off day when I would glide princess-like up the aisle to the strains of Lohengrin's wedding march ("Here Comes the Bride") in a beautiful white gown and veil, on my father's arm, to be delivered to my dashing Prince Charming, with my mother in the front pew, surrounded by friends and family. Our Danish Lutheran minister would officiate. Only the groom remained a mystery. The rest of the roles were cast.

As a little girl I was angry at my mother for not having had a proper wedding. She had no fancy white wedding dress and all that should accompany it: veil, flowers, a church, a fancy tiered cake, bridesmaids, portraits.

I didn't understand things like the Great Depression. All I knew was that she should have had all those things …… for me. How could she not have given any thought to *me* when planning her wedding? Didn't she imagine that someday she'd have a sentimental daughter who would want to wear her mother's wedding dress? And didn't she care that I would suffer from not having her wedding portrait to swoon over?

I vowed not to be so cruel to my daughters. *I* would have a beautiful wedding gown that they would want to wear for their weddings. *I'd* marry in a pretty little church, and have glamorous wedding portraits for them to sigh over.

So the planning for my wedding began long before I met my groom.

In Mama's cedar chest was an embroidered organdy blouse Grandma

Petersen had worn as a girl in Denmark in the 1870's. It was form-fitting, had a high collar, long sleeves and lots of little buttons. I loved to play dress-up in it. Grandma was tiny, and since I grew up to be little too, it fit me. From time to time, even as a teenager, I'd put it on. I liked the way it felt and the way I looked in it.

Another influence was Scarlett O'Hara. When introduced to *Gone With the Wind,* I decided I was born 100 years too late. I loved the long full skirts the ladies wore, and of course, their ante-bellum plantation lifestyle. I envisioned myself in a Scarlett-like hoop skirt.

So it was decided. On my far-off wedding day I'd be a hybrid of Scarlett O'Hara and my Danish grandma.

In the summer of '54, Prince Charming would graduate from Fresno State College on June 5, and a week later we'd be married. His mother nearly had a stroke, nor was his father thrilled. We were too young. I was not Spanish. I was not Catholic. And, as his mother declared in outrage, "She has no *family!*"

The biggest bugaboo was that I wasn't Catholic. If we didn't marry in the Holy Roman Catholic Church we and our children would burn in hell. John's parents would disown, and our children would have no grandparents. He had no doubt they would make good on their threat and couldn't let that happen. I didn't realize then that his mother would always win, but found it out over the next many years.

My biggest problem was that if we did marry in the Catholic Church I'd have to promise to raise our children Catholic. I couldn't do that.

John pleaded, "Just say it. For my mother …… for me. We'll raise the kids however you want."

"It would be a lie. I can't start our marriage with a lie."

We were deadlocked.

No one in John's family was a practicing Catholic. Aside from eating fish on Fridays there was little evidence of Catholicism. They went to mass once a year, if that. Yet John's mother insisted that we marry in St. John's Cathedral – a gloomy stone fortress that gave me the creeps.

This dilemma consumed us for several weeks, his parents unwavering, John cajoling and pressuring, and me digging in my heels and resisting.

I repeated, for the hundredth time, "I can't start our marriage with a lie."

"Just cross your fingers behind your back and say the words. It's between you and God; forget about the priest. Do it for me. Please. You don't have to mean it."

By then I was beaten down. I had no one to back me up. So, finally, I said the damnable words without meaning them. Then, silently, "Between you and me, God, I'll do my best to raise fine moral children -- without the Catholic Church." My god would understand.

I refused to marry at St. John's Cathedral, though. John's mother let that slide since she'd won on the larger issue. I chose Our Lady of Victory, a smaller, less oppressive Catholic Church. It wasn't pretty, like my little Lutheran church, but it wasn't creepy old St. John's either.

We started meeting with the priest, whose job, of course, was to convert me. That didn't happen.

My sister and I went to the Bay Area[7] to shop for material for the dresses my attendants and I would wear for the wedding. I got bolts of white embroidered organdy. I planned to make mine, but was overwhelmed with finishing my freshman year at Fresno State, planning the wedding, working part-time at Coopers Department Store, and cooking and keeping house for my stepfather. I even came down with the mumps during this time.

I found a seamstress. She would make it for just $25. She was amazing. She designed it from my crude sketch and Grandma Petersen's blouse, artistically incorporating the material's embroidered pattern into it. She even covered each of the 53 tiny buttons – 37 down the back and 8 on each sleeve – placing a small embroidered flower in its center.

When the date was set, the church reserved, and the invitations ordered, John's stunning 14-year-old cousin, "Maria Elena," who bore a striking resemblance to Elizabeth Taylor, "had to get married". Just the immediate family went to Carmel for her hurry-up wedding in a charming non-denominational chapel. John's mother was so enamored of it that she begged us to get married there, too.

"It's not Catholic," I pointed out.

"If you get married there you don't have to marry in the Catholic Church."

---

7. While there, Kitty took us to the horse races at Tanforan race track in San Bruno, where we ran into Mom's old boyfriend, Dean Livergood. Bitter irony: although 20 years older than she, he was still alive and well while she was in the cold, cold ground.

She actually offered me a way out. Although I considered it briefly, in the end I decided against it. I didn't want people to think I "had to run off and get married," like Maria Elena. Also, it was important to me to be surrounded by my family and friends, and I couldn't ask them to absorb the expense of an out of town wedding.

John and I should have simply eloped, or married in Carmel's charming chapel. But I denied my principles and better judgement in favor of having the wedding of my dreams.

June 12, 1954. The big day arrived.

My cast of characters had changed. Although I wished it could be otherwise, Tracey took the role of father walked me up the aisle. Aunt Bill sat in the Mother of the Bride's place in the front pew, on the left side of the church. Father Kevin Cleary, whom neither bride and groom knew well, officiated.

In the foyer, before I entered the church, someone put a penny in my shoe … for luck. A family tradition. One at a time, my three bridesmaids, Nina, Kathleen, and Frances, did the slow *Step, pause...... Step, pause......* up the aisle, followed by Pat, my Matron of Honor, and then Debbie, the flower girl. When Debbie had nearly completed her slow journey to the front of the church, Tracey stepped into the aisle.

Not yet! It's too soon! Debbie's not there yet.

Ready or not, I was going to make my princess-like entrance.

My right hand on Tracey's arm, I started off on the "right foot" – the one with the penny. I began the *Step, pause...... Step, pause......* in a regal manner, smiling as Britain's Princess Elizabeth did in newsreels.

Tracey had no patience with this *Step, pause...... Step, pause ......* nonsense. He bolted up the aisle. I tugged on his arm to slow him down, but he marched on, hellbent on getting this thing over with as fast as possible, ignoring my repeated yanks and tugs. His long legs made short work of it as we tramped the length of the aisle in record time. We had to pull up short and come to a standstill to avoid running over adorable Debbie who, of course, had everyone's full attention.

So much for my grand entrance.

John's punishment for marrying a non-Catholic was that we weren't allowed anywhere near the altar. The priest came down to our level. The ceremony was the abbreviated version. The processional and recessional music I was accustomed to and insisted upon were disallowed; they weren't Catholic religious music.[8] The soloist sang a Catholic hymn which meant nothing to me. Post-ceremony formal portraits were forbidden – only candid shots during the ceremony.

Adding insult to injury, during my recitation of vows, which included "… to love, honor, and *obey*," the priest inserted, "I will always submit to my husband." I gulped, gasped, and nearly choked on the words. There were no equivalent statements for the groom, not even something like, "I will be kind to my wife."

After all the weeks and months of preparation and all the years of dreaming about it, the wedding was over in a flash. Just as Tracey had sped me up the aisle, the priest rushed through the ceremony, presumably unwilling to spend more time than necessary on someone who refused to convert.

After a brief kiss, John grabbed my left hand and we hurried down the aisle. My right hand – the one with the bouquet – grasped my veil to keep it from sailing off. My old fashioned bouquet of white roses and Esther Reid daisies covered my eyes. Blindly, I lurched in high heels down the aisle and out of the church.

How appropriate – I actually stumbled blindly into marriage. It was all very un-princess-like. Nothing was as I'd imagined it.

My wedding dress was about the only thing on which I had any say at all. Maybe that's why I'm still hanging onto it all these years later – why I still drag it from house to house and state to state as I journey through life.

As it turned out, John and I never had any daughters to sigh over our glamorous wedding photos or wear my wedding finery.

And our three sons couldn't care less.

---

8. Lohengrin's Wedding March is from an opera by Wagner. And the composer of the celebratory wedding recessional, Felix Mendelssohn, was a Jew.

Spam Roast

"Early Salvation Army" is how John described our furnished studio apartment behind a garage. The furniture was a hodge-podge. It was what we could afford. The rent was $50 a month.

John had graduated from college with a major in Journalism and a minor in Sociology, but couldn't get a job in either field. While in college he had gotten deferments from the draft, which was reinstituted during the "Korean Conflict". Now out of college, with no deferment, he was "draft bait." No one would hire him. He continued in his job as printer's devil in Ernie Benck's print shop, where he'd worked part-time through college.

In addition to janitorial work, the job consisted of melting lead in a huge vat in a small windowless brick building behind the print shop, then skimming off the dross and pouring the remaining lead into "pigs" to cool and form into "pig iron" for reuse in the following day's print jobs. It was unbearably hot, filthy, and strenuous, lifting lead weights above his head and throwing them into the vat, keeping the fire beneath it stoked -- just the kind of job he went to college to avoid.

I worked in the accounting office at Cooper's Department Store. Neither of us made much money.

When we got married I'd been the family's cook for several years, ever since Mom got sick. And before that I loved being in the kitchen, cooking with her. I was accustomed to cooking for a family, a group, a gang, not just two, so I had to scale down and I had to be creative. One of the dinners-for-two I came up with was Spam Roast.

SPAM ROAST

Glaze: Mix:
  $^1/_4$ cup syrup from can of sliced peaches
  $^1/_4$ cup brown sugar
  1 teaspoon prepared mustard

Cut Spam into 4 sections, to within $^1/_4$ - $^1/_2''$ of the bottom:
Place in baking dish
Insert canned peach slices in slits
Bake at 350° for $^1/_2$-hour, basting frequently with glaze.

It was the early days of commercially frozen foods, so the menu was completed with a half-package of Bird's Eye frozen peas, green beans, or baby lima beans, baked potatoes, and a fresh garden salad.

Nothing went to waste. For dessert, I'd do something with the remainder of the canned peach slices and syrup -- maybe a small peach upside-down cake.

Before long, John got fed up with being unemployable. So he "volunteered for the draft". That was different from enlisting in that a draftee served a two-year commitment rather than an enlistee's four. He just wanted to get it over with and get on with his life as a journalist, for which he'd prepared.

When he went off to basic training at Fort Ord (Monterey, CA) I moved back "home" where I resumed my cooking duties. Spam Roast was insufficient for more than two people. (My sister had moved back too, and Stan was in the Army in Korea.) I forgot all about Spam Roast and don't know that I ever fixed it again.

Back then, in 1954, we thought it was pretty good. But then we also enjoyed Creamed Tuna on Toast. To say that we weren't sophisticated is putting it mildly.

Note: The above story was written in 1995, 41 years after the fact, when I lived in Colorado. My good friend, Marilyn Sisler (Petaluma, CA) sent me an article from the San Francisco Chronicle featuring my son Alex, titled, "Hawaii's Love for Spam is Handed Down". Alex was Executive Chef at a fancy 5-Star restaurant on Maui. The section mentioning him began, "Putting Spam aside . . . "

As I read the article, our newlywed days and this simple dinner came to mind.

I taught a weekly memoir-writing class at a Colorado Springs senior center. Everyone, including me, was assigned to write something, on any subject, and read it aloud in class.

I wrote up the story of "Spam Roast" and read it at the next class meeting.

The following week, every single student brought his or her own Spam story. All were completely different, their only commonalities being Spam itself and the era in which it was part of everyone's diet.

Who would have thought?

A Hick from the Sticks

Nineteen years old I was, and such a hick from the sticks you wouldn't believe.

New York City's heat blasted me as I stepped outside Grand Central Station that July day in 1955. On virtually my first foray out of the San Joaquin Valley I was en route halfway around the world to Germany. John was stationed in Darmstadt, the capital of Hesse, in the center of the country.

Surrounded by my mismatched luggage, I carried everything I couldn't cram in it: a heavy wool coat and oversized traveling purse draped over one arm; my camera and huge binoculars hung from the other shoulder. With my free hand I hailed a taxicab.

A sunflower-yellow cab with a black-and-white checkerboard stripe stopped before me. The driver sat behind the wheel, looking at me, like, "Ya want dis cab or not? If ya wannit, openna damn door and get in."

I opened the rear door, struggled to get my heavy suitcases and all my stuff in the cab, climbed into the backseat and sat down, closing the door behind me. I gave the name of my hotel and off we drove.

"Where ya from?" he asked. "Yer first trip to New Yawk?" he wondered. "Whadda ya heah fawr?"

Trying not to appear the proverbial hick, although craning my neck to gape at the city's skyscrapers, I answered absently.

Once again, in front of the hotel, he just sat there behind the wheel, making no move to open my door or offer assistance with my bags, all of which was standard procedure back home.

The meter read $1.55. I handed him two one-dollar bills and held out my hand for change. His jaw dropped. Looking him steadfastly in the eye, I jiggled my hand to indicate I expected change.

"I gotta eat, lady."

I kept my hand in the same demanding position.

He dropped a nickel in it. "I got kids at home, ya know."

I just stared him in the eye, holding my open hand in his face. Continuing to plead his case, he deposited one nickel at a time until I finally had the full 45¢, whereupon I declared, self-righteous as all get-out, "A tip is for *extra* service, not for just doing what you're already getting paid to do!"

I was downright proud of myself for not letting this city-slicker cab driver take advantage of me. In a huff I unloaded my belongings onto the sidewalk. He drove away shaking his head.

Two days later, en route to the ms Hollendam for the trans-Atlantic voyage, I returned to Grand Central Station to collect the rest of my baggage: a steamer trunk and a footlocker. The ride to the station was the same as before -- no assistance from this cabbie either.

I asked him to wait while I collected my things from the baggage dock. A Redcap loaded them onto a cart, which he pushed through the station and out to the sidewalk. After he lashed my bulky gear to the rack on the back of the cab, I handed him a generous tip -- a couple of bucks.

He held up his hand like a traffic cop, shook his head, and set me straight. "The standard charge is a buck-fifty *per item*. ... *Plus* a tip."

"Oh!" I flushed hot-flash fuschia. *I have a feeling we're not in Kansas anymore, Toto.*

I gave him the full amount, plus a bit more, and got back in the cab. When we got to the Holland America pier in New Jersey where the Hollendam was moored, I gave this cabbie his full tip and some extra.

Thus did I learn my first lesson in the ways of the world.

Seeheimerstrasse 22

I *must have lived here in another life.*
The ancient village of Jugenheim *a.d. Bergstrasse* felt like home from the very first minute as we drove through it to our new home. In fact, it felt more like home than any other place I've ever been.

It may have been its ancientness -- the cobblestone streets, the shops' stone doorsteps worn concave by centuries of shoppers, the medieval German buildings. But maybe it was more than that. It was all delightfully familiar: the sights, the sounds, the smells -- everything about it.

If I *had* lived there in previous life it must have been a happy one.

John wouldn't say anything about the place he'd rented except, "You're going to like it."

The mansion -- *Seeheimerstrasse 22* -- we arrived at was surrounded by a high stone wall with protective glass shards on top, and a cast iron gate. We walked through the gate and turned the bell-knob on the heavy front door. A woman in her mid-thirties answered. Blond and beautiful, effervescent and ebullient, Frau Annelore Gaetcke wore an apple-green dirndl, the bodice lacing up the front, over a snowy white blouse. She graciously invited us in, vigorously shaking our hands.

Annelore introduced her mother, Frau Olga Lindner, whose grey hair was held in a bun on the back of her head with oversized tortoise-shell hairpins; her father, Herr Dr. Lindner, in a dark suit and tie, his gold-rimmed glasses resting on his nose; and her son, Klaus, a gangly, gawky 15-year-old giant.

Frau Lindner took one look at me, clasped her hands to her bosom, and exclaimed, "Ach, she's young enough to be my granddaughter!" She quickly became *meine Omi* --my German grandma. These lovely people were my family for the next year-and-a-half, my dear friends forever.

Annelore escorted us through our new home, virtually the entire second story of the house. Our bedroom alone was the size of a small cottage. One entire wall was windows, looking over a pear orchard. It was furnished in elegant marble-topped walnut antiques. The linens, trimmed in hand-crocheted lace, were turned back over a green silk damask eiderdown coverlet.

Our living/dining room had a huge carved antique sideboard, a china cabinet with rounded glass and gracefully curving legs, a dining table and chairs, and in the parlor area, two comfortable chairs and a round cocktail table. The rich, dark tones and intricate patterns of an antique Persian carpet added to the *Gemütlichkeit*. The best part, however, was the balcony overlooking the Rhine Valley. We were on a hill and, on a clear day, could see the Rhine River.

My basement kitchen had been the family's summer kitchen in better times, i.e: before the war. It was inconvenient but I could adjust. I shared it with Hannelore E. who could not. She commuted to and from her job in Frankfurt and lived in a tiny garret in the attic. I often "borrowed" her pot holders or utensils, having left mine upstairs, and then would, of course, leave hers upstairs too. She pounded on our door with her the heel of her fist, like the Gestapo, demanding her things.

In Germany in 1955, refrigerators were rare-to-nonexistent. *Seeheimerstr. 22* had none, so I adapted my shopping and food storage habits. There were no supermarkets (i.e: one-stop shops), but rather, one store for eggs, milk and cheese, another for meat, the third a bakery, and there was a greengrocers' for fruits, vegetables, and staples such as flour and sugar. In order to prepare a meal one had to shop at several stores. German *hausfrauen* spent their mornings shopping and gossiping in various stores around the village before going home to cook. I shopped locally for perishables a couple of times a week, which enabled me to get acquainted with some of Jugenheim's shopkeepers and residents.

Hot water was a seasonal thing, i.e., winter only. Heated by the coal-burning furnace *im keller*, water ran through pipes and radiators to heat the house. In summer, my bath water had to be heated on the gas cookstove in the cellar, carried up two flights, and poured into the bathtub, where it cooled on contact, before I could run down and back with the next pot full. (John showered at the base before reporting for duty.)

The house at *Seeheimerstr. 22* was built in 1870, before indoor plumbing. By 1955 an upstairs bedroom had been converted into a bathroom, with the biggest bathtub I'd ever laid eyes on or laid down in. That's where I did laundry, too, including thick towels and huge sheets. It was a real chore, but I had no choice. There were no laundromats, and laundries were not in our budget.

Downstairs, just inside the front door, a broom closet had been turned into a tiny *toilette*. This mini-bathroom was very well-placed. Many times I made it from the commissary in Darmstadt on the *Strassenbahn* (streetcar), walked a mile or so up the hill carrying a couple of weeks' groceries, struggled with the antique skeleton key, and made it to that tiny *toilette* in the nick of time.

The house was set on nearly an acre. Mature pear trees were surrounded by gooseberry and red currant bushes. It was untended and filled with nettles. In the yard ran a Banty rooster and his harem. He was a tyrant who flew at me with beak and claws every time I ventured outside my cellar kitchen. I kept a rake beside the door to fend him off, but never figured out how to hang clothes on the line while clutching the rake to defend myself.

Der Keller was a treasure trove, including, among other things, an antique wicker pram, which Frau Lindner *u.* Frau Gaetcke used for hauling things to and from *dem Strassenbahnhof*; a washboard I was delighted to find and very grateful for (it was a wash day godsend), a toboggan on which we careened downhill a snowy day or two; and *Omi's* bicycle on which she, at 70, went shopping in the village. In good weather I occasionally borrowed it and went off on my own excursions.

John was absolutely right. I loved it. This was my place.

A couple of weeks before I was to arrive he placed an ad in the newspaper -- *Darmstadter Echo*. All the other responses were for downtown apartments renting exclusively to Americans. He knew I'd hate that. If I was going to live in a foreign country I'd want to live in a foreign country, not a "Little America". So when this response came in, a suite of rooms in a charming country home, he grabbed it. I'm so grateful.

Our American friends pestered us, "When are you going to move into town?" to which we answered, "What for? We love it here." We were the only Americans living in Jugenheim, which suited me just fine. I was delirious.

John's experience was less benign. He had to wear his uniform -- that of the conquering army. He got what he interpreted as hostile glares from the other passengers on *der Strassenbahn*. As the only American soldier on the streetcar for most of the 15-20-mile trip, he bore the full brunt of the antagonism of the conquered people toward their conquerer. At least that's what he felt.

It was not a problem for me. I'm a very different person, more outgoing and secure. Also, I could "pass". Unlike John, I'm northern European, with fair skin, green eyes, and light brown hair. And I didn't have to wear an American army uniform.

Whenever John and I went out sightseeing, sometimes with his army buddies, sometimes just the two of us, at some point we got thirsty or hungry and stopped at a *Biergarten* or *Gasthaus*. Invariably, the waitress came to me for the order, assuming I was *das kleine Fraulein* out for a good time with *American Soldaten*.

As I went through the days, weeks and months, I kept my ears open and picked up the German I needed to shop in the village and ride to and fro on the *Strassenbahn*. But I heard one phrase over and over. *"Ich weiss es nicht."* Since I heard it so often I knew it must be important. I started asking friends and strangers alike, "What does it mean: *'Ich weiss es nicht.'?*"

They shrugged. "I don't know."

Over and over I asked, and over and over I got the same answer.

That's strange, I thought. *Everybody says it but nobody knows what it means.* Finally, in a flash of belated brilliance, it dawned on me. *"Ich weiss es nicht"* means "I don't know".

And so it is with languages and cultures. Sometimes the most obvious is the most obscure.

Thanksgiving in Jugenheim

My penchant for thinking I can *do any*thing, and jumping right in and doing it, has gotten me in trouble more than once in this life. Such an occasion was Thanksgiving, 1955. It was just three weeks after my 20th birthday, and I had never cooked a Thanksgiving dinner. In fact, no one in my family had. Parts of it, yes, but the whole thing? *Nein.*

In my family, holiday dinners were a cooperative effort, with everyone pitching in. There was a reason for that, as I was about to learn. But that year in far-off Germany there was only me.

Accustomed to a large extended family on holidays, I insisted that John invite a few of the guys from his company. I wanted people to share our dinner with us. I wanted John's buddies to have a home-cooked Thanksgiving dinner rather than an Army dinner in the mess hall. And, of course, I planned a soup-to-nuts dinner. I don't do things by half-measures.

I knew how to cook. What could be so difficult?

I borrowed a few things from Frau Lindner's kitchen, such as a food grinder for the cranberry/orange relish, and a roasting pan for the turkey. I told her and Annelore about our Thanksgiving holiday and its typical menu, including pumpkin pie. Pumpkin pie? They'd never heard of such a thing. They knew of pumpkin soup, but pumpkin pie?! *Nein.*

"What's in it?" they asked, incredulous.

"Pumpkin, of course, and eggs and cream, sugar, cinnamon, nutmeg, cloves."

They shook their heads. "I can't imagine it."

Then I said, "Pumpkin soup?! I've never heard of such a thing. What do you put in it?"

"Onions sauteed in butter, chicken stock … thyme … sometimes curry powder or nutmeg, salt and pepper, and thick cream. *Sehr gut.*"

That was beyond my imagining.

I promised them a piece of pie in exchange for a sample of their next pumpkin soup. We often shared *kleine bisschen* (little bits) of food with each other.

One day, Frau Lindner, who spoke no English, knocked on my door, asking if I liked *Spargel mit Schinken*. Not understanding, I got my English-German/German-English dictionary. She flipped through its pages until she found it. Reading the English translation of *Spargel*, she smiled and said, "Ahh! Ahs-per-*AHH*-goos." When I assured her that I liked ahs-per-*AHH*-goos, she brought a plate of lovely white asparagus spears wrapped in thin slices of ham for me to try. "*Ein klein bisschen*," she said.

I'd never seen or tasted white asparagus before. Never even heard of it, in fact. My palate was getting an international education.

I got started early Thanksgiving morning to bake the pie (limited by my one pie plate), make the stuffing and get the turkey stuffed and in the oven. About pie baking in Jugenheim: I had no pastry flaker, no rolling pin, and no breadboard. I cut the shortening into the flour with a fork. My "rolling pin" was a wine bottle, and I rolled out the crust on my dining table. To make matters worse, I'd forgotten about my mom's fail-safe pie crust recipe and used the not-fail-safe one from my cookbook, all of which made the task enormously frustrating.

Every time I made a pie I told John, "You damn-well better enjoy this pie, 'cause it's the last one you're ever going to get!" And I meant it. But then I'd get hungry for pie and do it all over again. Whoever made up the saying, "easy as pie" didn't have a clue.

That Thanksgiving day, I must have climbed up and down all those stairs a hundred times. The food preparation had to be done upstairs since my cellar kitchen had no table and practically no counter space, and the cooking had to be done downstairs where the stove was. So, up and down, down and up, all day long.

I made the stuffing from scratch -- everything had to be from scratch to be true to my family's tradition -- and stuffed it in the bird. While it was in the oven I went to work on the other parts of the dinner: cheese-stuffed celery stalks, vegetable soup, yams, carrot coins in butter, mashed potatoes; I don't remember what-all. I whipped cream for the pie and set it in our "icebox" (the space between the inner window and the storm window, looking out to the balcony). The stone walls were 12 inches thick, so there was room for a small bowl of whipped cream.

Also, while the turkey was roasting, I set the table as festively as I could, then ran back downstairs to take the bird out of the oven, the stuffing out of the turkey, and make gravy before our guests arrived.

Dinner was served with me running down to my cellar kitchen and back up to the second floor, putting the finishing touches on the next course and hauling it upstairs. Our guests seemed uncomfortable about my running up and down, huffing and puffing, transporting stuff. I'm sure I looked harried and exhausted from trying to get everything on the table hot and beautiful. They joked with John about it, trying to shame him into helping or letting them help, I think. I'm sure I told them, "No, sit still. You're guests."

In John's Spanish culture one's gender determined what one could/should do. Cooking and serving, and all forms of housework were the domain of females. It would have been demeaning for him to do "women's work". He'd be shamed by it.

Wellman, Ole, and Tom were very complimentary about everything. The dinner was a success and I was proud I'd pulled it off. Platters and bowls were practically licked clean, and nary a crumb of pie was left. Frau Lindner and Annelore would have to wait 'til next time.

I was pleased I'd gone to the trouble of making a home-cooked Thanksgiving dinner for John and his army buddies. That is, I *was* pleased until the Armed Services Radio announcer waxed poetic about the fabulous Thanksgiving dinner the Army served in the base mess halls. The men who dined there had everything I'd served, and then some. And it was probably a lot better, having been cooked by *chefs d' cuisine* rather than a kid just three weeks out of her teens.

At the end of the day, after the guys left, I collapsed into a cushioned chair in the living room and proclaimed, "If **anyone** ever tells you that cooking isn't **hard** work, they're **lying**."

I feel sorry for people who don't think they can "do *any*thing" or haven't the confidence to jump right in and do it. There's a whole lot of things I'd never have done if not for that trait -- things I'd be very sorry not to have done, including cooking that crazy Thanksgiving dinner.

But then, there are things I wish I *hadn't* jumped right into too.

Frohe Weinachten

Christmas in Germany. How wonderful! How special! How romantic! Except that John was a lowly Specialist 3rd Class -- that era's Buck Private -- the lowest paid in the Army. There was always too much month left over at the end of the money. Christmas comes at the end of the month and we were flat broke. We agreed to simply ignore Christmas that year, not an easy thing to do, since Germany is the birthplace of Christmas as we know it, and the Germans go all-out. Every *Strasse* and *Platz* was decorated to a fare-thee-well, as was every shop.

But we had no choice -- we had no money for gifts for each other, much less anyone else. Or a tree and ornaments. We wished our families back home a *Merry Christmas,* explaining there would be no gifts from us that year.

The Lindners and the Gaetckes had invited us for dinner on Christmas Day, so that was taken care of. We'd have to come up with some small gifts for them. We did: an embroidered fine linen handkerchief each for Frau Lindner and Annelore Gaetcke, and a long-playing vinyl record of trumpet classics for Klaus, who was learning to play and was crazy for American jazz trumpeters, e.g., Louis Armstrong, Miles Davis, Dizzy Gillespie, Harry James, Al Hirt. They were all on it.

It was the best we could do.

By the time Christmas rolled around we'd bought a car. We'd taken all our worldly assets -- $600 -- out of savings, and made monthly payments for the rest, which added to our state of broke-ness.

The Saturday before Christmas, Frau Lindner asked us to drive her to Heidelberg where she could sell one of her few remaining expendable assets, a

WWI Luger pistol. She directed us through the center of Heidelberg, past the *Platz* in the medieval town's center, which was decorated with lush green boughs hung with huge red ribbons, and enormous candles. It's the most beautiful and Christmassy city I've ever seen, to this day.

It was getting harder and harder for me to deal with the fact that we'd have no Christmas, other than that provided by our landlords. I was really going to miss it. Even in our poorest times we'd always had a gathering of family and friends at our house on Christmas Eve, with homemade cookies and cakes and open-faced sandwiches and drinks. And Christmas carols.

As the holiday got closer the tension in me grew.

Finally, the day before Christmas Eve, I decided I was not going to stand still for no Christmas. I just couldn't. We had to at least have a Christmas tree.

Like a maniac I searched through every pocket in the closet, our dresser drawers, the bottom of my purse, under cushions, and raided our piggy bank for loose change. In the end I had nearly $5 in German coins. I put on my button-less wool coat (I clenched it shut with one hand), my gloves and scarf, and my warmest shoes -- saddle oxfords -- with bobby sox. This California girl had come ill-prepared for a German winter. I headed for the Jugenheim village *Platz* where, according to Annelore, someone was selling Christmas trees -- *Tannenbäume*. There I purchased a perfectly shaped 1-meter (3') tree for 4DM ($1).

I asked them to hold it for me and headed for the *Strassenbahnhof* at the bottom of the hill.

I was on a mission. En route to the Post Exchange on the base to buy lights and ornaments, I got off at the usual stop, hiked up the hill, and entered the PX, only to discover that a single string of lights cost more than I had.

Not yet discouraged, I descended the hill, caught the next streetcar to the *Kaufhaus* department store at *Luisenplatz* in the center of Darmstadt. Maybe I'd do better there.

No Christmas tree lights were to be had at *Kaufhaus*. Germans didn't put lights on their Christmas trees. Instead, they used candles in little tin candle-holders that clipped onto branches. Surely something as exotic at that would cost a lot. And I'd still have no ornaments. Now I *was* discouraged.

That was not the case at all. I was able to get four dozen candles and candle holders -- three dozen more than I needed, it turned out. My thinking was that we'd need as many candles as there were electric lights on our tree back home. Wrong. I got two boxes of ornaments and some tinsel, and still had enough to buy ingredients for Christmas cookies. After shopping for those, I returned to the *Platz* in Jugenheim for *meinen Tannenbaum.*

When John got home I told him what I'd done and asked him to invite some of his Army buddies out for Christmas Eve. The next day I set up the tree and decorated it, sparing him that task. (He hated all activities surrounding the purchase and trimming of the Christmas tree. After the tree was up and decorated he enjoyed it, though.)

Then I set to work making cookies, mixing them upstairs, baking them downstairs. I made a couple of old favorites, then two new ones from my Betty Crocker Cookbook: *Berliner Kranzer* and Russian Tea Cakes, which I still make every year. I produced a couple of platters of open-faced sandwiches. This was more like it.

When our guests arrived -- the same three as for Thanksgiving, plus a couple more, we lit the candles on the tree and passed goodies around. The tree was pronounced beautiful and the refreshments were a hit. The guys seemed to be enjoying themselves. I was getting ready to say, "Okay, it's time for caroling. Let's start with "Deck the Halls," when someone knocked on the door.

Annelore invited us to the illumination of her family's *Tannenbaum.* We blew out the candles on our little tree, gathered up the goodies, and followed her downstairs, through the living room and into the dining room.

On the large Persian carpet stood a dining table that comfortably seated 20-24, an antique sideboard, a magnificent grandfather clock with carved stag heads and curlicues, and an upright piano with two brass candle holders to cast light on the sheet music between them. A grand Christmas tree -- the *piece d'resistance* -- stood before the bay window, nearly touching the 14' ceiling, covered with fanciful antique glass ornaments, tinsel, and unlit white *Weinachtskerzen* -- Christmas candles.

Joining our hosts at the table, we added our refreshments to theirs. Our guests got acquainted with Herr Dr. *und* Frau Lindner, Annelore and her physician husband, Herr Dr. Gaetcke, visiting from Hamburg, and their son Klaus. The always mirthful Hermann Gaetcke kept the gathering's joviality at a high level.

Then it was time for the "illumination ceremony". Each of us took turns lighting a candle on the tree until all were lit. Magic filled the air. Electric lights can't hold a candle to that. (Sorry. Couldn't resist.) We learned that in Germany, the candles on the tree were only burned on Christmas Eve, and it was a ceremony. No one's attention strayed from the beautifully lit tree, so there was little danger of fire.

According to tradition, the tree, fully decorated, was delivered and set up that afternoon by St. Nicholas while the family was at Christmas Eve services at the *Kirche*.

Annelore sat at the piano and played Christmas carols, which we sang in both German and English. My dream come true.

Presents were exchanged. We gave our pitiful gifts -- our G.I. friends seemed embarrassed for us -- and received a fantastic *Bowlem Schüssel* (a ceramic punch bowl), with six medieval Rhine castles in *bas relief* on its circumference, its lid topped with a knight in armor. We were overwhelmed. It is one of my most treasured possessions, and I've often served from it on Christmas Eve. Only on Christmas Eve.

When it was time for our guests to return to the base, we wished each other goodnight. *Gute Nacht.* Merry Christmas! *Frohe Weinachten!*

John and I went back upstairs where we relit the *Weinachtskerzen* on our little tree and reveled in the beauty of the moment. I was awestruck that Christmas had actually happened, and that it had happened so wonderfully . . . so beautifully . . . so perfectly. My heart overflowed.

It was a magical evening. And one of the two best Christmases in my life.

Should've Married Ole

Y ou should've married Ole," John would say, shaking his head. "You're just like him."

Before marrying me, John had never lived with people who didn't seriously overreact to everything (in my opinion), and he didn't know what to make of my un-hysterical reactions. We had a few months together before he left for the Army. And in Germany, before I got there, he'd lived in the barracks for a few months, enabling him to observe his buddy, Ole -- Magne Olson -- and make note of *his* lack of hystericalness.

"You should've married Ole," he often told me.

There were times when I agreed with him.

I'd never been around such excitable people, who acted as if everything were a crisis or catastrophe. And now I was married to one. And I didn't know what to make of that. I was joined in holy matrimony to a man whose first response to almost everything was to yell. And swear. And sometimes punch whatever inanimate object was handy. His nerves were always on edge. Whatever happened, he yelled. And swore. And sometimes punched.

He hadn't acted that way before we were married. Except for a few times, which I forgave and forgot about when he calmed down. I was, after all, a teenager in love.

John was the most honest, moral, and ethical person I've ever known. As Editor of The Collegian -- and later, as a reporter and newspaper editor -- he crusaded for truth, equality and justice. His college friends nicknamed him "Crusader Rabbit" after a cartoon character always on one crusade or another. (By the way, they called me "Sparkle Plenty," after a Dick Tracy comic strip character.) John was a sweet, caring man whose heart was in the right place. That, in large part, is why I fell in love with him.

He'd go out of his way to avoid offending or inconveniencing anyone or calling attention to himself. He was shy and quiet, respectful and deferential ... in the outside world. He saved up all his frustration, anger and need to control for the ones he loved the most -- first me, then me and our children.

John lacked confidence and self-esteem. He almost seemed to feel that he didn't deserve the space he took up on the planet. His parents had made sure of that. He'd been ridiculed and denigrated his whole life, and threatened with abandonment if he wasn't who they wanted him to be. "If you believe (x-y-z) you're no son of ours!" they'd declare. (To their way of thinking, he went to college merely to qualify for a white-collar job, not to learn how to think.) They wanted their son to be perfect, and by ridiculing, denigrating and threatening him, constantly drove home the point that he wasn't.

I'm sure it wasn't their fault. It must have come down through the generations.

To John, life itself meant stress. At that point, being in the Army was stressful. Later on, it was being a newspaper reporter and editor, with the constant pressure of deadlines and split-second decisions. Having children was stressful. Having a wife was stressful. Even being a neighbor was stressful. Just being in the world seemed stressful to John.

Naïvely, I believed I could make him whole. I would build up his self-esteem. I would enable him to feel worthy. I would provide a calm, loving atmosphere in our home. I would make him happy, and then he'd be less uptight and less likely to freak out. (This was long before I ever heard of "codependency".[9])

Ole, a Minnesota Swede in John's outfit, and he became good friends. Like John, Ole was a recent college graduate serving his two-year military obligation. Both liked to read and discuss books, movies, politics, and ideas, and joke around. John had a good sense of humor.

Ole, a humorous, positive person, was happier in the Army than John, to whom the two-year stint was a most unwelcome interruption, a chunk of life stolen from him. Ole griped about Army life – it was customary – but he took it in stride. Instead of resisting and resenting it, he was delighted to be in Europe

---

9. Codependency: a condition that results in a dysfunctional relationship between the codependent and other people. Codependents are addicted to helping others. They need to be needed.

at the Army's expense, steeping himself in its history and culture, enjoying the educational and cultural aspects of its museums and cathedrals, its concert halls and plazas, as well as its *Biergärten* and *Gasthäuser,* of course.

He and I were alike in that way. I absolutely loved being in Europe with all it offered. All John wanted was to be out of the army and back home with his family and familiar surroundings ASAP, getting back to his life.

Ole was a frequent guest in Jugenheim. He became friends with our landlord and landladies, and was invited, along with us, to their parties. He occasionally accompanied us on outings, sometimes with other guys from the company, sometimes just the three of us.

We enjoyed a pleasant friendship. Our second summer in Jugenheim, Ole's sister and her friend, bicycling from Stockholm to southern Italy, stayed with us.

Occasionally, when I made a statement or cracked a joke that demonstrated I had a functioning brain and perhaps a little wisdom, it elicited an expression of approval from Ole. John discounted or dismissed whatever I said or, worse, ridiculed it, making me feel like the lowly high school graduate I was, out of my league in the lofty company of college graduates. Once we were alone, he'd demand, "What'd you say that for?" (This continued throughout our marriage.)

Ole, on the other hand, was complimentary and appreciative. He often told John, sometimes in my presence, "You're a lucky man."

But mostly, what prompted John to say "You should have married Ole" was our moderate, even temperaments and positive outlooks. John never did learn to appreciate the fact that I reacted, even to crises, with calm equanimity. Or that I rarely got mad -- I'm slow to anger and slower to confront. Or that I could find something good in nearly every situation. He often chided me for being a "…goddam Pollyanna".

John didn't *get* me at all. His family's way was the right way; I was abnormal. Something was wrong with me. (I felt the same way about him and his family.)

A case in point: One time, when our youngest child, Alex, was about 15 months old, we were at the kitchen table. Alex sat next to me in his highchair. Now Alex, while not hyperactive, was super-active. Perpetual motion was his *modus operandi.* It still is. He was all over his highchair doing baby acrobatics.

Up and over he went, falling toward the floor. I reached out and grabbed him by an ankle and pulled him onto my lap in a warm mommy hug. No point in upsetting him.

John was up, out of his chair, ready to scoop a fractured infant up off the floor. But when he saw that I had the situation well in hand, he stopped mid-lunge and roared, **"God damn it, Carol! Don't you *ever* get upset over *anything?!*"** (This was after 12 years of marriage. He'd had plenty of time to observe my reactions to all sorts of events, and was still of the opinion that I was abnormal, my actions weird and unnatural.)

I've always felt that "calm, cool and collected" was a better response in most situations than "freaking out". I've always said, "I'm a good person to be with in a crisis." And I am.

But to my husband, I was freakin' unnatural. (And to my way of thinking, he acted like an over-the-top lunatic.)

During the time we were in Germany and Ole was our friend, John had someone to compare me to, someone as unnatural as I. It's possible that when Ole reacted calmly to a situation which sent John over the edge, John would tell him, "Carol should have married you." That idea might have been planted in Ole's mind too.

Whenever John erupted in anger and rage, when his fear turned to fury, when he ridiculed me or put me down, I'd wonder what it might be like to be married to a calm, cool, collected man who appreciated me. And since John so often said, "You should've married Ole," he was the one I wondered about.

When the time came for Ole to be released from the Army, a month or two before John's discharge, he came out to Jugenheim one last time to say goodbye to our landlords, have one last dinner at our table, and bid us farewell. At the end of the evening, we said goodbye, knowing we'd probably never see each another again.

John preceded him down the stairs while I stood in the doorway. At the landing, Ole turned and looked back. Our eyes connected.

I felt mine fill.

Then he was gone.

Our 1956 VW Bug
Biography of a Car

W e needed a car and justified its purchase thusly:

Spec 3 John Purroy Jr. didn't qualify for base housing, so we lived "on the economy" at the end of the *Strassenbahn* line, 15-20 miles from the base. A car would eliminate his daily *Strassenbahn* ordeal.

Winter was approaching. There'd be plenty of snow and ice and chilly weather in northern Europe, a real concern for us California kids who had barely even ever seen snow. Our house was at least a three-quarter-mile walk up a fairly steep hill over cobblestone streets, from the *Strassenbahnhof.* A car would make winter survival a lot easier. (As it turned out, that winter was Germany's worst in over 100 years -- *Ach. Schrecklich!)*

Also, knowing this was probably a once-in-a-lifetime opportunity, we wanted to travel through Europe as much as our meager income and John's limited leave time would allow. A car would better enable us to.

We ordered a brand new top-of-the-line tan 1956 VW "Bug" -- Export Model. It arrived by rail from the north Germany factory in late autumn 1955. We got it right off the railroad car in Darmstadt, direct from the factory, for about $1000 US.

What a great day that was! We were giddy. To celebrate we went out to dinner at *Gasthaus Tannenberg* in Jugenheim. The following weekend we took our first drive into the countryside, where someone took our picture with our brand new VW. (Page 364.)

Germans love flowers. They even have fresh flowers in their cars, in cute little vases attached to the dashboard. John thought it was silly, but I had to have one. Most were attached by nut-and-bolt, which John absolutely vetoed, but I found one that stuck on with a suction cup. I cannot tell you how much pleasure it gave me to have fresh flowers in the car as we buzzed along the *Autobahn* and over cobblestone streets, and later on, through other countries. I wish I still had my little auto vase.

I had sort-of learned to drive before leaving the States, but hadn't gotten my license. Germany had no speed limits, and its accident and death rate was the world's highest, so I didn't fight it too much when John declared I was *not* going to drive in Europe. "Wait 'til we get home," he said.

While having a car made his day-to-day life a lot easier, it didn't change mine much. I still walked or took the *Strassenbahn* wherever I went. Except that every couple of weeks, when I went to the commissary and PX, I could lug the groceries only as far as my good friend Inge Van Dervoort's apartment in base housing and wait for John to pick me up. That was a blessing.

During my 18 months in Germany (John was there 3 months before I arrived), we took three major trips in our little tan bug. Since petrol's very expensive in Europe -- 3-to-4 times what it is in the States -- we filled as many 5-gallon gas cans as we could fit in the car before leaving. When that ran out we'd have to pay European prices. (On the base, gas was 15¢ a gallon.)

Our first trip, through Switzerland and Italy to Rome, via Pisa, Florence, Milan and Venice, was in March and April, 1956. We would arrive in Rome a few days before Easter. Unworldly as we were, it hadn't dawned on us that it might present a problem. We had not made reservations.

On the highway, maybe 60 miles outside of Rome, we were stopped by a man in uniform. He held out a pole with a *D'Arresto* (Stop) flag in front of our car. Assuming he was the *Policia,* we stopped. It turned out he was a hitchhiker -- an Italian soldier "thumbing" a ride home to Rome for Easter. He squeezed in with our gas cans and sleeping bags, and off we went. We spoke no Italian and he spoke no English, but John spoke Spanish, which is first cousin to Italian, and I knew some German, so we three spoke "hodge-podge" and more-or-less made ourselves understood.

He told us that during Easter week there was no chance of finding a place to stay within a seventy-five-mile radius of Rome. Oh. We envisioned sleeping in the car or the park.

Once in Rome, however, our grateful hitchhiker made some phone calls and arranged for us to stay in a spare room in the home of a friend. We were not allowed to bathe there, though, so our hitchhiker told us about the public baths at the train station. That's where we bathed during our Roman Holiday. That was just one of the differences between us and the team of Gregory Peck and Audrey Hepburn.

In the neighborhood of our makeshift hotel we parked on the street. As soon as we got out of the car, street urchins appeared, offering to guard it in our absence -- for a fee -- insisting it was necessary. Certain that if we didn't hire them they would slash our tires or bash our windows themselves, we hired one of them.

Driving in Rome was a real challenge. Round-abouts were everywhere, with cars and motorbikes zipping 'round the three- or four-lane streets, honking and threatening. John, timid soul that he was, was greatly intimidated. The more he hesitated, the more he frustrated the other drivers, so the more they honked and gestured in a threatening manner.

And then there was the problem of which street to get off at with cars whizzing by at the speed of light. Frightening! He did a lot of yelling and swearing at the other drivers. Being Italian, they were all honking, yelling, swearing and gesturing at each other. So his yells and curses landed on my ears alone.

Rome was like a movie set. Handsome young guys sang operatic arias and ballads on street corners. Bright flowers enlivened ancient ruins. Statues and fountains and Roman antiquities welcomed us and beckoned us to return.

Then came our trip back to Jugenheim. A blizzard had just passed through Switzerland. The roads were icy, the mountain passes virtually impassable. For starters, we had to get up over a very steep Alp in the Dolomites. Several cars lined up ahead of us: a Mercedes or two, a Buick, an Oldsmobile, a BMW. One by one they started out and made valiant efforts, but backed down the mountain in defeat. We doubted that our Bug, with its sewing machine engine, would make it, but had to try. It could do no worse than those big cars. We started up the mountain and, *putt putt putt putt putt putt,* up and over we went. Our little Beetle was okay, after all.

Our next trip, in July of 1956, was through France to Spain, where we visited John's aunts, uncles and cousins. Our first major stop was the fishing village of Bermeo, on the Atlantic coast south of San Sebastian, his mother's ancestral home. Spain was a poor country and in Bermeo everyone's fortunes were tied up in fishing boats. It was a town of empty streets -- empty of cars. Several of his relatives -- adults, and even old people -- had never even sat in an automobile. So I stayed behind while John took everyone for rides. He crammed in as many as would fit in each load, and off they went to the neighboring town of Guernica. You'd have thought they were at Disneyland, they were so excited.

Then, after visiting Bilbao and Madrid, it was on to Pamplona, now thought of as "Hemmingway country," for *Fiesta de San Fermín* and the running of the bulls. Pamplona is the capitol of Navarra, where John's father was born and grew up. We spent an afternoon at the bullfights. Once was enough for me, but John and Tio Carmelo went back every afternoon. It was interesting being in a place where there were other Purroys. In California we were the only ones. In Pamplona, "Purroy" was on office buildings, shops, and cafés. One day we drove up to the family home in the village of Navasques, where we picnicked in the rolling green hills with Tio Carmelo, Tia Yolanda and their five kids, John's first cousins. What lovely, kind people they were. They didn't even snicker when I answered their *"Gracias"* with *"Granada"*.

Our third trip, in late September, was through northern Germany to Denmark, Holland, Belgium, England and Luxembourg. We visited the town where Grandma Elsa Petersen grew up -- Haderslev, Denmark -- and met distant cousins, including my penpal, Anne-Karin Henning. We drove through Odense and saw Hans Christian Andersen's home, and, in Copenhagen, the Little Mermaid. My main discovery was that the Danes as a people are so marvelously jovial, and love to laugh, joke and tease.

Coming south, we took the ferry from Calais to Dover, with the car down below in the hold. And, in England, we had our first experience of driving on the left side of the road. Far more terrifying than the round-abouts of Rome!

When it was time to return to the States we had the option of flying from the east coast to California, with our car going by slow boat through the Panama Canal, or picking it up in New Jersey and driving across country. Since, before going to Europe, neither of us had ever been outside California, we decided to drive across the USA. After Thanksgiving in New York City, we headed west. It being winter, Route 66 was our choice. Another grand adventure.

The following spring, the VW Bug took me to St. Agnes Hospital for the birth of our first child. And we brought him, Steven Ernest, home in it. We soon moved to Turlock, a couple of hours away, so we made frequent trips to Fresno to show him off.

We had two more babies, both born in Santa Rosa, CA. Before Martin's birth, I was driven to the hospital in my obstetrician's car -- and a wild ride it was, running red lights, screeching around corners, *et cetera*. But that's another story. Martin did, however, come home from the hospital in the VW.

When Alex was about to make his grand entrance, we drove to Memorial Hospital around 11 pm. Since our medical insurance didn't cover Maternity, we sat at the curb in the VW until 12:01 a.m. to avoid paying for another day. He arrived at 2 am. One-and-a-half days later, the VW Bug carried him home to Franquette Avenue.

We continued making trips to Fresno in the Bug. Packing it was a challenge. When we unloaded at the other end, everyone's eyes popped. It was reminiscent of the circus car with a jaw-dropping number of clowns piling out of it.

There were the five of us, of course -- John and me and the three boys, and our clothes. Then there was all the baby and kid paraphernalia. We took a highchair, stroller, diaper pail, usually the crib mattress (which fit snugly in the back seat and made a play area for the kids), plus toys, books, clothes, snacks and drinks, and Schatze, our black and tan dachshund. One time, Schatze's four puppies, almost ready for new owners, went along. We had no external luggage rack, so all this was inside the car.

Before Martin was born, I declared it was time I learned to drive and got my license. John was adamantly opposed to it. He was afraid that if I had a driver's license and access to a car, I'd be off and running. And he knew that if I became a driver, I'd kill myself and the children.

I wanted to be able to go to the grocery store and take my time shopping. As it was, with him driving me to the store, he'd wait outside in the car, tapping the steering wheel impatiently, checking his watch every few seconds, wondering what was taking me so long. Aware of this, I tore through the store like a tornado. And I was tired of it.

I wanted to be able to take the kids to the park once in awhile, Story-time at the library, or over to a girlfriend's.

It was a fight. Each of us was determined. It was the first time in our marriage that I didn't cave -- the first time I stood my ground. In the end, he taught me to drive. I got my license -- *and* had the car one day a week.

Mercifully, I don't remember the learning-to-drive process. (Must've blocked it.) But I do remember the day I went for my licensing test. John drove me down to the DMV and kept little Stevie while I took the driving test. Steve was not quite two, and we were into toilet-training, hoping to get it done before the new baby arrived. As the examiner and I walked toward the car, I remembered that Steve's back-up training pants were in my purse.

"Oh!" I said, turning back toward John. "Here," I handed them to him, explaining, "in case of an accident."

The examiner gasped, his eyes bulged. "You're *expecting* to have an *accident?!*" he exclaimed, his voice ratcheting up an octave.

I explained that *I* didn't expect to have an accident, but my toddler might. John held up the training pants for visual reinforcement.

"Oh," the DMV man heaved a sigh of relief.

Then we started off in the Bug for my test. I passed.

Not more than a week or two later, I did have an accident. I was on the way to the store. John was home after work, so Steve was with him. I drove down Sebastapol Road toward town. A train was going by, so a string of automobiles was stopped ahead of me. I pulled up and stopped, too. In my rearview mirror I saw a car coming up behind, and its driver wasn't paying attention. He was not going fast, but it was obvious he wasn't going to stop. I stepped on the brakes to keep from bashing into the car in front of me.

<u>*Blam!*</u> He plowed into my VW's cute little rear end.

We both pulled over to the curb and got out. When my very pregnant self emerged from the VW, the expression on the other driver's face was one of pure terror.

"Oh! Are you all right? Oh, my god! Here, sit down! Are you okay?" He was shaking. "It's my fault. I wasn't looking. Oh, I'm so sorry! Here's my insurance information." He offered it in his quivering hand. "Oh my god. Please sit down." The poor man was in way worse shape than I was.

After assuring him that I was unhurt and I was not going to give birth as we spoke, we exchanged names, phone numbers and policy information. I got into my crippled VW Bug and limped back home.

Not enough time had elapsed for me to get to the store and back.

"Forget something?" John asked.

"No," I said, still shaken. "I had an accident."

"I knew it!" he exploded. "I knew this is what would happen if I let you get your license!"

I was so stunned I couldn't breathe. I felt faint. I had to sit down. I'd been foolish enough to expect something like, "Are you all right?" or maybe a comforting hug. His instantaneous, automatic assumption that I was at fault, and his lack of concern for me and our unborn baby were almost more than I could bear.

That may have been the beginning of the end.

We had our 1956 VW Bug for another 6 or 7 years -- a total of 10. It got decrepit. Although Volkswagens -- "the people's car" -- were designed so people could do their own repairs and maintenance, and many VW owners did, John was not mechanical. When it came to wrenches and pliers, he was clueless. As was I. Our beloved Bug went into decline.

And with three kids we needed a bigger car. We traded it in on a white 1966 Dodge Dart station wagon.

When the time came to say goodbye to the VW Bug, I shed a few tears. I wished we could have kept it -- and had the station wagon, too. But we were a long way from being a two-car family. We had to be practical. Our one car had to be the station wagon.

I wish I still had that little VW Bug. Just thinking of it makes me smile.

A Ship of Fools

It was late November, not the best time to cross the North Atlantic. John and I had traveled by train from Darmstadt to Bremerhaven, then transferred onto an army ship. *An **army** ship?*

It was obvious this was not a Navy ship or an ocean liner since it was anything but "ship shape". It was butt-ugly, it was dirty, and it was slow.

Since John was an enlisted man, we were separated during the long voyage home. He bunked with hundreds of other enlisted men down in the ship's hold while I shared a "stateroom" with other enlisted men's dependents. It had two sets of metal Army bunk beds under which we stored our suitcases. No closets or lockers, no dressers. My cabin mates were two women and a little boy, all of whom had been stationed in France.

This mid-winter crossing of the North Atlantic from Bremerhaven to New Jersey was everything you might imagine. During storms, icy winds blew with hurricane force, huge waves crashed over the ship, sending it rocking. The hatches were battened and the decks were off-limits to keep us from washing overboard. Even when there was no storm, the sea was rough, pitching and tossing us like a toy in a rambunctious child's bathtub. Everyone, as a matter of course, carried waxed-paper-lined barf bags everywhere they went, and after the first day or so, used them in polite company without embarrassment.

Walking was a real challenge, with the ship heaving this way, that way, and every other way. We staggered like drunken sailors, bumping into everything, including each other, trying to remain upright while moving forward.

Because John was "married and traveling with spouse", he was allowed to come up to the common room for part of the day. Other enlisted men who were single or traveling sans spouse had to stay down in the hot, airless hold the entire voyage. And, according to John's description, it was putrid.

Everyone down there was seasick all the time. A garbage can stood in the center of the room, with guys shoving each other out of the way so they could throw up in it. According to John, it sounded like a room full of gigantic frogs, all making frog noises as they puked up their guts.

I was four months pregnant and expected to be sick throughout the crossing, due to both morning sickness and seasickness. I'd always gotten car sick as a kid. But I wasn't. The fourth or fifth day out I stopped carrying a barf bag.

I was one of the few who could eat during this rough voyage. Mostly, plates went back to the galley full or nearly full. Some folks didn't make it to the dining room at all. John was not eating since the below deck mess hall was so unappetizing, so I'd stuff fresh oranges and pastries into my oversized traveling purse for him. We weren't supposed to but nobody stopped me.

Even in the best of circumstances, an ocean voyage can be boring, and this was not the best of circumstances. A recreation room with board games and a small library offered a few diversions to occupy us during those long days and evenings.

A couple of times during the thirteen-day voyage there was a show, sort of an amateur night, MC'd by one of the officers. And once or twice, a movie was shown. We were easily entertained.

One day, another ship passed us, causing great excitement. Everyone who could get out on deck did. We waved and hollered to the passengers of the other vessel who waved and hollered back, while the ships whistled and tooted at one another. The only problem was that the ship passing us was going the same direction we were. It just glided past as if we were standing still. It would probably cross the sea in half the time we would!

It was white and pretty like a passenger ship is s'posed to be, with colorfully striped smokestacks. Ours was olive drab and ugly. Obviously, there were a few differences between an army boat and a real ship.

We left Germany just after the Hungarian uprising and were concerned we'd be held up by it: our government *had* promised to help Hungary's "freedom fighters" if they would revolt against the communists. All the men aboard this vessel had been poised to go to Hungary to fight if the US government had kept its promise. But it hadn't. So we were going home, fully expecting the ship to turn around and go back should the powers-that-be change their minds.

Cut off from the world, we were hungry for news: It was November 1956.

Just before we sailed, Dwight Eisenhower and Richard Nixon were re-elected, which probably meant *status quo,* but you never know. The guys wanted news of football games. Elvis Presley was the hotter than hot; any news of him was titillating. Movie star Grace Kelly had recently married Prince Rainier of Monaco; we gals were eager for news of this fairytale couple.

A few days out there was a "news bulletin" — news more startling than anything we'd imagined. Elvis Presley had died. Word of it spread with the speed of light, sending shock waves through the ship. It was alarming, in part, because he was one of us, our contemporary. Elvis and I, and probably half the people on that boat, were just 21 years old. He had risen like a meteor. We all lived vicariously through his rapid rise to fame and wealth.

No details were offered, so there was a great deal of speculation as to the how, why, when and where of it, creating a diversion. The ship buzzed with it.

We rolled on, one storm after another, one Parchesi game after another, one shivering walk around the deck (weather permitting) after another, one boring day after another. Interspersed with all this were our reminiscences of Elvis, including his songs: "Heartbreak Hotel", "You Ain't Nuthin' But A Hound Dog", "Love Me Tender Love Me Sweet", and "Don't You Step On My Blue Suede Shoes". A lot of head-shaking accompanied any discussion of him. We couldn't believe it.

Eventually, my cockiness regarding barf bags caught up with me. I was in the Rec Room one day, in the midst of a group of people, when all of a sudden, without warning, I erupted like Mt. Vesuvius. By that time, everyone was blasé about barfing and seeing others barf, but this was too much. Now this huge room was full of gigantic frogs -- heaving, green and miserable -- puking up their guts.

From then on I carried my barf bag like everyone else. I never needed it again, but kept it handy just in case.

Finally, the long voyage neared its end. We hauled our bags out on deck. A tugboat escorted us into the New York harbor where the Statue of Liberty welcomed us home. By that time, we were celebrating about getting off that damn boat as much as about getting back to "the land of round doorknobs" -- the good old USA.

We were soon to rejoin the world and learn what had happened since we had, for all intents and purposes, left it two weeks earlier. Now, whoever had circulated the story of Elvis' untimely death saw fit to reveal the rest of the story.

"Elvis had a heart attack and died …………when his hound dog shit on his blue suede shoes!"

Oh no! We'd been duped. This was indeed a ship of fools. But we also had a good laugh out of it.

……………………………………………………

Fast forward. August 16, 1977: Elvis and I were 42, twice the age we'd been when his death was prematurely reported, but still too young to die. This time it was for real, though. Elvis Presley was dead. Really. This news bulletin was not by word of mouth. It came over radio and TV.

This time shock waves went around the world.

When I heard the news my first thought was: *Yeah, his hound dog shit on his blue suede shoes!*

And I'm willing to bet that everyone else who was on that ship had the same reaction.

My Happiest Time

When asked, "What was the happiest time of your life?" I didn't have to think about it. Without a second's hesitation, I answered, "When my children were small."

My friend, a professional psychic, nodded. "When I asked that question I 'saw' you hanging clothes on the line."

I said, "Yes, that's it. I love hanging clothes on the line -- the feeling of the air on my skin as I shake out a piece of laundry with a sharp snap and hang it just-so, next to another piece that's similar in shape. I feel good when I step back to look at the neat clothesline, my laundry fluttering in the breeze. The era when I did that routinely *was* when my kids were little."

I was told more than once that I was the only stay-at-home mom who really enjoyed her kids and wasn't always wishing she was somewhere else, doing something else.

I was very aware that I had the world's most important job -- nurturing, teaching, and raising the next generation. The future was in my hands. To me, it was the most rewarding and fulfilling job. I'd always adored babies and little children and was thrilled to have my own.

As a kid, whenever a baby was anywhere near, I simply took over. Their mothers were happy to let me. I was trustworthy, and it gave them a break. I did a lot of babysitting, starting at age-9, and always had more jobs than I had time for.

So when my first baby, Steven Ernest, was born (May 8, 1957; 6 pounds 14^1/$_2$ ounces), I was delirious. I finally felt I was living my purpose. And I could not believe how much I loved that little bitty guy. He was the most gorgeous thing I'd ever seen, and the smartest, and the sweetest. And he was the best baby in the world. He started sleeping through the night at two weeks. He had lots of red hair and enormous blue eyes that lit up with delight and recognition from his very first day of life, astonishing everyone. He did everything way ahead of schedule: walked *and ran* at 9 months, and by his first birthday had a small but clear vocabulary.

John's (Catholic) mother warned, "Don't have a second baby. The next one couldn't possibly be as smart as this one. It would suffer by comparison."

We didn't listen and 23 months later Martin John was born. (April 8, 1959; 7 pounds 7 ounces). He proved her wrong. He was every bit as smart, and gorgeous, and sweet. He started sleeping through the night even earlier -- at one week. He had light brown hair and huge blue eyes with long dark lashes. And he never cried. He was the happiest baby and little boy anyone ever saw. He, too, did everything earlier than most babies. Once again, I was flabbergasted by the love flowing through me when I held him, fed him, touched his satiny skin or smelled that sweet baby smell.

I simply loved looking at my little boys, touching them, stroking them, hugging and kissing them .... and playing with them.

As Steven grew into a little boy he loved books -- storybooks and poetry -- and was passionate about learning. And music. He still is.

As Martin grew into a little boy, he was both sensitive and tough. He rarely cried, even when a door slammed on his fingers. Every time he went outside he brought me back a handful of flowers. When he saw someone in pain or distress, empathetic tears welled in his eyes. And he was funny. A natural comic, he made people laugh even before he could talk. A true comedian, his delightfully off-the-wall sense of humor is still a very important part of him.

So, according to (Catholic) Grandma, we definitely shouldn't have a third. We'd already pushed our luck beyond the limits of probability. We couldn't possibly be lucky enough to have a third child so amazing.

But my little boys were so wonderfully happy and well-behaved, such model children, I scoffed, "I've got this *Mother* thing down! Piece o' cake."

As a matter of fact, we almost didn't have a third, although we wanted to. Hypothyroidism prevented conception. But it was discovered and treated in time.

Alexandre Nicolas was born on October 14, 1963. (8 pounds 2 ounces.)

This one had dark hair, gigantic dark brown eyes, and was so beautiful he stopped traffic. His coloring was like his Spanish dad's, whereas Steve and Martin, as children, resembled their English-Scandinavian mom.

He woke up every 2 hours for at least 7 months. He was a wiggle-worm beyond belief -- never still for a second. One of our babysitters said, "Trying to hold him is like trying to hold onto an eel." That was true. The only time I could cuddle him was when he was asleep. And he had a mind of his own. He was a wonderfully good little boy, but on his own terms.

He was just as bright and sweet as his brothers, and an amazing athlete from day-one. Perpetual motion personified, he tested the limits constantly.

We might have had more children. I would very much have liked to have a daughter. But when Alex was born, my roommate in Maternity at Memorial Hospital had just given birth to her eleventh boy, trying for a girl. That cured me. Three was enough.

Besides, each baby was approximately a half pound larger than the previous one. This could get out of hand.

I was living my purpose. My three sons were my reason for being. And they were the most wonderful kids.

I was part of a babysitting club in which a group of young mothers took turns caring for each others' children. Everyone wanted to sit for me because my kids were so delightful. The boys played host to the sitter, serving refreshments and entertaining her with intelligent conversation. And when it was time for bed, they went willingly and happily.

One time when the kids were maybe 12, 10 and 6, they and I went to Fresno where we stayed with Aunt Bill for a few days. She told everyone, "Carol's boys are the most even-tempered children I've ever known. They're a delight to have around."

And they've grown up to be just as wonderful, just as smart, just as much fun, and just as delightful -- my three favorite people on earth.

He's Our *President!*

President Kennedy fielded questions from reporters. "Do you think it's safe to go to Dallas?" Dallas, Texas was known to be a city in which hate-filled, anti-Kennedy ultra-conservatives abounded.

"I'm the president of all Americans. One American city is like any other, so far as I'm concerned." (Paraphrased.)

When the Today Show ended at 9 a.m. on November 22, I turned off the TV and went about my day as usual. A little later, my neighbor Dee Taylor called inviting me over for a cuppa. I bundled up Martin, $4\frac{1}{2}$, and Alex, 5 weeks, and went next door. Steve was in First Grade at Village Elementary School. Dee and I sat at her chrome and formica kitchen table, looking out over the neighborhood's bare trees and brown lawns that winter day, chatting and drinking hot tea. Alex snoozed in his plastic InfantSeat while Martin and Dee's two little girls ran around trying to out-shout the television. No one paid it any mind.

All of a sudden, though, something caught my attention. Nothing overt, just a change in the announcer's tone. "Shhhhh." I waved my hand out in front of me. "Shhhhh." Leaning toward the living room, I strained to hear. I knew something portentous was coming. The kids quieted.

Newsman Walter Cronkite stated in shocked solemnity, "President Kennedy has been seriously wounded. Perhaps fatally."

"Oh my god!" I gasped. "Oh my god!" My hand flew to my mouth, my heart stopped. We moved into the living room, closer to the TV, and watched in disbelief.

"Don't you think you should call John and tell him?" asked Dee.

"No, he knew it before Cronkite. He's on the Wire (services) Desk."

We stood paralyzed, barely breathing. This couldn't be happening. Our eyes did not stray from the television.

Some time later, Cronkite announced, "From Dallas, Texas . . . . the flash, apparently official: President Kennedy died at 1 p.m., Central Standard Time -- a half-hour ago . . . " (From his autobiography, *A Reporter's Life*):

> The words stuck in my throat. A sob wanted to replace them. A gulp or two quashed the sob, which metamorphosed into tears forming in the corner of my eyes. I fought back the emotion and regained my professionalism, but it was touch and go there for a few seconds before I could continue.

"Vice-President Johnson has left the hospital in Dallas," he went on. "Presumably, he will be taking the oath of office shortly and become the thirty-sixth President of the United States."

It was surreal. I was numb, shaking inside and out. Tears streamed down my face. I felt empty. Gutted.

Dazed, I took my kids home and turned on the TV, which was normally dark during the day. I busied myself washing windows. I couldn't be still. I had to do something. Washing windows was as good as anything.

Later in the day, although I felt it somehow wasn't respectful, I let Martin go across the street to play with his little friend, John Kelly. He was just a little boy, after all.

Later, when he came home, he said, "I told Mrs. Kelly that President Kennedy got killed, and you know what she said? She said, "It's a good thing. I never liked him anyway." So I said, 'But he's our *president!*'" He was as righteously indignant as a four-year-old can be.

Yes, John F. Kennedy was our president. He was my president. Like so many others, I felt personally involved with and attached to him. He was the first president to elicit that kind of emotion, not only in me, but in millions of Americans. I felt as if I'd lost a member of my family.

I was so proud of my little boy, my wonderful Martin.

1000 DAYS, John F. Kennedy in the White House, by Arthur M. Schlesinger, the first book about the Kennedy presidency, was released early in 1965. I couldn't bring myself to read it then. "It's just too soon. Maybe in a year or so."

The "year or so" has turned into 47. It's now 2010 and I still haven't been able to read it.

Monkey Business

My kids laughed their heads off. Decades later, they're still laughing. This event is, without a doubt, their favorite childhood memory. They've passed it down to the next generation. When someone brought the subject up last Christmas my granddaughter Hannah knew all about it.

Montgomery Village, a one-block wide and eight-block long shopping center with a variety of stores, from a hole-in-the-wall candy store to Lucky's Supermarket, was a block from our house. At the far end, where Montgomery Drive crosses Farmers Lane, was Hal's Toyville -- "the center of the universe". Just up from Hal's was a pet store with all sorts of animals and pet paraphernalia.

Puppies or kittens were always on display in the front window to draw customers in. They were irresistible, so, of course, en route home from Hal's Toyville, the fabric store, or another shop at that end of the mall, we went in. The kids gave a kitten or puppy a quick nuzzle before looking around. From week to week we never knew what we'd find. The owner didn't seem to mind that the neighborhood kids came in to be entertained by his animal inventory.

We stopped at the aquarium to watch the tropical fish, then at the plastic pond where baby turtles crawled over one another, at cages of hamsters racing 'round in rattly wire wheels, or red-eyed white mice, colorful birds -- sometimes a parrot, snakes and lizards in glass boxes, and maybe furry tarantulas.

That week, at the back of the store, was a monkey -- a cute male rhesus -- in a cage. We gathered 'round. The boys mimicked the monkey's gestures and sounds, drooping their shoulders and scratching their ribs, their lower lips pushed out by their tongues, voicing monkey noises. "*Eeeee, eeeee, eeeee,*" aping the ape.

The monkey was not amused. He'd had enough of this nonsense. In fact, I think it pissed him off. He simply let fly and peed all over me. I was off to one side; he singled me out. He turned toward me and let me have it, in my face and hair and all over my torso and arms. He must have really enjoyed himself 'cause he did the thorough-est job imaginable.

"Ooooooh!" I screamed and shouted, "C'mon kids, let's get outa here!" racing for the door. Once outside, I took off running, assuming the kids were right behind.

They weren't. They were doubled over laughing. They laughed so hard they couldn't even walk, much less run.

I ran all the way home -- nine or ten blocks, stripped and threw my clothes in the washer, then got in the shower. I scrubbed and scrubbed with Fels Naptha, letting the water run over me until it was stone cold.

The kids eventually got their laughter under control and came home -- they knew the way and were old enough that I didn't worry. Steve and Martin always took good care of Alex, so I was able to concentrate on ridding myself of the odor of my misadventure.

For the next week I took shower after shower after shower, each one as thorough as that one. But the stench of monkey pee lingered. It was in my very pores.

Yes, this is definitely my three sons' favorite childhood memory.

Day of Revelations

I t happened on my 33rd birthday.
It was undoubtedly the most difficult day of my life, and definitely the most important. The information and guidance I received came from somewhere outside of me -- my "Higher Self"? My "Spirit Guide"? God(?), if such a thing exists.

I honestly don't know where it came from. To my surprise, I had real, out-loud conversations with not only whatever was penetrating my consciousness, but also with real people, 'though I was alone: John and his mother and father, who were among the living, but also my own mother and father, who were not. I cried, I railed, and in the end, I found my backbone.

The day started off like any other. John got up at 5:30 a.m., as usual, showered and shaved, coffeeed and toasted, and left for work at the Press Democrat where he was City Editor. I supervised the children's morning rituals. Steve and Martin dressed, had breakfast, and walked the three blocks to Sequoia School. I picked up Alex's carpool pals and drove to Franklin Park Pre-school, then came home to read the Chronicle over a pot of tea at the kitchen table, as always. I was barely aware of it being my birthday. It was a day like any other.

Then it started. My Day of Revelations. My awakening commenced. I don't know how else to describe it. All of a sudden I began a dialogue, the one described above. I began connecting with things I knew without knowing I knew them, and getting flashes of new information from somewhere outside myself.

This information -- this knowing -- was mostly about myself: my character, my victimhood, my responsibility, my strengths, and my innate wisdom. But there was also instruction and enlightenment about the world, love, the nature of life and death, and God.

By then I had been married 15 years and 4 months. In that time I had learned something about cultural differences. I, of Danish/English American heritage, had married a Spanish Basque American. I had not realized what a huge difference there was between our two cultures. Both he and I were, after all, born and reared in Fresno, California, attended its public schools, listened to the same radio programs, saw the same movies, and played or watched the same sports. So we had a shared culture. But when I married into his family, I could have been on another planet.

I never knew people could be so mean-spirited, or would accuse a totally innocent person of heinous acts. To exert control they used anger/rage, jealousy, worry, mistrust. They -- John and his family -- insulted, demeaned, belittled, denigrated, degraded and discounted me as if I were a lowly, worthless, immoral creature. In fact, they treated me as if I was a slut.

And they were excitable. There was constant turmoil: screaming, shouting, suffering, agonizing. And double messages abounded. They said one thing and meant the opposite.

I really thought these people should be placed in a padded cell, and the key thrown away.

I often felt that John forgot who he was married to. His mother was the one whose approval he sought, the one he considered far more than me. Nearly every decision we ever made had to be presented to his mother. If she disapproved he didn't want to do it. She ran huge guilt trips on us. And when she didn't get her way she became "deathly ill" and took to her bed for a full week or until we gave in, whichever came first. It usually worked on John, which I didn't understand. Why doesn't he see through it and just say No?

When she attacked me (which was not infrequent), John's obtuse reaction was, "I don't know why you can't get along with my mother." And when her behavior toward me was so terrible he couldn't help but notice, he'd say, "She *is* my mother and you *will* get along with her."

The only times he openly defied her were when she forced him to choose between her (his mother) and me (his wife). This happened on at least three occasions. To his credit, he chose me and our little family. But after one such occasion we were banished from the family for over two years.

John's mother honestly believed it was her God-given right to run her children's lives, which also affected their spouses and children. John and his mother "forced" me to do things I didn't want to do and "prevented" me from doing things I did. They accused me of things of which I was innocent, and disbelieved me when I told the truth.

I spent a great deal of time during those first 15+ years of marriage resenting them and their attitudes and behaviors. I blamed them for treating me so miserably.

I put up with it because I thought I had to. I felt trapped -- powerless. I believed I had no options. I'd made my bed and must lie in it. No one ever promised me a rose garden. Back then, unless your husband beat you regularly and horrifically or you caught him "in the act" with another woman, divorce wasn't an option. It carried a huge stigma.

Also back then, females were socialized to be perceived, even by themselves, strictly in relation to others -- as someone's daughter, someone's wife, someone's mother -- and only in terms of what they could do for those close relatives. It never occurred to most of us that we were persons in our own right, that we were important too; that our feelings, opinions, thoughts, ideas, values -- and very culture -- were as valid as anyone else's. Or that maybe someone could do something for us. It was the woman's job to make the marriage work, to keep everyone happy.

It never occurred to most of us, if we were in a relationship with a man, that we could be equal partners or had any control over our destiny, which was determined by our gender. And (generally speaking) it didn't enter the heads of the men in our life, either.

I felt I had to accept John's and his mother's treatment because I had no way to support myself and my children. Also, since my parents were dead, family was extremely important to me. I did not want to deprive my children of a close relationship with their father and grandparents.

In effect, I'd sold myself out. I sold out my self-respect and self-esteem day-by-day in return for *Family* for my children.

On this turning point day I began to see things differently. I realized for the first time that no one can do anything to me that I don't allow them to; I "cannot be a doormat unless I lie down" (Ann Landers' wisdom), thereby inviting them to walk all over me; I am responsible for my life, and even for the way people treat me. I understood that if I respect myself enough to demand respectful treatment from others, chances are good I will get it. I don't have to be a victim.

More importantly, I realized that if someone did not treat me well I could get along without them. This was the greatest revelation on that Day of Revelations. If necessary, I could survive on my own. Somehow. I need not be dependent: financially, emotionally, or any other way. That was empowering.

That was the day, my 33rd birthday, that it came into my conscious awareness. I *got* it.

That was the day I became an adult. That day I took responsibility for my own life. That day I began to know that I always have choices, and can re-choose if my previous choices aren't working, that each day is a new start, with new possibilities and potentials. I can recreate myself and my life however and whenever I wish.

When John came home that afternoon he found a new wife -- very different from the one he'd left that morning, just 9 hours earlier. I have no doubt that it scared the hell out of him. I told him of the day's many revelations. Our relationship began to change ...... some.

. . . .

Note: None of the events of my Day of Revelations was ever mentioned to John's mother. But from that day forward she didn't even attempt to mistreat me. Somehow she sensed the change in me and intuited that her abuse would not be tolerated.

As a result, I surmise that prior to that day there must have been something in me, in my attitude and demeanor, that not only told (certain) people they could abuse me, but perhaps even invited them to.

Peter Peter Pumpkin Eater

I forbid it! You were born a woman to take care of your husband, your children, and your house. Period."

There it was. John finally said it. That explained a lot. Over the years he had acted on that belief in many ways but never actually voiced it.

The topic of the above discussion was my returning to college. Sixteen years earlier, when we got married and he insisted that I quit school, he promised I could return and finish college someday.

With his above statement, it became obvious he thought "someday" would never come.

After the first year of our marriage he had never let me have a job of any kind. "People will think I can't support my family," which *was* an issue. But if I were out of the home, working for someone else, I'd not be taking care of the Big Three: Husband, Children, House. Even if I were to do day-care at home, taking care of other people's children would diminish the care I could give our children and our house. (*And* demonstrate that he couldn't support his family.)

But the main reason he demanded that I quit college when we got married was that he was certain I'd meet someone on campus who I liked better than him and he'd lose me. Or I'd cheat on him.

The same thing was true when it came to getting a job. There were bound to be men in the workplace. In Spanish culture, women cannot be trusted. If I were working with men I'd surely be having sex with them.

This was especially true when we lived in Germany. I could have gotten a secretarial job in some office of the Army. We had no children, I had nothing but time, and we definitely could have used the money. But he forbade it. I was not even allowed to stop at the PX Snack Bar for a Coke when I finished grocery shopping at the base commissary, because men would be there.

Throughout our marriage, when we went to any kind of social gathering -- which was infrequent due to his intense introversion -- if I spoke to or even made eye contact with a man I heard about it for the next two or three weeks. "I guess you'd rather be with _____. You'd rather be having sex with _____."

Huh?

He usually sat in a corner, watching. (Mind you, this was *his* circle of friends -- *his* co-workers -- the only people we socialized with.) He berated me for not sitting in the corner with him. He interpreted any conversation or eye contact with a man as flirting, and insisted that I should be sitting in the corner, flirting with him. *Why go to a party if I could only interact with my husband? I could do that at home.* Besides, I wasn't a flirt. I just wanted to have conversations with adults.

Even though I was home all day every day with the children, he didn't trust me, imagining I was having sex with the mailman, door-to-door salesmen, the meter reader. His fear of being cuckolded was even greater than his fear of me leaving him. A Spaniard, he'd have died of humiliation and disgrace.

But he *was* terrified I'd leave him, so he did his best to make sure I couldn't or wouldn't. He imagined that if I had any self-esteem I'd leave, so he convinced me I was stupid, unattractive, totally lacking in sex appeal. No other man would ever want me, and I couldn't make it on my own.

He also imagined that if I had any money I'd leave. That was part of his not allowing me to have a job.

If I wanted to buy him a present I had to ask for money. After awhile (before my Day of Revelations), I started skimping so I could squeeze $5 a week out of the grocery money. (A week's groceries cost $15 - $18.) I gave new meaning to "rubber chicken". I could stretch a chicken so far it snapped back. And I had 1,001 hamburger recipes. I'd learned to cook beside my mom who, 'though poor, was a fabulous cook. I knew how to do it.

I opened a secret bank account, squirreling away $5 a week, so I'd have a little money to call my own, and be able buy John a present now and then without having to beg.

But I digress.

His idea of "take care of your house" went so far as to forbid me to garden, which is outside and therefore "men's work".

One day when he came home from work I was in the backyard pulling weeds, which for me is therapeutic.

"What are you doing?" As if he couldn't see.

"Pulling weeds."

"Is everything in the house perfect? -- Your job is to keep the house clean. You can work in the yard only if everything inside is done."

When we went on a trip we couldn't leave until the house passed a white-glove inspection. The summer Steve was five and Martin was three, we were ready to leave for Disneyland when it got really ridiculous. "We're not leaving until this house is *clean!*"

John had us all turning the house upside down -- turning over the couch and chairs -- pulling dressers out from the wall -- re-vacuuming under all the beds -- scouring the house for errant Cheerios. The kids and I were eager to get going. But the start of the trip was delayed more than an hour while we searched *everywhere* for that wayward Cheerio he was certain I'd missed.

"Why does it have to be so all-fired perfect?" I demanded. "No one's going to be here. Nobody will see it."

"What if a burglar comes in?" he asked.

And he was serious! He got teased about that for awhile.

Since I wasn't a *House Beautiful* kind of homemaker, I was a failure as a woman and a human being. Years later, when my good friend, Judy Rivers, told me, "You're such a perfectionist,"[10] I couldn't accept it. I'd bought into John's opinion that if I wasn't good at housekeeping I wasn't any good, period. It didn't matter what else I excelled at.

And I do have a number of skills and talents. I'm often asked, "Is there *any*thing you can't do?" I answer, "I don't know. I haven't tried everything yet." But back then, the only thing that mattered to John, other than being a good mom and cook (which I was), was, Does she keep an immaculate house?

I've since concluded that I need a wife -- the kind John envisioned for himself -- who would cheerfully wash the same dishes every day, make the same beds, mop the same floors, wash, dry, and fold the same laundry, and keep everything picked up and organized, with no expectation of anything else -- so I can focus on other things -- creative things. In a perfect world, everyone would have a "wife".

10. She said it watching me knit a very intricately patterned a sweater.

John didn't allow me outside in the front yard alone: he had no doubt someone would snatch me up and run off with me, or have his way with me right there on the front lawn. He didn't want me to go anywhere alone either. If I couldn't get a girlfriend to go shopping with me, he strongly objected to my going. Again, mistrust and jealousy; his certainty that I'd cheat on him or leave him if given the chance.

He'd have been very happy if he could have locked me up in the house. He reminded me of this children's nursery rhyme:

> Peter Peter Pumpkin Eater,
> had a wife and couldn't keep her.
> He put her in a pumpkin shell,
> and there he kept her very well.

It wasn't that he couldn't keep me, but he imagined he couldn't, which was just as bad. And it wasn't that our marriage was unhappy. As long as I was "the good wife", and did everything his way we were fine.

When I opened the discussion about my going back to college, I had no intention of leaving him. I really thought it would strengthen our marriage, since I would be learning fascinating things and would be a more interesting person.

"Someday" had arrived. My full-time Mommy Career was coming to an end. Alex, our youngest child, was about to start Kindergarten. I could dash out and take a couple of classes and be back before he got home.

John put his foot down.

So did I.

He refused to budge.

So did I.

We were in a stalemate. It was our biggest struggle ever, and it lasted several weeks. I knew I risked my marriage if I persevered. I also knew I had to.

"It feels like you're buying a ticket out of my life," said John when I applied to enroll at Santa Rosa Junior College. The same old fears cropped up: I'd meet someone I liked better *and leave him*: I'd prepare myself for a job with an earning capacity *and leave him*. Also, there was the powerful and persistent fear that I'd betray him with another man.

I had to let that be his problem.

I enrolled at SRJC. Three classes, nine units. I started college the same day Alex started Kindergarten.

An Idea
Whose Time Had Come

Bizet's opera, Carmen, set in Spain, opens with a visit to Corporal Don José by his sweetheart Micaëla, at his military camp. He's thrilled to see her, all the more because she's brought a letter from his sainted mother, who covered it with her sweet kisses. While practically ravishing Micaëla, he sings a *really* long aria about how much he loves and misses his mother.

That's right, *his mother.*

The opera ends with Don José, who has left poor Micaëla and run off with Carmen, a gypsy who changes lovers as often as most folks change underwear. Don José learns that Carmen's affections have turned to Escamillo, the Toreador. Having declared his love for her, Don José believes she belongs to him. He flies into a jealous rage and stabs her to death.

Bizet nailed it. He really knew Spanish culture. He knew that a Spanish man's first, last and forever loyalty and devotion are to his mother. She is his one true love. And Bizet knew that a Spanish man believes he owns his woman and must control her. Society expects him to. A man can change lovers -- as Don José had, but his woman is *his.* Bizet knew that to a Spaniard, jealousy is proof of love; the more intense the jealousy the more intense the love.

By now, the 21st century, it may have changed, although I doubt it. Culture runs deep.[11] But back in the 1950s, when I married a Spaniard, it was alive and well. And I didn't know what hit me.

---

11. Having spent a good deal of time recently in Puerto Rico and getting to know many women, I know it hasn't changed there.

It wasn't until we'd been married 17 years that I took an anthropology class on Hispanic culture at SRJC, in which I learned that in Spain (and other Hispanic countries) Don José's behavior (short of the murder) is normal.

Any woman who marries a Hispanic man needs to know this.

In that anthropology class, I learned that a Hispanic man's first obligation and undying loyalty are to his mother. That shocked me to the core. And it explained a lot. When it was time for John to get out of the Army, he could have gotten on at Stars & Stripes, which was headquartered in Darmstadt. It would have been a good career move. But he declared, "We owe it to my mother[12] to be near her when our first baby is born." That was crazy to me, but he was in charge, so we came home.

I also learned that in Hispanic cultures, women are divided, psychologically if not physically, so as to be easier to control. According to the instructor, every woman in this culture is pitted against every other woman. Women are taught to mistrust and despise one another. The despicable nature of women, which is a given, is a constant theme in the literature, songs and jokes, as well as other aspects of the culture.

I learned that in the Spanish culture, there are only two kinds of women: the Slut/Whore/Hussy and the Madonna/Angel/Saint. And that every woman is a whore, except one's mother, who is a saint, and one's daughter, who's an angel -- unless or until she proves otherwise. The expectation is that every woman will, the minute she's out of her parents' or husband's sight, go forth and sin.

So, in bygone times, girls/women of good families were never allowed out of sight of someone responsible for them. When the culture was established, unmarried women were accompanied everywhere by *dueñas,* older women chaperones. Nor could married women leave the home unaccompanied. Like nuns, they went everywhere in twos. Although it's changed in Hispanic countries in the past 50-60 years, this is the culture in which John grew up and into which I married. Every woman is suspect by the nature of her gender, hence, the need for watchful, rigid control.

I also learned that it is the custom for a man in this culture to choose a very young girl as his intended bride so he and his family can get her under their

---

12. To her dying day, she manipulated him by shrieking, "You owe me! You owe me. You almost killed me when you were born. You owe me!"

influence before she gets any ideas about independence and self-sufficiency. I was just 16 when I met John, barely 18 when we became engaged, and four months shy of 19 when we married, so we fell right into that cultural pattern.

In addition, the male responsible for a girl or woman must be in full control of her -- her whereabouts, her dress and demeanor, her behavior. Hispanic men are easily disgraced. In this culture in which a female was either a Madonna or a Whore, there was no middle ground, no gray area. And there was no going back, no redemption. If you escaped his control even once you were a whore, and your father (uncle, guardian, husband) was forever disgraced.

In this class I also learned that pre-menopausal women are not taken seriously. They are dismissed, discounted, ignored. I'd experienced this over and over from John's family, but it also happened in this class on Hispanic culture. More than once, I gave a spot-on answer to the instructor's question. My teacher, himself from Mexico, who had taught us about this typical behavior, demonstrated it perfectly. He acted as if I hadn't spoken, as if I were not even present, turning to the next person, a guy whose answer wasn't as good as mine, and praised him for it. I'm sure he wasn't even aware he'd fallen into that deeply ingrained cultural pattern. Culture runs deep.

Currently in the U.S., where, over the last century, the nuclear family has become the norm, and we've become a very mobile society, we are no longer surrounded by the extended family to exert pressure and control over us. This must be crazy-making for a husband mired in 14th-century Spanish tradition, as John was. He's certain that while he's at work his wife is having sex with everyone whose pants zip up the front. If she has a job, she's cheating on him with every man in the workplace.

Even from a distance, his parents do their best to undermine her confidence, convinced she is a whore -- because every woman is. Over the years John's mother told him time and again, "She doesn't love you." Her "proof" was, I didn't scream and cry and beat my breast when he left for Germany. This was 1955, ten years after the end of WWII, when Germany was the best duty in the Army. And I'd be joining him in a few months. Another "proof" was, I didn't name our first-born son after his daddy. (I thought John Purroy III was a bit much.)

John's mother was absolutely convinced our third child was not John's. What she based this on is a mystery. The day Baby Alex came home from the hospital I spoke with her by phone. She asked, "What does he look like?"

I said, "He looks different from the other two."

That's all she needed. That was her proof. She didn't listen long enough to learn that Alex, with the dark hair and eyes of a Spaniard, looked like John. The other two resembled me.

In that class I came to realize that my husband and his family were not crazy, as I'd imagined. Rather, they were culturally appropriate in a bizarre culture.

I had married into the culture of the enmeshed family.[13] It was also a closed society. If you weren't born into it, you could never get in. Even after I was married to John more than 20 years, his mother would say things like, "Don't talk about this with your wife. This is a *family* matter."

Speaking from the European perspective, it seems that the closer one gets to the Mediterranean and the Islamic cultures of the Middle East, the more macho (male-dominated) the culture is. Spain gets credit for it, though, perhaps due to its lengthy occupation by the Islamic Moors.

However, my own culture was male-oriented too. Tracey's behavior toward my mom wasn't all that different from what I've just described.

I was raised by a strong, independent woman who had betrayed herself (and her daughters) when she knuckled under to her domineering second husband. While proud of my strong, independent nature, she inadvertently, by example, prepared me to squash it in deference to a husband.

But now, in my 30s, I was ready to reclaim my inherent nature. John blamed the change in me on The Women's Movement, in general, and

13. Excessively enmeshed family systems make it difficult for children to develop any autonomy, individuality, or privacy. Everything is "everyone else's business", and family members "stick their nose in" where it isn't wanted or needed, wanting to know everything about what each member is doing, feeling, thinking, considering. No action of any member is considered trivial; everything is invested with deep significance or "hidden meaning", and sends ripple effects throughout the system. Indirect communication (triangulated messages) may be frequent as members "talk behind each other's back". Marlowe C. Embree, Ph.D.

Betty Friedan's *The Feminine Mystique*, in particular.

Au contraire. The Women's Movement was an idea whose time had come. Many, many women, like me, had their own private consciousness raising sessions. It may have been an example of the "100th Monkey" concept. (When enough citizens in a community learn a skill it reaches "critical mass" and spreads throughout the population.)

Betty Friedan's book helped spread awareness of female subjugation and victimhood, but she did not invent it. She did not invent our resentments, frustrations, anger. She did not invent our need to be recognized as equal human beings rather than as a lowly sub-category of beings.

Friedan and others in what came to be known as "The Women's Movement" spoke for those of us who lacked the courage or skill to speak for ourselves.

My new realizations from that anthropology class, *The Feminine Mystique*, Women's Studies classes, and publications such as *Ms. Magazine,* were enlightening and empowering.

I learned that our culture's male-orientation was reflected in *our* language too. I learned not to refer to both sexes as "he", as was customary.

For the first time, I heard the sexism in "I now pronounce you *man* and *wife*".

I learned that "woman" is an Anglo-Saxon word that originally meant "wife of man". So if a female wasn't somebody's wife she remained a girl.

I became sensitive to marriage vows, such as, "… love honor and *obey,*" required only of females, not males.

I became aware that females were discriminated against in every segment of our modern-day American culture, that there were very different expectations of females and males.

As I shared all this with John, and as he saw his American culture changing, his intellect battled his emotions. As an educated man and a liberal progressive, he embraced the notion of equality for women in the abstract. Just not for *his* wife.

However, he was rapidly losing control over that situation. That ship had already sailed. Little by little I asserted myself. Little by little I advocated for myself.

Almost a Member of the Family

I 'd always wanted a grandfather clock, I don't know why. It may go back to the movies of my childhood in which families of substance always had one. It may have seemed to me that a grandfather clock in your home meant you were *Somebody.*

Both John and I sprang from working class families in which "necessities only" was the rule. A grandfather clock was hardly a necessity and he wouldn't hear of it.

Then, one day in 1971, Judy Rivers told me about this guy, "Jay", who had brought a whole slew of antique clocks, including "grandfathers", from Europe and was selling them at bargain prices.

"I want one," I said.

John's reply, as expected, was, "No. Absolutely not." He had all the usual reasons. "We can't afford it." "Where would we put it?" and "Things like that are for rich people, not people like us."

I would not be dissuaded. "We could at least go look, and see if we can afford one." "We can put in the entry hall," and "We deserve to have nice things too."

Then he hit me with this one. "A grandfather clock is top-heavy. It'll fall over and kill one of the children."

I guffawed. He had the good grace to look sheepish.

"I *really* want a grandfather clock. I've *always* really wanted a grand father clock. We can bolt it to the wall if it'll make you feel any better."

He relented. I could go look, but he set a limit of $200.

When I went to look at the clocks, Jay wasn't home, so his wife took me out to the barn. The smell of hay and dust reminded me of Grandpa Petersen's barn.

Seventy-five clocks, maybe more, sat on sheets of painters' canvas covering part of the dirt floor. Wall clocks, mantle clocks, grandfather clocks, grandmother clocks. Some simple, some ornate. In every size, shape and design. How to choose?

Many were eliminated by my $200 limit, but one grandfather was in my range. Jay's wife said that one was $150. It was one of the smaller, plainer ones.

That's probably why it's so cheap, I thought. "I'll take it."

Jay drove up and entered the barn. When his wife proudly told him of her sale he reddened. "No way!" he declared. "That's a really good clock. It's a Gustav Becker.[14] It's even got his label on the back. It's worth a lot more."

"But," I asserted, "she said I could have if for $150."

He shook his head. "That's one of my best clocks. Besides, somebody already put a deposit on it." He seemed to waver. "But ... that was a month ago, and ... and she hasn't come back for it. I'll tell you what, we'll split the difference. You can have it for $350."

My shoulders slumped. I shook my head. "I only have $200."

He sighed and grimaced, hemmed and hawed, staring at his shoes. "Okay, $200."

Then he told me about the woman who had put the deposit on it. "She brought a tape measure and measured it top to bottom, side to side, and front to back. She was going to use it for her coffin! So," sighing deeply once again and nodding slowly, "if you want it, you can have it."

I think he was relieved to have saved it from being de-clocked and buried six feet under, the woman's stony face framed by the round window where the clock's face ought to be.

He delivered it and set it up in our entry hall, the very center of the house. "Keep it level, polish it once a week with Old English Red, and enjoy it."

We have. It is the heartbeat of my home, its pendulum swinging steadily, rhythmically, day in and day out, its chime mellow and melodious, pealing on the hour and the half-hour. And it is lovely to look at.

It quickly became almost a member of the family, standing there just inside the front door, a loving "grandfather" welcoming us all back home from our wanderings.

Years later, when John and I separated, I told him, "You can have whatever you want. Take *every*thing, *except* . . . "

"The clock," John finished my sentence.

"Yes. The clock."

---

14 Gustav Becker, Clockmaker, who set up his workshop in Freiburg, Silesia, Germany, in 1850.

The Candidate

T he Candidate," with superstar Robert Redford, was being filmed in and around Santa Rosa. Camera crews, equipment trucks, and movie stars were right in our neighborhoods and neighborhood shopping centers. The whole town buzzed with excitement.

"I just saw Peter Boyle at The Hilltopper. Having a Caesar Salad."

"No kidding! Melvyn Douglas was at the Topaz Room the other night. He sat at the bar, just like a regular guy, talking to everybody and signing autographs."

We hadn't had this much excitement in Santa Rosa since Iva Kroeger's murder trial.

"The Candidate" was a film about politics and the campaign of a particular candidate. Robert Redford was producer, director, and leading man. Peter Boyle and Melvyn Douglas were among the cast members.

A crowd scene was scheduled to be shot at Howarth Park. It was supposed to be a 4th of July picnic, somewhere in the Midwest. Extras were needed. Redford had put the word out to local organizations, including the Democratic and Republican clubs. Telephone trees were activated and the news spread.

Extras would not be paid, but a picnic lunch would be provided. My friend Char Ginsberg planned to go, so I went too. Like a lot of other parents, we kept our kids out of school that day, rationalizing it would be educational. They might learn more there than at school that day. It would be something different, anyway.

Since it was supposed to be July, we were told to wear summer clothing. I don't remember what month the scene was shot, but it was so cold we could see our breath. Throughout the day we huddled in coats until just before the shooting started. Some of us cheated by wearing sweaters under summer cottons, but still shivered. Those who wore Hawaiian shirts or sundresses -- sans sweaters -- were placed up front, in direct view of the cameras. My kids and I were sent to the rear of the crowd.

The year was 1971. At 36 or 37, Redford was boyishly handsome, with sun-streaked sandy hair, sparkling blue eyes, and a flashing smile. He's shorter than he appears on screen, but with that light-up-the-world smile of his, who cares?

He let it be known early-on that we were there to work. He was all business.

Several cameras shot each scene from every angle. The actors went through it multiple times for various reasons. Sometimes they stumbled or flubbed their lines. Sometimes the cameramen didn't get the shot the director wanted. Sometimes the lighting was wrong. Sometimes the extras were out of place. And sometimes the director wanted the scene shot again just because. Each scene was shot over and over and over, with the actors repeating the same actions and the same lines again and again.

We extras mostly just stood around. Coats on; coats off. Boredom. "Look interested." "Stand here." "Stand there." "We don't need you now." "We need you now. Quiet on the set!"

Eventually, it was time for the lunch break. A Montgomery Village restaurant catered the affair. The groaning-board was set up amid all the movie-making hoopla, under pine trees with Lake Ralphine in the background. There were fried chicken, cold cuts, chips, potato salad, green salad, Jell-O salad, rolls, chocolate cake, and soft drinks -- like a real Midwestern picnic.

Redford announced he would sit with the kids on the platform that was the speaker's podium in the movie. He would not be giving autographs. "Don't ask." Nor would he engage in conversation with the adults.

Everyone crowded around the buffet loading up their plates. I was last in line. Concentrating on my food selections, I was unaware that someone had come up behind me. A male voice asked, "Where are the soft drinks?"

Without looking up, I pointed. "That tub, over there."

"I see it. Thanks."

I recognized that voice. I turned to look into the face it had come out of. Superstar Robert Redford, himself, stood right next to me, but quickly moved off in pursuit of a soft drink.

Oh no! I'd missed my chance. If only I'd known, I'd have taken him by the hand and led him to the soft drink tub. I'd have handed him a Coke or a 7-Up. I'd have opened it for him. I'd have wiped it dry for him. I'd have . . . Oh, heck, I don't know what I would have done, but I would have done something!

He took his plate and drink and sat on the wooden platform, surrounded by a dozen or so kids. He was relaxed, asking them about themselves, happy to answer questions about himself, Hollywood, movie making, his previous movies, and so forth. He chatted awhile longer with the kids, then spent the rest of the lunch break with them, tossing a football. All that charm wasted on kids!

Then it was time to get back to making a movie. The afternoon went much as the morning had. Coats on; coats off. Boredom. "Look interested." "Stand here." "Stand there." "We don't need you yet." "We need you now. Get in your places. Quiet on the set!"

At the end of the day, the very gracious Robert Redford thanked us for our participation and told us to look for ourselves on screen when the movie came out.

I was right. It was an educational experience. We learned a lot about movie making that day.

We learned it's not much fun to be a movie actor. It's not all fame, glory and stardom. An actor has to do the same thing over and over and over and over. And there's a lot of merely standing around, waiting while other people do things, like setting up props, changing camera positions, adjusting lights, and touching up make-up. Bo-ring.

What would be fun, in my opinion, is to be the director. The director gets to do something different all day, and gets to tell everybody else what to do, and how and when to do it.

We learned that making a movie takes all kinds of people you never think about: lighting people, sound technicians, make-up artists, prop people, costume designers, camera operators, lighting technicians, set designers and builders, etc.

And we realized what a tough and important job the editor has, deciding which of thousands of takes to use, then piecing them all together to produce the final product.

We'd never watch a movie in quite the same way again.

But the best part is that ever since that day in 1971 I've been able to brag:

- Robert Redford bought me lunch.

     True. He was the producer so it came out of his pocket.

- Robert Redford and I had a conversation.

     Well, we did. It was short, but it *was* a conversation.

- I was in a movie with Robert Redford.

     So what if I wasn't exactly his co-star?

When "The Candidate" opened at the theater across Summerfield Road from Howarth Park, we rushed to see it. The scene that took all day to shoot lasted only a couple of minutes in the actual movie.

We looked for ourselves in it. Although I have seen "The Candidate" several times and searched that crowd scene over and over, I have never found myself or my kids in it. I guess we didn't exactly end up on the cutting room floor, we were just unrecognizable pinpoints at the back of the crowd.

Give Peace a Chance

I'm going to march in today's protest," I announced. I had waited 'til the last minute to tell John.

"The hell you are!" he exploded.

"Yeah, I am," I said quietly but firmly.

"No you're not! I'm a newspaper editor. I have to be objective. I'm a journalist, goddam it."

"But I'm not."

"No, but you're my wife. You represent me. If you protest in public, you'll compromise my objectivity. No one will believe I'm impartial."

"Look, I'm not you and you're not me. I have a right to speak my own mind. If people can't see that we're not joined at the brain it's not my problem."

"No, it's mine," he said, chagrined. But he was not finished. He played the Motherhood Card. "You have children to take care of. And you could get arrested!"

"That's irrelevant. It's time to stand up and be counted. I'll do more for my children by protesting the war than by staying silent. I'm marching."

"You could get beat up. You could get shot! Then what's to happen to them? To me?"

"I'm not going to get shot. This is Santa Rosa, not Vietnam. Or Kent State. And I *am* marching!" I sounded more confident than I felt.

"You can't. I won't let you." He pounded his fist on the table.

"Excuse me? You won't *let* me?!"

"That's right! I forbid it!" He stamped his foot.

"Didn't you learn anything the last time you used that 'F-word' -- forbid?"

He grimaced. The last time was when he forbade me to go back to school. I was in now in college -- a full-time student.

It was a major turning point in my life. Going to college in the late '60's and early '70's was significant. As a college student at that very crucial time in America's history, I was exposed to the discontent of its youth. I was in a unique position. In my mid-30's, a wife and mother, I sat in classes and the cafeteria with kids whose contemporaries were fighting in Vietnam or dodging the draft in Canada or Sweden. I listened to their rage. Very few still supported U.S. participation in the war. Even most of the Vietnam veterans attending college on the G.I. Bill had concluded we should not be at war in Vietnam.

A cultural revolution was underway across the land. It was a time of galloping social change. Women's Liberation was happening. The Sexual Revolution was happening. The Civil Rights Movement was happening. The Drug Culture was happening. The Counterculture was a significant segment of our population -- that is, "Flower Children" -- Hippies. The Generation Gap was happening. The Environmental Movement had begun.

And the war in Vietnam was happening.

The country was polarized as it had never been except during the Civil War. This time the split was roughly along generational and educational, rather than geographic, lines. Few stayed neutral. Passions were inflamed on all sides.

The elders, by and large, clung to the old ways. They knew what was right. And they didn't question the government. They had come through World Wars I and II, when that would have been unthinkable. As my mother-in-law said, "Don't you think the 'higher-ups' know best? They have information we don't, so we have to trust them."

Young people, in general, weren't so sure the old ways were right, weren't sure their government could be trusted, and were coming up with their own solutions, their own culture. One of their catch phrases was "Never trust anyone over 30".

Better-educated people also were more likely to question what was happening and embrace new ways. They'd been taught to think for themselves, not just accept what they were told.

By May of 1970, when that protest march took place, the war in Vietnam had been going on for several years. By then, a great many Americans questioned U.S. involvement. It was becoming more and more clear that things were not right. Although protests had been going on for some time, I had stayed on the sidelines. I wrote letters to the president and my congressmen, and I wore an anti-war pendant (*War is Not Healthy for Children or Other Living Things*), but that was about the extent of it.

Things had changed. Now shocking headlines screamed at us about our soldiers massacring whole villages, about American soldiers committing atrocities. *My god! What has this war done to us?! Americans are supposed to be the good guys!* There were headlines about the war illegally expanding into Cambodia and Laos. The final outrage was when four Kent State University students were shot and killed, and nine others wounded, on campus by National Guardsmen for exercising their constitutional rights of assembly and free speech.

This was too much! I could stay on the sidelines no longer. I had to make my small voice heard. I had to march. I had to protest.

"If you get arrested, I'm not going to bail you out," said John, resigned to the inevitable. It wasn't that he didn't agree with me. He did. But, a typical journalist, he was an observer, a recorder of life, rather than a full participant. And he didn't want me to be one either. He was accustomed to being in control of his wife, a situation that was rapidly changing -- had already changed.

Our three sons begged to be allowed to march with me. John said No and we gave in to his paternal authority.

I joined hundreds of other protesters. Mendocino Avenue had been blocked off from the SRJC campus to Courthouse Square in the center of town. Huge numbers of police lined the street. Men in suits, probably FBI agents, took everyone's picture. Every attempt was made to intimidate and dissuade protesters.

Among the protesters were, of course, plenty of frowzy-haired hippies dressed in rags. But there were others, as well. There was a contingent of Vietnam veterans wearing fatigues, some pushing others' wheelchairs. There were whole families, including small children. There were middle-aged and middle-class folks, like me. And there were elderly people.

Some protesters carried hand-lettered signs screaming, *Make Love Not War!, Hell No, We Won't Go!, What if they had a war and nobody came?* and *Nazi Ovens in 1944; US Napalm in 1970.* Some bravely carried American flags.

I say bravely because the hawks, who regarded themselves as True Americans, claimed the flag for their own and would deny it to the doves, whom they considered traitors.

On the sidewalk along the parade route, with hordes of helmeted policemen armed with rifles and billy clubs, and FBI guys with their cameras, were incensed pro-war activists lobbing insults. Their placards read, **America, Love It or Leave It** and **My Country, Right or Wrong**.

We marchers were solemn. This was not a frivolous thing we did. We were dead serious. We knew it was important. We held hands or linked arms. Someone started singing "All we are saying is, Give peace a chance."[15] Softly, timidly, we joined in and sang along. Over and over we sang it as we made our way up Mendocino Avenue. It became a mantra, a chant, a plea. Many of us had tears streaming down our faces.

The march ended at Courthouse Square where there were speeches. Before dispersing, we sang a couple more choruses of "Give Peace a Chance". It was our fervent prayer. *Let there be peace on earth.*

Well, I didn't get arrested, and I didn't get beat up or shot. I merely got photographed for my FBI file. I went home and resumed my normal life. But "normal" was in transition. I had changed and would never be the same. I had defied my husband for the second time in roughly a year. And I had publicly stood up to my government. I was no longer a passive, submissive, obedient wife and citizen.

That week was the turning point in public sentiment about the Vietnam War. Americans outraged by our government's actions at home and abroad had reached a critical mass. We could no longer be ignored.

We could be ridiculed. We could be castigated, vilified and berated. But we could not be ignored. The tide had turned. More and more ordinary Americans — not just easily discounted drugged-out hippies — were now "fed up", were now willing to question their government's policies, and demanded to be heard.

Colleges and universities across the nation shut down for the rest of the

---

15. Lyrics and music by John Lennon.

semester in protest.

Finally, but not nearly soon enough, the war ended. It had accomplished nothing except the huge loss of lives and the emptying of America's coffers.

Oh, it had changed our American culture. It had robbed us of our innocence. It had damaged our self-image as Americans: as a people who banded together in troubled times, who in both war and peace were honorable, who trusted and respected our leaders.

Our country had changed and would never be the same.

. . . .

Postscript: Robert MacNamara, Secretary of Defense during John F. Kennedy and Lyndon Johnson's administrations, published his book *In Retrospect* about it. In it he acknowledged the war in Vietnam was a big mistake, and that the 'higher-ups' in the government knew it all along. He admits they lied to get us into the war and kept lying to keep us in it.

Ass Prints

Sonoma State College
Anthropology Department
Class: Culture Change
Spring 1971

W
e never knew what to expect in this class. I suppose that was the
point, since its title was "Culture Change", and in real life, change
most often happens in unexpected ways.

I entered the classroom that day with a couple of classmates who arrived
at the same time as I. Instructed to move the desks up against the walls, we
complied.

In 1971, the SSC campus (like most college campuses) looked like a rag-
pickers' convention. Our instructor -- "James Avanti" -- had just returned
from two years in Afghanistan as a Peace Corps volunteer. Like most college
and university students and faculty members at that time, he was long-haired,
bearded, and wore ragged, faded clothes and scuffed Army boots. Like many
other instructors and a large percentage of the student body, he was said to be
stoned most of the time.

His teaching methods were non-traditional. On the first day of class he
said something like this: "The only education worth having is that which you
get for yourself. I am not going to be your teacher. You are. You are responsible
for your education."

When pressed about grades, which he held to be irrelevant, and our
preoccupation with them tediously *bourgeois,* he said, "You have two options.
You can take over the class for a day and teach. Whatever you want. Or you can
write a paper. You will grade yourselves and I will abide by that grade."

Needless to say, we'd all get A's.

He fielded questions about what kinds of things were acceptable to teach and what types of presentations were expected or preferred, avoiding giving guidelines, always throwing it back on us. We were responsible for our education. The teaching calendar was established and the semester began.

In this back-to-basics hippie era we had an assortment of hands-on learning experiences by idealistic students, e.g., a sheep shearing and wool spinning demonstration, bread baking, high-density gardening. We had art projects: weaving, basketry. We had music: acoustic guitars, dulcimers, recorders. We had demonstrations/lectures on Native American philosophies and culture. We had anything anyone wanted to offer and never knew what to expect.

So that day, when told to clear the center of the room, we thought nothing of it. That day's teacher -- "Jane" -- and several student assistants, busily prepared the room for the lesson. On the bare floor, in the center of the room, they un-rolled a long wide sheet of white paper. Someone covered the glass pane in the door of the windowless room. That was a first and it got everyone's attention.

"Hmmmm. Wonder what that's all about. What are they hiding?"

Jane and her crew took paint pans, rollers and brushes out of brown paper grocery bags and filled the pans with water-soluble paints of various colors.

Checking the clock and giving latecomers an extra couple of minutes, a guard was stationed at the door(!), and class began. In the center of the room, Jane, her accomplices, and Professor Avanti undressed, neatly lining up their well-worn Birkenstocks or scuffed Army boots against the wall. Folding their faded, torn, crudely mended jeans, shirts and Army Surplus fatigue jackets, they stacked them on a file cabinet in the corner.

Now naked, Jane stood in the center of the room. "We're going to do an art project."

Another girl without a stitch on produced a camera.

Jane and her All-togethers invited the rest of us to join them in their nudity. "Every one of you is a participant, whether you join in or sit and watch, cover your eyes, or walk out. Whatever you do, *that* is your participation."

The Starkers encouraged, prodded, cajoled, and tried to shame the rest of us into joining them. Not a single person moved to do so. Everyone's clothes stayed put. On the other hand, no one left. We were in for the duration.

Jane announced that our art project was "Ass Prints". The Nudies divided into two factions: painters and paintees. The painters, one or two at a time, picked up rollers or brushes and dipped them into the paint, whereupon one or two paintees bent over, presenting their posteriors to be smeared with bright colors.

The paintees, carefully positioning their brilliant backsides on the paper on the floor, rolled from side to side to fully register their derrieres, much like the thumb printing process at the DMV, carefully and firmly imprinting tush on paper.

The artists switched roles and continued until each had made his or her own mark on the paper, which probably would end up as a mural on some wall at the college. We speculated on its potential title. Several possibilities were offered: "Em-Bare-Assed". "The Arse Farce". "Fancy Fannies". "The Butt Glut".

As the class drew to a close, the professor apparently decided his rump print wasn't enough. James Avanti announced he'd add a penis print. His partner obliged, dipping the paintbrush into bright green paint, and applied it down one side and up the other. Meticulously positioning himself on the paper, Avanti executed a pelvic thrust to ensure a good impression.

Through the entire class period, the bare-assed photographer snapped photos of the artists at work, and the rest of us as well. Everyone in that room, at his or her level of participation, was thoroughly photographed.

In my small group in the corner sat Al Wahrhaftig, Anthropology professor. Fascinated with the Peace Corps returnee, he'd picked that day to sit in on Avanti's class. Occupying the corner opposite the door, we coped with our nervousness by wisecracking and making bad-ass jokes.

I imagine the assumption among the nudie-cuties was that everyone in college in that era was as free-spirited as they, especially a college like Sonoma State, a.k.a. "Touchy Feely U" and "Granola State".

Maybe they didn't imagine that, in this ostensibly hippie school, most students would cling to middle-class values as well as their clothes, and participate only as observers. It's possible that the day's "teachers" were as shocked by their classmates' reticence as the other class members were by their leaders' naked shenanigans. It's also possible that there were a lot of "wannabe hippies" around. They dressed the part, but.........

All over the room, most students merely sat and watched -- or averted their eyes -- smiling nervously from time to time. Except for our little group in the corner, there was silence. I imagine no one wanted to appear disapproving, and were fascinated with the goings-on. One couldn't appear overly interested in the naked antics, nor could one look away. It was clearly a test of group reactions and peer pressure.

In my small randomly selected group were: Dawna, the class' youngest student -- a shy freshman who lived with her parents and was yet to go out on her first date; a couple of veterans in their mid-20s; Al, the visiting professor; and me, a 36-year-old middle-class housewife and mother. As a matter of fact, I was nearly as naïve as Dawna. Until that day in that class my husband was the only man I'd ever seen naked.

With my tendency to wisecrack in tense situations, I may have been responsible for our small group's temporary cohesiveness. Also, my intention was to allay the discomfort of Dawna the Innocent. From the first day of class she had gravitated to me, the class mom, perhaps the only student in this class of apparent vagrants she could relate to. She seemed to seek me out for comfort, so I felt protective.

In any case, our little group did a lot of cutting up and chuckling through this unique event.

I'd had misgivings about attending Sonoma State. It scared me. It was "a prophet without honor in its own land". The farther one traveled from Sonoma State, the more highly regarded it was. Students came from all over the world to attend SSC, especially its Psychology Department. But in Sonoma County itself, where I lived, SSC, especially the Psych Department, was scorned.

When, at age 34, I started college, it was at the more traditional setting of Santa Rosa Jr. College. That terrified me too, because I so lacked confidence, having been "just a housewife" for so long, reading books for pleasure, not information. I adjusted and adapted, though.

Then it was time to go on to a four year college . . . or quit short of my goal of a college degree. The only school available to me was Sonoma State, and to tell the truth, it scared me. Its reputation was very far-out and local folk disparaged it. Come to find out, its reputation far exceeded its actuality. Until this spring day in 1971, probably the most outrageous thing that had occurred was a little skinny dipping in the campus' lake.

Nothing before or since ever equalled the Ass Prints incident. But the activities in that class that day were exactly what the local populace thought standard at SSC.

As class ended, the *artistes au naturel* toweled off each others' rear ends, dressed, gathered up their art project, and removed the paper over the window in the door. The desks were set back in rows and we left on schedule with ten minutes to get to our next class.

My next class was Genetics Lab. I arrived in class, got my fruit flies from the brooder and joined my usual group. When I mentioned the goings-on in my last class, everyone already knew about it.

My lab partner, a woman about my age, was outraged. "Damn!" she exploded. "*You* were in that class?! It's not fair! It's not fair! I'm about to graduate. I've been here four whole years and nothing like that has ever happened to me. I've waited all this time and it never happened. And you," she sputtered, ". . . in your first semester! It's not fair!"

The Ass Prints class was the talk of the school the next couple of weeks. Avanti was called on the carpet. There was a hearing; he was fired on the spot, asked to gather his things, and leave the campus, *post haste*.

At the time of the official hearing, John, now News Editor at the Press Democrat, deemed it a legitimate news story and sent a reporter to the college. The story appeared in our local paper, then the wire services -- United Press International and Associated Press -- picked it up and broadcast it worldwide. The Press Democrat got phone calls, as did the college. People around the world wanted details. They wanted pictures. They wanted everything they could get. They couldn't get any more than the story in the local paper, though. The class' photographer maintained there was no film in the camera. (I don't believe it for a second.)

Chagrined college administrators did what they could to keep the scandal low-key. The furor soon died down and the ass prints incident was forgotten. Sort of.

California State University, Sonoma
Psychology Department
Fall Semester 1981

Ten years later, after graduating with a BA in Anthropology and getting teaching credentials, I was back at Sonoma State for a Master's degree in Psychology. It wasn't a lowly college anymore; it had been upgraded to a university. The era of explosive change of the '60s and '70s was behind us and Sonoma State had more or less lived down its outrageous reputation.

One day in a Psych class, the instructor told about his sabbatical leave in Australia in the spring of 1971. In a Sydney newspaper he saw an article about a college class in northern California in which people took off their clothes and made ass prints. He quickly scanned it. To his relief, although it was his college, it was not his department.

"I've always wanted to talk to someone who was in that class, to find out what really happened," he said. "But I've never been able to find one."

I smiled, raised my hand, and confessed that I had, in fact, been "a participant" in that infamous class.

Finally, his quest was ended. Now he could get to the bottom of it, so to speak. The spotlight was mine and I told my story.

To quote Dave Barry, I am not making this up.

The End!

Motherless Children

The closer I got to the age at which my parents died (38 and 44) the more keenly I felt my own mortality. Very early-on I learned that there are no guarantees in life. *What if I don't live any longer than my parents did? What if I leave my kids without a mother?*

Neither they nor John knew the first thing about cooking, shopping, or keeping house. The kids had small chores, such as keeping their rooms (sort of) picked up, rinsing their dishes and loading them in the dishwasher. Along with raking the lawn and carrying in groceries, that was about it.

By the time my mom died I was a survivor. At 16 I could cook, I could sew, I could do the things necessary to physical survival. I wanted to make sure my kids had survival skills in case they had to finish growing up without me.

Picking up the pace in my last year or so at CSU, Sonoma, I took 22 units a semester. What with commuting to and from school, sitting in class, and doing all the homework and housework, I was busy . . . and exhausted.

I called a family meeting. Steve was 15, Martin 13, Alex 8. With the five of us around the kitchen table, I began. "We're all busy. Each of us has a job. Dad has his at the newspaper. You kids all have school and homework -- that's your job. It's mine too. We all work hard at our jobs. *And* I do all the work at home. I cook all the meals, do all the laundry and most of the cleaning, all the shopping, and so forth," I started.

"How would you feel about everyone pitching in to keep the household running?"

They wanted to know what that meant.

"We can all keep our own things picked up around the house, and do laundry when it's needed during the week. With the automatic washer and dryer, that's easy. On Saturdays, we'll do the vacuuming, dusting and tidying up. And since there are five of us, how about each of us taking one night a week to fix dinner? I'll take one night, and I'll do the cooking on weekends. You can make whatever you like. If you tell me what you need from the store before I go shopping on Saturdays, I'll get it for you. If not, you can walk down to Safeway and get it yourself."

"But we don't know how to cook."

"It's time you learned," I replied. "I'll help you. Let me know what you want to fix and I'll write out instructions, if you need them. And I'll show you whatever you need to know."

John had come a long way since declaring that anything inside the house was women's work, and he or his sons would be disgraced to do it. He and the kids agreed to this new arrangement. Each one prepared dinner one night a week. Steve, the eldest, was the most adventurous and provided the greatest variety in his meals. Martin did very well too. His favorite and most frequent meal was "hot dog goulash". Alex knew how to make Sloppy Joes and hot dogs, so he fixed Sloppy Joes one week and hot dogs the next, then back to Sloppy Joes. I don't remember what John fixed, but he did his share and didn't complain.

I think they were pleased with their new skills and their contributions to the household. They did their cooking stint even if we had dinner guests on their night to cook. And they learned to operate the vacuum cleaner, dishwasher, washer and dryer.

I was enormously proud of them. This new program worked well. And my anxiety about leaving motherless children was somewhat allayed. All of them are now excellent cooks, and enjoy cooking. Alex went on to become a *chef extraordinaire*. He now has his own restaurant -- *Dóce Lunas* -- in Kenwood (Sonoma County), California.

My birthday:

I was not prepared for the intensity of emotion that slammed me on my 45th birthday. On that day I was older than either of my parents ever got to be. I think, subconsciously, I didn't expect to make it to 45, so when I did, I was overcome with a confusion of emotions.

I felt the heavyheartedness of sadness and loss. I've missed my parents every day of my life. This day served as a powerful reminder of what my children and I had missed.

I also felt elated that maybe I'd live to see my children grown after all, and maybe have grandchildren one day to hold and snuggle, and if I were really lucky, watch them grow up.

I felt so very fortunate, so grateful to be alive. What a glorious gift life on this beautiful planet is! I renewed my commitment to live each day in appreciation and gratitude.

I felt close to both my parents and my children; I was the link between them. I hoped I was able to pass along to my children some of my parents' character and wisdom, their values and ideals, their humor and spirit.

Having made it to my 45th birthday, I may live forever!

The Mini-Skirt

In preparation for a family vacation in Mexico the summer of 1973, I made some traveling clothes, outfits I thought appropriate for a young wife and mother: slacks and tops, a casual skirt or two, and a suit: a knee-length skirt, shell top, and jacket of compatible fabrics.

Like most kids in 1973, the boy's wardrobes consisted of raggedy jeans and Army Surplus shirts. So each got a pair of decent jeans, dress slacks, and a couple of nice shirts. All three declared, "I'll never wear these again!"

"Fine. But you *will* wear them while we're in Mexico."

Mexico did not look kindly on hippies. Anybody who looked like one was not allowed in. It was perceived as disrespectful to their country.

Steve was 16, Martin 14, Alex almost 10. They had longish hair and absolutely refused to let me cut it. We'd have to live with that.

The day before leaving, I was packing when my friend Char Ginsberg stopped by. I showed her the clothes I planned to take. She looked aghast. "That's *so* middle class!" In that era, "middle class" was a pejorative.

She had on a little cotton knit dress. "Here, take this," she said, taking it off and handing it to me. I gave her something of mine to wear home and tossed her dress in my suitcase.

The mini-skirt was new and daring. This little dress, which ended considerably north of mid-thigh, qualified. John, who maintained I should be the poster child for **Modesty**, objected to it. But it was the style, so I wore it. In fact, it was so comfortable I wore it and wore it. Nearly everything else stayed neatly folded in my suitcase.

Martin was the first to fall prey to "Montezuma's Revenge" and was sicker than a dog. In the end, only Steve and I escaped it. The others' terrible trots and mighty miseries slowed us all down but didn't stop us.

The highlight in Mexico City was the *Museo de Anthropologia,* which alone was worth the trip. The best museum I've ever visited, it chronicles life among the Mayans and Aztecs, ending with the invasion of the Conquistadors on April 21, 1519. Even the kids loved it.

Before moving on to the beaches at Mazatlan, we took a bus tour to the Teotihuacán Pyramids. I slipped into Char's little dress and off we went. When I saw that people were climbing the pyramids, I wanted to too.

Eying the hemline of my skirt, John reacted as most husbands would.[16] "You stay here. The kids and I will go up." (Photo, page 354.)

"I don't want to just watch other people have fun. I'm going too. "

"Not in that dress you're not!" he snapped. "It barely covers your underwear. Why didn't you wear slacks?"

"Well, I didn't. And I'm going."

As I moved toward the man-made stone mountain John's jaws tightened, his cheek twitched.

When I started the climb, he followed on the step immediately below me and stayed just behind me all the way. His breath riffled my hair. His body heat smothered me.

By the time we reached the top I wondered why I'd insisted. My heart was about to explode. My lungs were on fire. My legs shook. Why did I think this would be *fun?*

The spectacular stone pyramids, completed around 200 AD, were religious structures. Evidence shows that humans were sacrificed atop the Pyramid of the Sun: victims' hearts were carved out of their chests and, still beating, offered up to the gods. If my heart was any indication, those victims' hearts were pounding to beat the band.

On the way down John stayed right in front of me. The chiseled stone steps were narrow, short, and uneven, forcing us to take hundreds of teeny-tiny steps and making walking difficult. There was no space between us. The toes of my shoes banged the backs of his ankles at every step.

He stuck to me like wallpaper. If I hung back, he hung back too. The kids and I laughed at his doggedness in guarding my modesty. But that didn't stop him.

He said, "N*obody* is going to look up *my* wife's skirt!"

---

16. I acknowledge this in retrospect.

Having Kids Was Starting to Pay Off

teve stepped forward and offered without waiting to be asked. "I'll drive there for you!"

In October 1973, OPEC (the Organization of Petroleum Exporting Countries) announced an oil embargo, causing gasoline shortages in many Western nations. Arab countries would not deliver oil to countries that supported Israel in the Arab-Israeli "Yom Kippur War", including the U.S.

Gas prices spiked from 38¢ a gallon to 55¢; rationing went into effect. One had to get to the gas station first thing in the morning and wait in long lines every odd or even day, according to one's license plate number, for just a couple of gallons. We had two cars, one odd and one even.

Fortunately, Steve was 16 and had gotten his license on the earliest possible date, his 16th birthday. He looked for any excuse to get behind the wheel and go someplace. He volunteered to drive to the closest gas station, at Highway 12 and Middle Rincon Road, every day – or as often as needed -- around 5:30 a.m., when the lines formed.

Having kids was starting to pay off. Steve happily ran errands, drove his brothers where they needed to go, and occasionally, drove the family car on a date.

On Thanksgiving, we drove over the hill to my sister's house with our half of the dinner, unloading the multitude of dishes in front of her house. Once inside, we discovered we'd forgotten something. Steve offered to go back for it and we were happy to let him. Over the hill, across the valley, then back across the valley, and up and over the hill he drove. Only upon arrival back at Pat's house did he discover that the Tupperware mold of "For Goodness Sake Salad" had made the trip -- both directions -- on top of the station wagon. We had set it up there when unloading from the first trip and forgot about it. That proved he was a careful driver.

At Christmas, the boys wanted to go get the Christmas tree themselves, without parental interference. Tossing a saw and hatchet in the back of the station wagon, they set out on Christmas Eve day. Inasmuch as we continued observing the German Christmas Eve tradition of illuminating the tree with candles, we always waited until just a day or two before Christmas to get one. That way it was fresh.

The kids were gone until late afternoon. I have no idea where they went – I probably don't want to know -- but they came home with big smiles, muddy shoes, and a perfectly shaped tree, its full branches evenly spaced, just right for candles. They hauled it out of the station wagon, brought it in the house and proudly set it in the middle of the living room. The house was perfumed with the essence of pine.

The furniture disappeared under its branches. Their beautiful tree touched all four walls of the large room, with at least 12″ of its top bent over at the ceiling.

"Wow!" they exclaimed in amazement, laughing. "It didn't look that big out there!"

"Well, company's coming in a couple of hours," I said. "We've got to trim the tree. And I do mean *trim* the tree!"

The kids got pruning clippers out of the garage and went to work shaping the tree to the proper size, putting candle holders, candles, and ornaments on it while I finished the party preparations. When our guests arrived, no one was aware that the tree wasn't as nature intended.

OPEC lifted the oil embargo on March 18, 1974, and Steve went back to sleeping in.

Death of the Dream

The one who made the decision to divorce gets the blame, rather than the one who made the decision necessary.

My big mistake was in not making that decision at least ten years sooner. I loved John. My heart bled for him. We'd probably still be married if he'd picked on only me. But he didn't.

Before we got married he absolutely vowed, "I'll never do to my kids what my parents did to me." And he meant it. He loved his three sons more than anything and was the best father he could be. But when push came to shove, he couldn't help himself. His parenting imprint was so thorough and so insidious that he was powerless *not* to do to his kids what his parents had done to him.

Martin, our most sensitive child, was the most frequent target. Martin couldn't do anything right. His dad was on his case constantly. He'd done nothing wrong, but got chewed out and put down for anything, everything, and nothing.

Steve wasn't immune. But until close to the end, Alex was exempt.

John didn't realize he was doing it. And he certainly didn't mean to. He was simply on "automatic pilot", acting and reacting as he'd learned in his formative years.

For nearly twenty years I'd tried to get him to go with me to family counseling. A few times he agreed, but we never got there.

I should have left when the emotional abuse first started, but I knew how much he loved his kids.

I should have left ten years earlier, but the kids needed their dad.

I should have left a long time ago, but didn't want to hurt him.

I should have left, but was a coward.

One day, when we'd been married more than twenty years, Steve (18) and Alex (12) came to me. "Mom, you have to do something. Dad is destroying Martin."

That did it. God knows, I'd tried. But nothing I did or tried to do had changed anything.

Steve and Alex weren't suggesting I divorce their father, but they didn't know I'd already tried everything short of that. It wasn't a slam dunk, though. I tried again to get him into counseling. I tried to make him see what he was doing to Martin -- to all of us.

The more stressful his job was, the more stress he brought home. He seemed angry at all of us, criticizing us, yelling at us -- especially Martin. I sympathized with him. I knew he was having a tough time at work.

But our family was in crisis. Martin was in crisis.

John's relationship with his own parents was Love/Hate. Their battles *royale* were legendary. But they *were* his parents -- you have to love your parents. Often, by the time we got back to Santa Rosa from Fresno, he had forgotten all about the horrific row they'd just had. For a long time I thought he was lying. *How could you forget something that intense? That traumatic? That recent?* Eventually, however, I realized he was telling the truth. He really didn't remember. To keep going, he had to erase it from his conscious mind.

I can't imagine his childhood, but I witnessed plenty of scenes when he was an adult. The incident that's most vivid in my mind was this one: Steve was taking guitar lessons. John said he'd always wanted to play the guitar, so I bought him one and encouraged him. He and Steve practiced together. I was so proud.

The next time we visited his parents, I mentioned it to them, thinking they'd be proud, too.

They laughed so hard tears spurted from their eyes. "Ha ha ha ha ha ha ha!" Pa slid off the couch onto the floor, laughing. "Play us a concerto, Juanito! Ha ha ha ha! Play a concerto!" They kept that up for several minutes. When their laughter died down, they wiped their tears and righted themselves on the couch, only to start all over again. "Ha ha ha ha ha ha ha! Play a concerto," they gasped, holding their sides.

John never touched the guitar again.

It has been suggested that perhaps, due to childhood traumas, he might have had PTSD -- Post Traumatic Stress Disorder. I've heard that PTSD can cause or exacerbate Alzheimer's Disease. Tragically, at 78, John is lost in Alzheimer's murky haze.

With great sadness, we divorced. I felt I had no choice. It wasn't what I wanted. I wanted a happy family, but we didn't have that. I had to do what I could to save our children. At 16, it might already be too late for Martin. My sweet, sensitive, funny, lovable Martin.

John accused me of being "cold". I had to be. Once the difficult, painful decision -- which I'd delayed for years -- was made, I had to stand firm. I'd been wishy-washy throughout our twenty-two year marriage. I couldn't be now. He never understood why I divorced him. He thought that's what I wanted.

Once he realized the divorce was for real, and, not only was he losing his wife, he was also in danger of losing his kids, he set about to win them over, and succeeded. However, in his pain and anguish, he portrayed me as the bad guy -- a bad mother, a bad person.

Mom was the one who made the Dreadful Divorce Decision, so it must be her fault.

In 1976, after twenty-two years, our marriage, with its "irreconcilable differences", was "dissolved" by the State of California. Our dream of a happy family and a happy life was shattered.

Steve, 18, was on his own. Martin, 16, and Alex, 12, lived with me, though John and I had joint custody. After a year or so, when Martin moved in with his dad, it broke my heart.

But I hoped John could now, finally, … not do to his kid(s) what his parents had done to him. I hoped this might give them a second chance, that both Martin and John would benefit and do some healing.

Single

A Wild Party

N ow single, with no husband to tell me what I could or couldn't do, I was feeling frivolous. I wanted to do something daring and different. I wanted to throw a wild party.

Alex's 12th birthday was coming up in a few weeks. I'd do it up right. And I didn't need anyone's permission. (I'd long since concluded that John felt the Husband/Father "job description" was to say No to anything his wife and kids wanted to do.)

Invitations went out to 7 or 8 boys, with instructions to "Wear play clothes". The morning of the party, while Alex was off somewhere, I filled 30-to-40 aluminum foil pie tins with Jell-O Whip & Chill chocolate pudding and stacked them in the refrigerator.

When all the guests had arrived I sent the boys to the park around the corner to play soccer. It was a brisk autumn day, warm in the sunshine, chilly in the shade. Pistachio trees and Virginia Creeper were a fiery red; oaks and liquid ambers a multitude of colors. Falling leaves swirled in the breeze and bright chrysanthemums bloomed in neighbors' yards.

While the boys were gone I placed the pies on the ping-pong table in the backyard and covered it over with a sheet. When they came back after their soccer game I fed them hot dogs, cake and ice cream. We sang "...Happy Birthday dear Alex, Happy Birthday to you." Then I sent them out back.

I pulled his good friend, Tom, aside. "Get Alex next to the table, then reach under the sheet and pull out a pie. And shove it in his face."

Tom's eyes widened in disbelief. However, with encouragement and reassurance from Alex's own mother he agreed to it. As the chocolate pie approached the birthday boy's face, his expression went from shock to incredulity to delight, all in three seconds. Then, pudding-faced, he roared with laughter.

I whipped the sheet off, revealing a table full of pies.

"Pie fight!" I shouted. "Have at it, boys!"

With yelps and shouts, whoops and hollers, the battle was on.

Steve, Martin and I stood back laughing as the younger boys raced around the yard throwing and dodging pies, having the time of their lives. When all the pies were thrown and the ruckus had died down, I brought a large plastic tub of warm soapy water, wash cloths and towels so they could clean up before going home.

They flat-out refused.

"No. We want to parade around the block." Dripping from head to foot with thick chocolatey yuck, they showed off their "battle wounds" throughout the neighborhood. Only then would they allow me to come near them with soap and water.

A good time was had by all. Especially me. I don't know if the other kids' mothers appreciated Alex's wild party, but their sons sure did.

My boys and I hosed down the backyard and scrubbed pie filling off the fence, deck, ping-pong table, trees and shrubs, restoring normality.

Knowing I can never top that party, I'm resting on my laurels.

The Gang of Ten
(Names are changed)

W e were the first non-Chinese to visit South China in more than thirty years, since Mao Tse Tung expelled all foreigners and sealed its borders.

An eclectic group, the "gang of ten" ranged from high school dropouts to Ph.D.s, from late-20s to late-40s. We were leftover hippies, rednecks, left-wingers, right-wingers, Christians, Jews, Atheists, adventurers and wannabe adventurers. Kelly was a hairdresser; Maya and Shirley, librarians; Helen, a professor; Kate, a nurse; Hal and Sue, dilettantes; Rod and Ted, "between careers"; and I was a travel agent. In the group was one married couple -- Ted and Kate; Maya was married but traveling solo; the rest of us were single.

Before leaving home we had a meeting in which Ted, our tour leader, strongly cautioned against any "hanky-panky" while in China. Its totalitarian regime was super-strict on morality. He warned that unmarried sex would get us kicked out of China. Immediately. No questions, no excuses, no appeals. I guess he felt it necessary to issue the warning inasmuch as, in the western world, the Sexual Revolution raged on, giving us freedom to behave like rabbits if we chose.

No worry. The two single guys in our group, Hal and Rod, seemed like the good-buddy/just-friends type. And we doubted we'd have either the time or opportunity to connect with a local, if so inclined.

At that meeting, we talked about food on the trip and agreed it would be best not to question what we were served. We'd eat whatever was set in front of us. This was an adventure.

After a frenetic week of shopping, sightseeing, and gorging ourselves in

Hong Kong's plethora of fabulous restaurants, we entered Communist China by train and spent one night in a Guanghzhou (Canton) hotel, best described by Sue in her declaration, "I've stayed in better jails than this!"

That evening after dinner, Helen produced a cassette tape on which she had recorded classic American jazz. Downstairs, just outside the dining room, she discovered a tape player, inserted her cassette, and pushed *Play*. An audience instantly appeared: hotel workers and guests, all Chinese. They listened with rapt attention, beaming while tapping their feet, some with tears in their eyes. They'd been denied all western music since Mao Tse Tung's takeover and the establishment of People's Republic of China. It was clear they'd missed it.

After breakfast the next day we piled into the white China Tourism Office van that had brought us from the train station the night before. Our guides, "Old Mr. Lee" and "Young Mr. Lee", would be super-glued to us throughout our China stay.

Our first day in China we spent in the van -- practically the only motor vehicle on the mostly unpaved roads -- dining at roadside eateries and stopping at hold-your-nose privies. Careening down the road, swerving to avoid people and farm animals, our foreheads were pressed to the van's windows. We didn't want to miss a thing. We felt as if in a time warp. China's farming techniques were 15th-century, at best.

We were impressed with the industriousness of the Chinese people, though. Constantly in motion, they worked, worked, worked. Men and women alike wore shapeless gray quilted pajama-like outfits. And everyone rode bicycles or walked wherever they went.

After lunch, all work stopped. Everyone simply lay down on the job and took a nap. Then, an hour or so later, they picked up their tools and went back to work. Very civilized.

We commented on China's seeming tranquility. Everything appeared extraordinarily orderly and serene.

At the end of the long day we settled into our hotel in Tai Shan where we spent the next week. My roommate, Helen, peeked into the bathroom.

"Thank God!" she exclaimed when she found that there was no splintery chunk of wood in lieu of toilet paper, as there had been in the Guangzhou hotel. We had an oversized concrete bathtub and a western-style toilet. We were thankful for that too.

Our room was Spartan but adequate: two twin beds with stone-hard mattresses, a small dresser over which a postcard-sized mirror hung by a string on a nail. The floor was bare concrete. There were no keys, nor were there locks on the doors. They would remain unlocked whether we were there or not. We were assured -- and reassured -- that we and our belongings were safe. "A hall guard is on duty at all times."

Our window looked out over a lake. In the center of the lake was an island, artfully landscaped with pine trees and boulders. It was linked to the mainland by a lovely arched stone bridge. Beneath our window lay a trail rimming the lake, so we awoke each morning to the sound of early-morning joggers. Their open-backed cloth slippers *shush shushed* as they made their way around the lake. And on the island, at 6 a.m. daily, a Tai Chi master led a group in the graceful movements of that ancient martial art.

Over the next week, our intense schedule took us to factories, schools, historical and scenic spots, dams and hydro-electric plants, as well as cultural and sports events. We had no free time, but asked to be allowed to wander through the local farmers market. Although China was a communist country, farmers were allowed to sell their over-quota produce and keep the money. There were no department stores, no boutiques, no shops. Aside from the government-run store in Guanzhou -- for foreign visitors only -- there was no place to buy anything and nothing to buy. So the outdoor market was lively.

One day in Tai Shan's farmers market, I wandered away from the rest of the group to get a closer look at something. I hadn't gone more than a few yards when I felt a vise-like grip on my upper arm. I turned to find a squat middle-aged Chinese woman, very stern, grasping my arm. "You go!" she demanded, pointing in the direction of my fellow travelers. "You go!" she threatened, dragging me toward them. She got no argument from me.

When the other nine learned of it we surmised that, to keep us in line, each of us was assigned a covert "escort" everywhere we went. We would see what they wanted us to see. And do what they wanted us to do. That's all. No more.

To fully appreciate their China experience, Helen, Shirley, Hal and Kelly hauled themselves out of bed every morning for Tai Chi on the island. The others went less regularly. I went once, but only to take pictures. (I am not an early morning person, nor am I an exercise person.) That morning, to my delight, this scene greeted me: Hal, my old buddy and honorary brother, was not getting the hang of it. The Tai Chi Master lost patience. Pointing at Hal, he roared, "You . . . move . . . like . . . *elephant!*"

That made getting up before dawn worth it.

The Gang of Ten took sick: colds, intestinal disorders, flu-like symptoms. Like the Ten Little Indians they fell, one by one. All except me. Every day I gobbled multi-vitamins, garlic pills, and acidophilus capsules. At first the others teased me, but as time went on each of them came begging for " . . . whatever you're taking."

The Misters Lee arranged appointments with a traditional Chinese doctor for anyone who wished. All nine jumped at the chance. The doctor took their pulse at the wrist and inspected their tongues. Each was diagnosed and prescribed a nasty, bitter tea. Each left the clinic with a sack of herbs, roots, seeds and bark to be steeped in boiling water. The resulting medicinal tea was to be consumed several times a day, every day, until it was gone. In spite of their rigorous adherence to the treatment, nobody got better.

They all continued on the China Tourism Office's killer schedule, though. No one was willing to miss anything.

By the time we'd been in Tai Shan a few days -- nine or ten days into the trip -- Rod and Maya began sitting together on the van, laughing too much at each other's jokes, and flirting across the dinner table. Hmmmm, maybe we'd misjudged ol' Rod. Maybe he wasn't only a "just friends" type of guy after all.

Before leaving Tai Shan we wanted to ride the bicycles parked in the hotel lobby. Everyone in China rode bikes and we wanted to, too. We told the Misters Lee of our desire. Their firm reply was, "No."

We pleaded.

"No."

We begged.

"No."

We implored.

"No."

Then somebody thought to ask, "Why not?"

With great certainty Old Mr. Lee answered, "American don't ride bike. Make accident. Make danger on road."

We were stunned. "Why would you think that?"

His answer amazed us. "American all drive car, not ride bike."

"Of course we ride bikes," we insisted. They didn't believe us. We continued to insist; they were steadfast. Finally, they relented to this extent: "We see you able to ride bike. You ride around lake. Two time," he said sternly, holding up two fingers. "We watch. Then we say."

It was only after circling the lake twice without incident that we were allowed on the streets and roads of south China. Of course, as soon as we had wheels we scattered, away from the watchful eyes of our guides and covert escorts. And we had a ball. It was the first freedom we'd had since entering China. Some of us took a right at the first intersection and went off into the countryside. Others rode toward town.

As it turned out, the Misters Lee were right. We did cause accidents. The bike-riding citizens of Tai Shan Province were so astonished to see non-Chinese foreigners on bikes that they crashed into each other willy-nilly.

As the first non-Chinese to visit in two or more generations, we were the objects of enormous curiosity. Everywhere we went a crowd gathered instantly. Everyone wanted to get up-close-and-personal. And their "personal space" is much tighter than ours. But we never felt threatened; they weren't unfriendly, just curious.

One day, Kelly begged off group activities pleading a stomachache. That evening she confided to me that she'd had a midday rendezvous -- an assignation. It seems she had a little romance going with a young man from the morning Tai Chi class. That afternoon she and her young man sat on the bridge by our hotel, dangling their feet over the edge, holding hands, having a picnic. I envied her the opportunity to connect with a real Chinese person. The closest I got was my covert escort.

After having shopped at the local farmers market a few times and noticing exotic items among the bok choy, pressed ducks, "coolie hats" and piglets, the more adventurous members of our group decided to buy a cobra for the hotel's chef to cook up for dinner. They located a vendor with a live specimen. Old Mr. Lee nodded his approval of it and the purchase was made. The seller reached into the basket and grabbed the snake just below the head, which he expertly whacked off, then handed its twitching, bloody body to Rod. With his usual swagger, holding it at arm's length, Rod carried it like a trophy through the streets of Tai Shan, all the way back to the hotel.

Cobra meat is believed to be powerful medicine, so it's very expensive. The cost, not included in the price of the trip, would be shared by those who ate it. I debated. It would be interesting, and it would give me bragging rights, but I felt squeamish . . . and couldn't justify the expense. I declined.

As soon as it was eaten I regretted my decision. *How often will you have the chance to eat something as outlandish as cobra?* I chastised myself. *You spineless ninny!* I decided that if I got another chance to eat an exotic delicacy I'd go for it.

One night toward the end of our stay in Tai Shan, after another exhausting day of sightseeing, Helen and I were awakened by the Inner Sanctum-creak of our door slowly opening. We heard the door click shut, then the quiet slap-slap of bare feet on the concrete floor. We bolted upright in the pitch-dark, our hearts pounding. We gasped in preparation to screaming, but before we could, our intruder spoke.

"Carol," he breathed. It was the familiar voice of my pseudo-brother, Hal. "Which bed is yours?"

In a whisper as loud as she dared, Helen shrieked, "What are you doing in here? Are you crazy?! Get out! Get out!"

Quietly but urgently Hal replied, "I need a place to sleep."

"You have a place to sleep!" I pointed out, wondering how much Chinese brandy he'd drunk. "Your room is next door!"

Helen whisper-screamed, "You'll get us kicked out of China! Get out!"

"I can't," groaned Hal. "Maya's in my room . . . with Rod. They're gettin' it on!"

"Oh my god!" Helen and I breathed in unison.

"Unbelievable!" Hal continued. "Like I wasn't even there! . . . . . . I can't stay in there with all that going on!"

"Oh, all right," I said, making myself as small as I could. "Come on. Get in bed." The two of us tried to get comfortable on the narrow bed. Helen calmed down eventually, after repeating several times, "We're gonna get kicked out of China!"

I guess we all got some sleep, I don't remember. And nobody got kicked out of China. Our hall monitor must have been on a tea break.

A couple of days before we would leave Tai Shan, our cobra-eaters, led by Rod and Maya, went back to the market to purchase a half-monkey (cut vertically), which would be that evening's main course for those who dared. *Here's my chance to redeem myself,* I thought. *I'll never have another chance to eat monkey meat. I'm gonna go for it.*

"I'm in. Tell the chef to set a place for me at the Monkey Table."

Monkey meat, like cobra, is thought to possess ultra-healing powers, so it too is exorbitantly costly. *What the hell!* I told myself. *It'll be worth it, for bragging rights, if nothing else.*

That evening, we adventurous monkey-eaters sat at one table, the spineless ninnies at another. Spirits were high. As usual, joking, teasing and laughing were in full sway. With longneck bottles of Tsing Tao beer we toasted one another and our friend the monkey, who would be our main course. *"Ganbei!"* We clinked bottles. *"Ganbei!"*

The chef emerged from the kitchen, beaming, carrying a clay pot in thickly gloved hands. He set it at the center of the table, and, with a grand flourish, lifted the cover. The entré was a sort of monkey fricassee. Up out of the gravy stuck a skinny brown arm topped by a hand -- a tiny hand that looked way too human.

I gulped, trying to overcome my revulsion, but reluctantly pushed my chair away from the table. "Sorry," I said. "I can't do this," and departed to the spineless ninnies' table.

That very pricey monkey meat, with all its curative potency, had no more effect on my ailing friends than had the cobra or their bitter tea. But they had bragging rights.

While in Tai Shan, we encountered a few citizens who were eager to tell us their stories; intellectuals who had been forced into slave labor or imprisoned and tortured during Mao's reign. Other Chinese bystanders smacked them on their heads and shoulders, shouting and gesturing, "Go away!" and telling us those people were crazy. We didn't believe it. Our storytellers seemed quite sane to us.

Hal invited one such man to our hotel. The man wanted to see our few books, touching them and turning their pages reverently. Mao's "Little Red Book" was the only book anyone in China been allowed to read or own for thirty-one years. He was thrilled to have a conversation about something other than that damn Little Red Book. He and Hal exchanged addresses and promised to write.

The China portion of the trip was coming to an end. We traveled by van to the China/Macao border. The Misters Lee would leave us there; they were not allowed to set foot outside of China. Once across the border we transferred onto a bus and were on our way. By this time everyone but me was seriously ill -- feverish, achy, pokey, shaky, snotty, hacking, raspy, and weak as new puppies.

As they crawled out of the van, Old Mr. Lee gestured for me to stay. When all the others were out, he said, "You not sick. You only one. You take care others. Make promise!" he demanded.

Oh great! I thought. *I have to be everybody's mother.* I envisioned myself carrying everyone's luggage, checking them in and out of hotels, and babysitting all of them. But what choice did I have? He wouldn't let me off the van until I promised.

Once out of China, my companions recovered quickly, so my Florence Nightingale stint was short-lived. We continued on to Macao, then hovercrafted back to Hong Kong where, a couple of days later, we boarded the plane for home.

Despite its difficulties, we had fallen in love with China, and had bonded with one another. We vowed to return -- together, if possible.

We were ten people, strangers mostly, bonded in camaraderie in an extraordinary adventure that can never be repeated. People change. Circumstances change. And the world changes. As Buddhism teaches, the only permanent thing is impermanence.

With lightning-speed, China has gone from 15th century to 21st. It became a superpower, a modern industrialized capitalist phenomenon, and a prosperous nation -- one The Gang of Ten wouldn't recognize. But then, we probably wouldn't recognize ourselves either. A lot of water under the bridge . . .

For one brief moment everything came together in a grand *tour de force,* creating the drama that could only have happened with those people, at that time, in that place.

Part III

Married Again

Isn't It Romantic?

Wayne rushed me into marriage. But I admit complicity. I thought it was terribly romantic.

> Isn't it romantic?
> Music in the night,
> a dream that can be heard.
> Isn't it romantic?

Later on, I figured out that he had to hurry me, before I got to know him; before I saw his Dr. Jekyll/Mr. Hyde swings; before I discovered his addictions.

Tall and handsome, tanned a deep bronze, with the muscled physique of an athlete, he swept me off my feet. Obviously, I wanted to be swept. I felt as if I were the female lead in a romantic novel or movie. Nothing like this had ever happened. At least, not to me. In my mind, I was still the plain, scrawny, awkward girl none of the boys in high school noticed; the woman John convinced had zero sex appeal; the woman no other man would ever want.

Our courtship was the stuff of dreams. Barefoot moonlit walks on white beaches, the warmth of the sand beneath my feet and his hand in mine sending erotic yearnings through me. Cocktails on the deck overlooking the azure Caribbean. As I splashed in the tepid water of Megan's Bay, he took his daily swim -- a mile out and another mile back, rising from the sea like Trident.

He was handsome. He was a college graduate, and had a good job. And he was spiritual. He said so himself, using all the right words to back up his claim. He talked the talk like an expert.

After three dates in Santa Rosa (where we met while he visited his sons over the holidays), several phone calls and letters, and less than a week with him on St. Thomas in the Virgin Islands, I was smitten. When he proposed, I breathlessly accepted.

I was a travel consultant at Creative Journeys. I offered to quit my job and move to St. Thomas. I'd get a job there. In his opinion, the only job I could get was that of bartender or waitress, working nights, which he vetoed. I don't know why, since he worked nights too.

His job as Night Watchman on St. Thomas' airport expansion project afforded him plenty of time to stroll in the moonlight, gaze at the stars, meditate, read, write letters, clip his toenails, snooze.

But he insisted on quitting this cushy job and coming back to California, where he assured me he could get any number of jobs. And if we wanted, he could be rehired by his current employer, Parsons, which had construction projects all over the world. Since I love to travel and live abroad, that prospect excited me.

He encouraged me to have a career, whatever I wanted.

He was outgoing and unthreatened by my gregariousness.

He was proud of my body and loved showing me off.

He seemed the very opposite of John.

I returned from St. Thomas to Santa Rosa aglow, with a ring on my finger. We'd spent less than two weeks together when he quit his job and returned to California, arriving a month prior to the wedding. By then the whole thing was in motion and, like the Bullet Train, damn near unstoppable. Not that I wanted to stop it.

Arrangements were made, invitations were in the mail, rings purchased.

Still on Cloud-Nine, I married Wayne.

They Tried to Warn Me

My mother used to say, "You never really know a person until you've lived with him."

I should have kicked Wayne out after the first month, or sooner. And I knew it. But I was too prideful. I didn't want to admit I'd made a mistake. And I didn't want to be a two-time divorcée. There was disgrace and failure in being divorced, increasing exponentially at being divorced more than once. I plunged into serious denial, which lasted much too long. Ten years.

After a few months I ran into Wayne's first wife, whom I knew slightly. "There are a few things you neglected to tell me," I accused.

Smiling slyly and shrugging, she responded, "You didn't ask."

That's true. I didn't.

Others had tried to warn me, though.

"He's a bum, you know," his former boss informed me.

"Don't you think you should wait awhile?" asked his brother. "Until you get to know him better?"

And,

"When is he going to start looking for a job?" my sister asked again and again. And again and again.

Stupid with "love", I dismissed them all.

It didn't take me long to figure out he was an alcoholic. But I was a lot slower in picking up on the fact that alcohol was merely a secondary addiction. Two other addictions ran his life.

I figure they dated back to a childhood bout with rheumatic fever.

Doctors advised that if he exerted himself in any way, his heart would give out and he'd die. So his doting mother, grandmother and two aunts showered him with sympathy, caring for him lovingly, filling his every need and whim so he'd never have to lift a finger and exert himself.

I believe that was what television psychologist, Dr. Phil (McGraw), refers to as (Wayne's) "defining moment."

That, and the fact that those four women were convinced he'd grow up to be CEO of General Motors or President of the United States -- without any effort on his part, of course, but just because he was so special. It wasn't difficult to persuade him of it.

So, on top of a galaxy-sized ego and his certainty that he was a superior being, which allowed for a mean streak a mile wide, he acquired two insidious and crippling addictions: Sympathy, with copious amounts of self-pity; and Sloth, with a prodigious sense of entitlement.

But, God help me, I loved him. I denied that I was absolutely miserable. Isn't the human psyche a marvelous thing, allowing us to **believe** what we **know** is untrue?

Good Things

h, there were some good things about Wayne. Among them:
- He washed both of our cars every Saturday.
- He kept us supplied with abalone.
- He was willing to go traveling with me.
- He fixed his own breakfast.

And for awhile that was enough.

Somewhere along the way, before meeting me, he had become Bi-polar -- a chemical imbalance formerly known as "Manic-Depressive" -- although it went diagnosed or treated. In his manic phase he was enthusiastic, eager to try new things and participate in life. It was always short-lived.

His manic phase ended on our wedding night. That night he went depressive. Hugely depressive. In his depressive phase he was self-pitying, morose, subject to weeping, cruelty and blame, doubting his life had worth.

Once again, it felt as if I'd landed in a looney bin. Different, but a looney bin all the same.

I suspect his self-doubts and self-pity, fed by Bi-Polar Disorder, is what set him on his spiritual path -- his search for God. When he came across the teachings of Joel Goldsmith, he'd found his guru.

Goldsmith's philosophy, like most (probably all) religions, is rife with shoulds and should nots, musts and must nots. In my opinion, its followers, by and large, feel vastly superior to us lesser mortals, suiting his need to feel exceptional. It took over his life. He hoped I'd be as taken with Goldsmith's Infinite Way as he was.

I began reading Goldsmith's first book. By the end of the first chapter, I wondered if we were reading the same book. My interpretation was very different from his. When I tried to discuss it, his response was, "It's not open for discussion. You can't intellectualize it. You just have to accept it."

That was it for me. An agnostic, I reserve the right to question and discuss everything, and to intellectualize the hell out of it if I want to.

I defend anyone's right to believe and practice whatever he or she wants. Just don't foist it on me.

I believe Wayne was an earnest seeker. He meditated faithfully first thing every morning, but never felt that he broke through. (My opinion: a typical addict, he was totally self-absorbed. The only thing he could focus on was himself, so he couldn't get out of his own way.)

Part of Goldsmith's belief system, according to Wayne, was that one mustn't go to medical doctors, but rather, God will heal you. And when the time comes to "make your transition" you should be so pure, so spirit-filled, your body simply vaporizes. So he rejected any suggestion that he get treatment for his Bi-Polar condition, or anything else, and made me promise that if he ever contracted something potentially fatal, like cancer, I would not arrange for medical intervention or pressure him to seek it.

Wayne's ego wanted him to be a spiritual teacher. While he idolized Joel Goldsmith, he wanted to *be* Robert Schuler (Crystal Cathedral). He wanted to be on TV, with millions of adoring followers watching him preach and philosophize, and sending him tons of money.

Be Your Own Guru

From Day-One, Wayne pressured me. "Be all you can be. Reach your fullest potential." At first I kind of enjoyed it. Having been married to John, who never wanted me to be anything -- never thought I could be anything -- this change was refreshing and affirming. He encouraged me to go back to school.

This was not an act of generosity. I was the one with money. As an independent divorcée, I did quite well on some real estate investments over the five years between marriages.

With him cheering me on, I returned to Sonoma State for an MA in Psychology, and then went on for a Ph.D. at a graduate school in the Bay Area. In the process, I also became a Certified Clinical Hypnotherapist, began seeing clients in private practice and presenting Personal Growth workshops.

Several of my clients and students asked if I were a Science of Mind minister.
"What's that?" I asked.
"Maybe you know it as the Church of Religious Science."
"Never heard of it."
I learned there's a group that teaches pretty much what I believe and teach, i.e., basically, positive thinking: "Change your thinking, Change your life." That was amazing. I always thought the regular religions -- Catholic, Baptist, Methodist, Presbyterian, Lutheran, Mormon, Judaism, Buddhism, Hinduism, Islam, etc. --were all there was. I never knew there were people out there who had reached the same conclusions -- more or less -- as I.

"You sound just like them," my clients and students told me.
When asked, I tell people I'm a universalist (small u). By that, I mean I

am non-religious. No dogma, no hierarchy, nobody controlling anybody, acceptance of all others. I believe in the universal commandments of love and kindness. And I believe in everyone's right to find his or her own spiritual path -- or none, if that's (their) choice. As for "God", I believe in a force of spirit -- but not something that's *out there* somewhere. I believe the God-force is within each of us.

In the course of being a therapist, I also learned that there are a lot of people who would be only too happy to give away all their power. To me. Only too happy to have me make all their decisions for them, happy to turn over all their responsibility.

To my astonishment, it happened over and over again. Clients or students expected me, begged me, to direct their lives. I can see where that would be a real ego charge to some people, and that some people might use it as an opportunity to misuse power.

When Wayne saw that people wanted me to be their leader he swung into high gear. He was willing to abdicate his own desired position in favor of me. Now he wanted *me* to be a Robert Schuler or Terri Cole Whitaker, with my own church, my own TV show, raking in the dough, becoming a multi-millionaire.

What he really wanted, in my opinion, was to live the lifestyle of the rich and famous, with no effort on his part. Practically from day-one, he'd said, "I wish you'd hurry up and get your act together so you can support me in the manner to which I'd like to become accustomed."

I had no desire to be a preacher of any kind. That was his fantasy. I led seminars, wrote books, and did some speaking engagements in addition to seeing therapy clients. He took that and ran with it. He wanted me to be a guru, but not the Ram Dass kind. He wanted me to be the kind who uses one's influence -- one's bully pulpit -- one's "spirituality" to become rich and powerful.

But that's not me. I don't require great wealth and fame. I don't want people's power. And I really don't want people to be dependent on me.

In the '80s, there was a book called *If You Meet a Guru on the Road, Kill Him,* and another, *Be Your Own Guru.* I totally agree with them.

My goal is to help people empower themselves -- become their own guru -- not to take their power or their money.

Many a guru is willing to sell "enlightenment" for as much as the traffic will bear. I believe the best things in life, including enlightenment, are free. That doesn't mean they come without effort, but paying big bucks isn't the answer.

This is Spiritual?

My understanding of "spiritual" is apparently vastly different from Wayne's. Proud he was so spiritual, he announced it broadly. The following are a few examples of "Mr. Spiritual's" behavior:

~~~~~

One September day, my son Martin brought a pick-up load of apples from the Sebastopol farm where he lived. I went to work peeling, chopping, stewing, mashing, spicing, and canning applesauce. When Wayne got home and saw what I was doing, he asked, "Why are you making so much?"

"So we'll have it for the next year, and Martin will have a good amount, and we'll have some for the other kids and some for our friends."

Within the next few days Wayne had eaten every last smidgen of that truckload of applesauce. I guessed he'd rather have a massive onslaught of the runs than share with anyone.

This is spiritual?

~~~~~

Zewdi is my "adopted" daughter. She and her husband Mehari and two of their children are Eritrean refugees from Eritrea. They're fine people, and I'm their "Grandma Carol". To point out the obvious, they're black Africans.

I once went with Zewdi and Mehari to speak on their behalf when they applied to rent a house. Wayne had a fit. "Why go out of your way to help black people?"

When they moved in they needed window coverings. I bought drapes for them at a garage sale. I think I spent $5. Before giving them to Zewdi, I washed them. Since I had no clotheslines, I took them next door to hang on my neighbor's line. My arms were loaded with damp drapes when Wayne came in. He asked about them. "They're curtains for Zewdi's new house. I washed them. I'm going to hang 'em out at Jeann's."

He waited until I was on my way back, then stood on the front deck reading me the riot act, yelling for all the neighbors to hear that I had no business spending our money on black people.

This is spiritual?

(I'd blocked this memory. Jeann recently reminded me of it.)

~~~~~

Miraculously, after returning from our big trip ("Our Odyssey" starts on page 223.) Wayne got another job requiring only his presence. He was in a holding pattern until a subdivision that he would "sit" got built. He meditated, read, loafed, snoozed, etc., . . . and got paid for it. The only trouble was, it was boring. Once in a while he sneaked off to an afternoon movie. He must have known his behavior was shameful because he never mentioned it to me. And he never let on that he'd already seen a movie I wanted to see, but went along as if it were brand new. I only found out about his covert afternoon entertainments from a friend who saw him at a matinée.

This is spiritual?

~~~~~

Wayne earned my three sons' hatred. Martin, 22, asked, "Mom, you're nice to his kids. Why can't he be nice to yours?"

"I don't know, honey. *(Sigh.)* I don't know."

This is spiritual?

~~~~~

Over and over, Wayne pointed out my spiritual inferiority, and by inference, his superiority. Here's one conversation:

Wayne: "You're not spiritual! You're not even searching for God!"

Carol: "Why should I search for something that isn't lost."

He harumphed and stalked away.

This is spiritual?

~~~~~

Outraged as I was by his behavior, I mostly overlooked it, continuing on, steadfastly in denial. Even while pretending (to myself as well as everyone else) I was happy, I did a lot of crying: laughing on the outside, crying on the inside. My learning curve was very flat.

We're all each others' teachers. I learned a lot from Wayne, not the least of which was, *Anyone who proclaims he's spiritual isn't.*

A Funny Thing Happened

A funny thing happened on my way to becoming a therapist. I thought hypnosis would be an excellent addition to my "therapeutic toolbox", so part-way through my MA program I registered for an off-campus class in Hypnosis for Professionals.

The day before my class began I visited Eeyore's Bookstore in Cotati, where a little paperback book jumped out at me. "Jumped" might be a bit too strong, but it did stick out from all the other books and attracted my attention.

What's odd about that is that on my previous visit to Eeyore's, the same little book had stuck out then too. The book was Dick Sutphen's *You Were Born Again to be Together*, which I think is a really dumb title. I'd have been embarrassed to let anyone see me with it, so I pushed it back in line with the other books.

But now it had happened a second time. *Maybe I should get that book. Maybe it's a sign. Maybe I'm supposed to have it.* I picked it up and flipped through its pages. It's about reincarnation, and past-life regressions to discover previous lives, and in this case, previous lives with a particular person. I hid it under my arm as I walked through the store and purchased it, hoping the cashier would ring it up quickly and hide it in a bag before anyone came up behind me.

I read it in one sitting and became excited, shouting, "This is fantastic!" and "I love this!" and finally, "Oh my god, I want to do this!" By the time I finished it I knew I wanted to include this type of therapy in my counseling repertoire.

At my class the next morning, when the instructor asked why we were taking this class, why we wanted to learn hypnosis, I announced, "I want to be a Past-Life Therapist."

I'm a bit impulsive. When I see something I want to do, I go for it. As I said earlier, there are a whole lot of things I'd never have done if not for that penchant -- things I'd be sorry not to have done. Being a Past-life Therapist is high on that list.

In my opinion, hypnosis is the most efficient and effective method of therapy. It's the closest thing to magic I've seen. It often works where nothing else does. Of course, it doesn't work for everyone in every situation. Nothing does.

Hypnotherapy is effective because it bypasses the conscious mind and goes directly to the subconscious, where memories of everything we've ever experienced live, where habits and addictions live, where fears and phobias live, where emotions live. So it's the means by which we can access them and solve a lot of problems. Under hypnosis, one is up to two-hundred times more open to suggestion than in the normal state of consciousness, so "re-programing" is effective.

Many times, over my 26 years as a psychotherapist and clinical hypnotherapist, I saw clients who had spent years and years with a psychiatrist or standard psychologist, but made little or no progress. With hypnosis, however, the cause of their problem was often accessed in the first session and quickly cleared up.

Very often, a decision made at a traumatic moment continues -- based on the information available at the time of the original event -- to direct one's behaviors or emotions throughout one's life. Locked away in the subconscious, it carries forward, regardless of one's changed circumstances, "protecting" him or her from whatever originally caused the problem.

As an adjunct to regular therapy, I often conducted regressions into a client's past to help overcome phobias, compulsions, blocks; recognize and alter behavior and personality patterns; decide upon plans for their future or determine one's "life purpose"; learn the cause or origin of an attraction or repulsion to a person, place or thing; determine the "origin" of or reason for, ailments, disorders, and surprisingly, even accidents.

Over the next year and a half, while completing my M.A. in Psychology, which included two counseling internships, I was in private practice as a Certified Clinical Hypnotherapist. I became well-known in the San Francisco Bay Area as a Regression Therapist -- a Past-Life Therapist.

When I the time came to write my Masters Thesis, I wanted to do it on that fascinating subject. I asked my Masters program mentor, Nina Menrath, for permission. She replied, "It's not standard psychological procedure, you know."

"No, but it should be," I insisted.

"Well," Nina shrugged, "it's all right with me. But you'll have to clear it with the Department Chair."

I tootled off to the office of Art Warmoth, Chairman of the Psychology Department, and repeated my request. "It's not standard psychological practice," he said.

I just looked at him.

"It's all right with me, but you'll need the permission of the president."

At the office of the university president, I asked again. "Well," said Pres. Holbert W. Burns, "it's highly unusual. But I guess it'll be okay." He nodded, lifting his shoulders. "Sure. Go ahead."

The following chapter is mostly from my thesis: *Past-Life Regression in Therapy: Expanding the Scope of the Unconscious.*[17]

Before a client came in for the initial past-life regression appointment I sent out a 60-minute cassette tape which explained and demonstrated the process . . . and answered frequently asked questions about hypnosis, regression, the subconscious mind, and the theory of reincarnation, as well as my credentials and experience.

---

17. California State College, Sonoma, 1984.

Four Case Studies

(The names have been changed to protect clients' identity.)

MOIRA

In her late twenties, Moira was attracted to Ron, her dance instructor. She wondered why. A happily married woman with two small children, she had quit college when she got married and was happy being a homemaker. Dancing was an outlet for her creativity and energy. Ron was a few years older than she. She felt an "overwhelming attraction" to him but had never acted on it and didn't know if he shared it.

After induction into the deep level hypnotic trance necessary for regression, I suggested, "Go to a previous lifetime in which you had a relationship with Ron, *if there ever was one.* If there was more than one, go to the one most relevant to this life."

Moira emerged in Stockholm, Sweden, a nineteen-year-old university student named Lyn, in the 1920s. Lyn was a brilliant, dedicated student, majoring in Biological Sciences, with a special interest in genetics research. She continued on at the university and completed her doctorate. Rolph was her professor. It was through his influence that her interest in genetics blossomed. He became her mentor and, eventually, her lover. She couldn't say whether they ever married, but after the completion of her education they lived together in a country home on a lake outside Stockholm.

She and Rolph worked together researching genetics and genetic engineering. They became well-known in their field, traveling and lecturing widely. They were happy together and fulfilled in their work.

Toward the end of the 1930s, the Nazis made their presence felt throughout Europe, threatening their neighbors on all sides, and occupying other countries as well. There was a great deal of talk of a "superior race" -- the "Master Race" -- by the Nazis. Lyn and Rolph were approached by Nazi agents to work for them and help create this "Master Race". They declined. At first they were courted, then threatened. Although they lived in a neutral country, they feared for their lives and felt they must escape. By this time, Nazis and Nazi agents were everywhere.

Lyn and Rolph attempted to escape on a train -- she wasn't sure where -- but never made it. The train was stopped and they were taken to a prison camp where both died.

While Moira was in trance, I asked if she could identify anyone in that lifetime as the person who is Ron in this life. "Yes. Rolph is Ron."

I asked if there was anything else to be learned from that lifetime that might be relevant to this one. She nodded. "Yes. Now I understand why I could never finish college. I'd always find reasons not to finish classes . . . . . I'd drop out before the semester ended. And then I got married rather than finish school.

"I must have felt that all that education was the cause of my early death. . . . I've sabotaged myself where college was concerned so I could live to a ripe old age. Maybe now, if I ever decide to go back to school, I'll be able to complete it successfully."

TROY

Troy, a student at UC Berkeley, had a "deadly fear" of tunnels and other enclosures with low ceilings. "I can't even sleep in a bunk bed. I feel like it's going to come crashing down on top of me."

After the induction, I told him to ". . . go to the situation or event that was the cause or origin of your phobia concerning low ceilings and small places."

He immediately began gasping for breath, writhing and struggling in the recliner chair in my office. "I can't breathe. I can't move. Get it off! Get it off! I can't breathe. I'm dying." He sucked in air and fought to get away from whatever was pinning him down and crushing him.

I quickly instructed him to go to the moment of his death, feeling no pain. "Your spirit has now left your body. Rise above your body and look down on it. . . . Tell me what you see." He immediately relaxed and quieted, looking peaceful. He said his body was crushed in a mine shaft when it collapsed, sending tons of rocks and dirt on top of him.

To learn more, I took him backwards in time: "Joe" was the oldest child of a wealthy Chicago attorney in the 1850s. He was expected to join his father's firm, but rebelled. He wanted to go off on an adventure. They quarreled and he left.

California's Gold Rush was underway and Joe went off to seek his fortune. He headed west and met up with two men who had the same idea; they became "partners". They found an abandoned mine shaft and began working it. That is, Joe began working it. His partners didn't want to go in; they "let" Joe go.

On his first descent into the shaft in search of gold, it caved in on him, ending his adventure, his dreams, his life. Joe was barely out of his teens.

Troy was ready to release his phobia now that he knew the cause of it. Several months later, when I spoke with him, he told me he is now having a much easier time of being in close quarters. He no longer feels the panic and fear.

LORRAINE

Lorraine is a very pretty woman, 27 years old. At the time of the regression she had been married seven years to a man of a different race and socio-economic background. They had two small children. It had been a stormy and difficult marriage from the beginning. Twice she had checked herself into a shelter for battered women, which is how we met. My internship was at a day-care center for children who were abused or neglected, or whose parents were in physically abusive relationships. Participation was often court-ordered, and therapy was required for the family.

Lorraine had allowed herself to be abused for many years before getting help. Deep down she believed she deserved no better. Her low self-esteem manifests itself in fat. She is 5'2" and weighs over 200 pounds.

Lorraine is very sweet, a giving person who always put others' needs and desires before her own. She teaches Sunday School.

I saw Lorraine for a series of counseling sessions in which I occasion-ally used hypnosis. In one, I regressed her into a "previous lifetime", "... to a situation or event that is the origin or cause of your weight problem." As I usually do, I asked her a series of questions to help her become oriented to the past-life situation.

"Are you indoors or outdoors?"

"Indoors."

"Is it daytime or nighttime?"

"Nighttime."

"What kind of room are you in?"

"It's a saloon."

"What are you wearing on your feet?"

"High heels."

"What are you wearing on the rest of your body?"

"A dress. Green satin."

"What are you doing in this saloon? What is your purpose in being here?"

"I work here."

"What is your job? What do you do?"

"I sell drinks."

"Anything else?"

"Yes. .... I go to bed with men."

"Do you like doing that?"

"No. But I need the money."

And so it went. "Sarah" lived in Ft. Worth, Texas in the 1840s. Except for the money, her job offered only degradation, humiliation, and abuse. She was determined to find a way out of it. She gave birth to a son, Johnny, continued saving her money, and plotted their escape.

With her savings she bought a horse and a buckboard wagon, and the two of them set out for Wyoming where land was free for the taking. It was far enough away that it was unlikely anyone would know of her past. She got a small plot of land and built a log cabin herself. She and Johnny lived and worked on the farm for a few years when she met and married a nice man, and soon after, had another child, a daughter. She was very happy.

I took her, still in a hypnotic trance, into her higher consciousness and asked her to look back over that lifetime to find any lessons that might be there for her. The lessons she found were: "I have to be strong. I have to take care of myself. I have to plan ahead."

I asked if there was anything else to be gained from reviewing that lifetime. She answered vehemently, "Yes! I am never going to be abused by a man again!" She shook with emotion.

I then asked, "What in Sarah's life caused you to be overweight in this life?" She repeated, "I'm never going to be abused by a man again!" adding, "I was too pretty. I'm hiding under my fat so men won't be attracted to me and abuse me."

"But that didn't work. You are fat, and you have been abused by a least one man. So that's not the answer."

"No. Not the whole answer."

It seemed to me that if she worked on the first three lessons from Sarah's lifetime (I have to be strong. I have to take care of myself. I have to plan ahead.), the weight issue would be taken care of. My objective was to help her strengthen her self-image and build her self-esteem so she would be strong enough to choose and/or develop non-abusive, healthy relationships.

In the nine or ten months since this regression, Lorraine has changed a great deal. She is still with her husband, Tom, who is also my client. Their relationship has changed to a degree unimaginable a year ago. She is becoming stronger all the time. She will no longer tolerate abusive behavior.

Tom likes the new Lorraine much better than the old one, and respects her more. Equally important is the fact that he likes and respects himself more.

I continued to be excited and thrilled by the efficacy of this type of therapy, to say nothing of the fabulous stories and scenes coming out of regression sessions.

I wrote my thesis, which was approved by the university, got my Masters Degree, and continued on toward a Ph.D. in Psychology. I led seminars and lectured, and occasionally appeared on radio and TV, talking about Past-Life Regression.

One day, I was interviewed on a San Francisco radio station. A woman racing down Highway 101 in Marin County heard the show. Her only writing implement was a tube of lipstick, and the only paper to write on, that morning's SF Chronicle. Scribbling my name and phone number on the newspaper in the passenger seat, she went home and talked it over with her family. Then she called me and we set up an appointment for her 20-year-old son, "Jerry".

JERRY

Over the past several years, Jerry's parents had taken him to every kind of doctor and therapist they could, including endocrinologists, acupuncturists, and psychiatrists. Nothing had any effect. At 20, he was still pre-pubescent. A big kid -- 6' -- he was apple-cheeked, had no facial or body hair, and, by his account, his masculine organs were those of an 8-year-old boy.

I asked if he were willing to see what we could find out through hypnotic regression, maybe exploring a previous life or two. By then he was willing to try anything. I was his last resort.

"Go to the situation or event that is the cause or origin of your delayed gonadal maturation."

Jerry looked around in the life in which he'd landed, and found his previous self, a young man named Nathaniel, on a wharf in 18th -century England -- in the office of his shipping company.

He was married to a beautiful girl and desperately in love with her. He loved her so much he spent most of his time down at the dock tending to business. He wanted to provide for her and fulfill all her material desires.

Upset that he spent so little time with her, feeling unloved and neglected, his wife sent him an angry note saying she was leaving him. "Don't look for me. You won't find me."

Nathaniel was devastated and, of course, went looking for her. His reason for being successful gone, he abandoned his business and spent all his time searching.

Jerry described the search -- the types of places Nathaniel looked for her.

Ultimately, he entered a house of ill-repute where a young woman beckoned. She wore a gown identical to his wife's. He eagerly followed her into her "crib". Something in him snapped; he grabbed a brass letter opener and stabbed her to death.

He ran. And ran. The police were in pursuit. Eventually, he was arrested, tried, convicted, and sentenced to death by hanging. On the day of the execution, an enthusiastic crowd gathered. In it was his brother, who, according to Jerry, is his brother in this life too. Their eyes met; his brother transmitting love and forgiveness through his gaze. Then a hood was placed over Nathaniel's head and the trapdoor dropped. It was over. He was dead.

I asked, "What are you experiencing now?"

"Peace. And guilt. I feel guilty. I did a terrible thing."

"Yes. Nathaniel did. But you're not Nathaniel. You're Jerry, and you haven't done anything bad. I want you to look back over that life and tell me -- your subconscious mind knows -- how that life is relevant to your current one, especially to your delayed maturation."

He was quiet for a couple of minutes. I didn't interrupt. Then, as if a light went on inside his head, his face brightened. "Oh!" he exclaimed, "if I remain a boy, I won't get into that kind of trouble."

"Ahhh. Your subconscious mind is protecting you by keeping you out of whorehouses?"

"Yes."

"All right. Thank your subconscious mind for protecting you all this time. And tell it you no longer need that kind of protection. Tell it you're not that person anymore, and the person you are -- Jerry -- would never do anything of that nature."

He did. We worked on relieving Jerry of any residual guilt and assuring his subconscious mind that it's safe now to be a man.

A few days later I sent him a cassette tape of his session, which I copied from my reel-to-reel recorder on which I recorded all my past-life therapy sessions.

Three months went by. Then a note from his mother arrived, saying something like, "It may be just a coincidence, but I thought you'd like to know that Jerry is now shaving every day, and the rest of his physical maturing has come along nicely, too."

Coincidence? Uh u-uh! No way, José!

After listening (at his invitation) to Jerry's session on tape, his parents were flabbergasted by the detail in it. They told me, "It has to be real, because in creative writing classes he can never get past the first sentence. He writes one line, then just sits there the rest of the class, unable to think of anything else to say. He has absolutely no imagination."

In any event, he provided me with my most dramatic past-life therapy case.

I was often asked, "But is it real?" or "Do you believe in that stuff?" My answer was, "Does it matter?"

As a therapist, all I cared about was the result. As a person, however, I do believe in "that stuff". It's what makes sense to me. It's the subject of another book.

My Spirit Guide

Although I'd done hundreds of past-life regressions, I'd never been regressed. And, of course, I wondered. *Who might **I** have been? How might it have shaped who **I** am now?*

But I didn't trust just anyone to regress me. I have huge respect for the mind and anything regarding it. Hypnosis, especially regression hypnosis, is not a parlor game; it should be taken very seriously. If I were to be regressed I'd want to be sure my therapist could calmly and wisely guide me through it.

I require that my regressionist be an expert, someone caring and wise, calm and competent and experienced -- at least as good as I.

I joined a professional organization called the Association of Past-life Regression Therapists -- APRT -- and went to several of their conferences. There were sessions on a variety of topics relating to past life therapy, taught by experts in the field, including psychologists and psychiatrists, most of whom kept their past-life therapy practice on the QT. It's not standard psychological practice, you know.

At these conferences, there were always a lot of "recognitions," relationships from previous existences. (You were born again to find each other at an APRT conference?) At one, a guy from Sacramento -- Larry -- "recognized" me. We must have known each other before, in some other life, right? He asked if he could regress me to find out. After learning his qualifications, experience and background, I said, "Okay." We found a couch in the conference lobby. In the few minutes before the next seminar, we barely touched on a past life, without delving into it, but got a possible "answer". Through the regression I "saw" myself, a boy, maybe 8 years old, on the desert. I was the "camel boy" tending to our group's livestock. Larry was my older brother in that desert lifetime. Cool!

As one of my clients said, "Past-life regression is Disneyland for adults."

Eventually, I went to a conference wherein participants broke into dyads and regressed one another under supervision. In one of my regressions I was a man -- a wealthy silk merchant -- in 12th century Persia. My "message" from that life was that it's okay to be rich.

In the second regression, I was a Native American -- a male this time too. In this one, our village or small tribe was about to be attacked. Too young to fight, I was sent off on horseback to bring help from a neighboring village. By the time I got back with reinforcements all my village's able-bodied men had been killed. Other than a couple of really old men, I was the only remaining male. I spent the rest of that life with the heavy responsibility of providing food and shelter for all my tribe's women and children.

On reflection, as I write this, *Maybe that's the reason I resist having people be dependent on me. Hmmmmm.....*

But back to the conference. The real biggie of the day was when I was asked, under hypnosis, to bring forth my "spirit guide".

S h a z á a m ! There he was.

At least 7' tall, a bronzed god, muscled, his upper body glistening, his lower body in full silk pantaloons. I don't remember if he wore a turban, but he looked like he'd stepped out of Arabian Nights. Only better. His teeth flashed Chiclet-white against his swarthy skin; his emerald eyes warm and loving. He was one gorgeous hunk of man.

We flew into each other's arms, holding each other tight. All these years later, I still go all quivery thinking about it.

He told me he's always taken care of me and always will. His long arms form a mobile fortress that surrounds me wherever I go. He runs interference, keeping me out of harm's way -- at least physical harm.

His name is Jamal.

Gawd, I love hypnotherapy!

Does Jamal exist? Is there such a thing as "spirit guides"? I can only hope so.

What's the Point?

At the pre-school day-care center where I interned, the employees and therapists were, of course, child advocates. Protectors of children. Guardians of children's safety. It was a sanctuary for children who had been abused and/or neglected by their parents, or whose parents' relationships were violent. Its stated purpose: "To break the cycle of family violence."

It was a wonderful place for those children. They were safe. They were nurtured. They were loved. They were entertained. They were educated. They were socialized in positive ways. The problem was, the children's parents were The Enemy.

The other therapists, as well as the children's caregivers, were all young. Idealistic. Outraged. Judgmental. When the parents of one of the children walked through the front door of this wonderful place, a solid wall of animosity and condemnation greeted them.

At the monthly meetings of the therapists -- interns and supervisors -- the view was that the children's parents were hopeless. "Those scumbags will never change." "They're criminals!" "They're beyond hope." Although they met with the parents in therapy every week, the foregone conclusion was that it was futile. Their attitude toward those parents demonstrated their view of them as despicable creatures.

The result, of course, was that the parents didn't change. It was a self-fulfilling prophecy. The cycle of violence was not broken. There had never been one case they could point to where their therapy worked. That was all the proof they needed that abusers can't change.

I had to wonder, *Then what's the point of the therapy?*

The parents were required to attend weekly therapy sessions. In most cases it was court-ordered. In others, parents voluntarily enrolled when they found themselves out of control.

When I began my internship I was 46 or 47, had children of my own, and had a great deal more life experience than any of the others. I was given three families to work with: a couple with two children; and two single mothers, one with three children, the other with two. I started seeing the parents at the day-care center, but quickly moved them to my office when I became aware of the hostility with which they were met in that setting. The day-care center that was so nurturing for their children was a toxic environment for them. (I continued working there with their children, though.)

It's all fine and well to provide sanctuary, but this place was only day-care, and it was just for pre-schoolers. What about when the children go home? They were with their parents nights and weekends. And they would be with them from day-one of Kindergarten until they turned eighteen. If we were to break the cycle of family violence, we had to do more than just provide temporary refuge for the children. We had to affect change in the parents -- the family.

In my opinion, we couldn't do that with disapproval and animosity. I tried to get that point across at the therapists' meetings, but was not heard. So I more-or-less divorced myself from the day-care center and did my own thing with my counselees.

I used every therapeutic technique I could think of, including a few not taught in "therapy school". My most effective "weapon" in the war against family violence was belief. My innate optimism guided me.

As I got to know my clients and they got to know me, I let them know I believed in them 100%. I believed they could change. I believed they *would* change. I believed they would learn self-control. I believed they would learn to like themselves. I believed they were worthy of having happy families and happy lives. I believed they were worthy of love.

I learned that the abusers had themselves been abused as children, so they were victims, also. We set about healing those devastating wounds.

In the nine-months over which I counseled them, the cycle of violence was broken in all three of my families. We proved they could change.

But nobody paid any attention.

Part IV

Odyssey

My Travels With Wayne

Three-quarters through my Ph.D. program, I became disillusioned with it. One night, after class, I came home and told Wayne, "I've been thinking. Your job at the subdivision is winding down, and I'm not happy with my Ph.D. program. We're never going to be any younger than we are now, we're strong and healthy, we have a little money, and we've got each other. We've both always wanted to go around the world . . . so why don't we just drop everything and take off for the next year or so?"

He thought about it for half-a-minute, then answered, "Okay, let's do it!"

Over the next three months I closed down my practice and Wayne finished up his job as subdivision salesman.

We had some ideas about things we hoped to accomplish on the trip. Foremost, we wanted to see the world -- learn about other cultures, see and feel places where historical events occurred, great classical art and architecture, some of the natural wonders of the world, eat ethnic foods and drink local beverages.

As a more specific focus, we wanted to visit places of spiritual significance, unsure what that even meant, sort of a course in comparative religions. We wanted to be exposed to the world's "high energy" spots -- places chosen as sites for temples and cathedrals; visit spiritual communities, from New Age enclaves to ashrams of various traditions; allow ourselves to experience different teachings and practices.

One could say that the purpose of the trip was to take an inner journey on our outward worldly journey.

Another reason for my wanting to take this trip was my upcoming 50th birthday -- to do something exciting and wonderful to celebrate it. This was not even thought of in the planning phase, but it must have been in the back of my mind all along. As the trip progressed and my half-century birthday came closer it became more and more important to me.

Despite all our reasons and rationalizations, we took this trip just because we wanted to and could.

We each took one piece of carry-on luggage: a soft-sided suitcase with shoulder straps. Aside from our major transportation expenses, i.e., a 'Round-the-World ticket on Canadian Air and Air India, trains and ships, we put our-selves on a budget of $50 per day, covering food, lodging, local transportation, and incidentals -- for the two of us. We knew there would be places where $50 wouldn't stretch, but hoped others would make up for it. On average, we'd spend no more than $50 a day. We would take only public transportation; no taxis or rental cars. We agreed this would be an "experiencing trip", rather than a buying trip. Our souvenirs would be photos and memories.

Following are some brief recollections -- a few of the highlights, and low lights, of our trip. Some are from my writings following the trip, some are new.

July 15, 1985
   ...Once aloft, with no turning back, a whole new set of anxieties opened up. How would we get along in countries where we didn't know the language? Where all the signs were unreadable? Where the monetary system was entirely different and the currency undecipherable?

We'd soon be landing in a city about which we knew virtually nothing. There was no one to meet us, no hotel reservations, prepared itineraries or schedules. This would be our *modus operandi* for the trip.

All of a sudden we realized how much we didn't know, and how "on our own" we were. Could we manage?

We were about to find out.

Amsterdam

We ventured out onto the streets of Amsterdam, this stranger of a city that would become a good friend in just a few days, embarking upon our new career: Walking & Gawking. Amsterdam is the perfect place for it, full of old-world charm and friendly people.

Our little "inn" was near *Rembrandt Plein,* the museums, the Heinekin brewery, lovely parks splashed with bright flowers, canals with picturesque draw bridges and an amazing variety of boats, including houseboats, and tightly packed houses with fanciful façades.

…To get to a recommended Indonesian restaurant, we had to walk through Amsterdam's famous red light district. Licensed prostitutes showcase themselves in display windows along the street, dressed scantily, often with bizarre makeup and hairstyles. Anything to attract potential customers.

…Amsterdam also has a lot of "Sex Shops". It's a little jarring, in a lovely old street lined with quaint old buildings, to see brazen neon signs shrieking "SEX SHOP". We never did find out what a sex shop is or what goes on inside one.

…The Dutch are very tolerant. Holland is a country which accepts all cultures and races without apparent bias. It was a refuge for hippies in the '60's and '70's. Like San Francisco, Amsterdam is a mecca for gays.

…A jovial Dutchman told us that the Dutch invented "Keeping up with the Joneses". To demonstrate their affluence each tried to outdo the other in their homes' façades, furniture, gardens, and even lace curtains, all of which makes this country totally delightful.

At night it transforms into a fairyland, aglow with millions of lights. Shimmering ribbons of light danced a ballet on the gently rippling water of the canals.

…A visit to Anne Frank's house was profoundly moving. The pulsating shriek of a European police siren chillingly recalled the scene in the play in which the Gestapo pull up to the building where Anne's family hid, then stomp upstairs to arrest the terrified group. Their emotion was still palpable in that building.

…Holland was our "shake-down cruise". We discovered we could cope with travel in a foreign country. It was the ideal place to start. Nearly everyone speaks English, they're marvelous hosts, and they actually like Americans.

The English Channel

…It was past midnight when our Amsterdam-to-London omnibus boarded the ferry at Calais. …After a sleepless night in painfully uncomfortable chairs, we watched as, over the ship's bow, the sunrise spotlighted Dover's white limestone cliffs rising out of the dark waters of the channel. At just that moment, BBC Radio (from London) played "The White Cliffs of Dover", which was broadcast over the ship's loudspeakers.

As the sun cast its early morning rays on those chalky white cliffs, Vera Lynn's throaty voice sang,

> There'll be bluebirds over
> The white cliffs of Dover,
> Tomorrow, just you wait and see.
> There'll be love and laughter
> And peace ever after.
> Tomorrow, when the world is free, *et cetera*.

I was just a child during the war but I recall the song and the emotions it elicited. Hearing it that morning, crossing the English Channel, my eyes filled with tears and my throat tightened. A wonderful, poignant coincidence.

London

At the Oxford Hotel, the "loo" was down the hall and the toilet tissue was like waxed paper. Useless!

This B & B, run by Pakistanis, had a TV-room/parlour on the main floor and a cheery breakfast room in the cellar. Cooking and serving "brekkie" was a delightful English mum who, it seemed, was the last English person in all of London. The streets were full of people from everywhere else on earth: India, Africa, the Middle-East, Asia, Southeast Asia, the Caribbean, the Continent, many of them in vibrant ethnic costumes. We couldn't help wondering, "Where are all the Brits?"

Our little hotel was about a half-mile from Buckingham Palace. The Queen was our neighbor. We were within walking distance of everything. But then we walked 10 - 20 miles a day, so a lot of things were in walking distance. A 4-day Rover Pass (unlimited bus rides) cost £2 (about $2.50) each. We saw the Houses of Parliament, No. 10 Downing Street, Big Ben, King James Palace, the Tower of London, London Bridge, Picadilly Circus, Hyde Park, Soho, the museums, Kensington Gardens, Covent Gardens, antique shops and flea markets.

Just to be in London -- the London of Dickens, the London of Mother Goose. What a thrill.

...One day, after many sightseeing miles, we arrived at Westminster Abbey, footsore and dry of throat. Tea was served in the old abbey garden -- we loved it.

...One day, near Victoria Station and Buckingham Palace, we saw quite a few elegantly dressed English people: ladies in lovely outfits complete with hats and gloves; the gentlemen were just as fine, some wearing dark suits, others in morning coats, striped trousers, ascots, and top hats. Some traveled by limousine, others by taxi, still others by bus -- and a few in opulent horse-drawn carriages with liveried coachmen.

...Later that day, from the upper level of a double-decker bus as we passed Buckingham Palace, we saw an open garden gate in the tall stone wall, watched over by uniformed Palace Guardsmen. Queen Elizabeth II was hosting a tea party. For this, the true Brits came out.

Craning our necks, we peered into the Queen's garden: guests milled and sat at umbrellaed tables as servants passed among them with trays of refreshments.

Pussycat, Pussycat, where have you been?
I've been to London to look at the Queen's tea party.

In my opinion, London is the world's largest and best theme park, with costumed people everywhere, fun rides, cool things to buy, eat and drink. It seemed as if the residents were part of the show, playing their roles to perfection.

. . .With this trip we'd jumped off the cliff, so to speak, and it was scary. Wayne reacted by becoming domineering and "take-charge". I let him. Why should both of us be uptight and over-organized? It annoyed him that I was carefree and relaxed, and it irritated me that he was uptight and controlling. (Sort of a replay of my childhood: my sister, organized and surrogate mother-bossy, and me, devil-may-care.)

Stonehenge & Salisbury

...Why here? we wondered. Why drag those humongous stones all the way here? What's so special about this spot? ...The history of Stonehenge is shrouded in mystery. No one knows who built it some 4,000 years ago. More than 80 stones, each weighing 4-to-50 tons, were brought from Wales, 180 to 240 miles away, depending on the route taken. Some claim it's a high energy spot.

…We took the first bus of the day. It arrived early, so the magical spot wasn't crowded. We took pictures and ambled around it, wishing we could get inside the ropes, into its center. Since we couldn't, Wayne was done. He was ready to leave. I needed to stay longer and be alone, so I invited him to wander off.

As I stood alone just outside the ropes securing the stones, strange vibrations raced through my body. I'd never experienced anything like this. It was pleasant: a quiet excitement, an inner arousal, like a small electrical charge coursing through my body, an energy surge. Interesting.

…Arriving back in Salisbury around noon, we went directly to the town square. The dignified, elderly lady of a city we'd seen the night before had transformed into a vibrant young girl on market day. Gaily colored umbrellas and awnings sheltered stalls and tables where fresh garden fruit and vegetables and merchandise attracted buyers. Enjoying delicious homemade pasty-pies purchased under a bright parasol, we wandered through the crowds, in living history.

…Our next stop was 13th-century Salisbury Cathedral, which boasts the tallest steeple in England and houses a copy of the Magna Carta. …In the cathedral that day, several choirs competed in a choral festival. The vaulted chambers reverberated with voices making a joyful noise unto the Lord.

Glastonbury

It was dark and rainy when we got off the bus in Glastonbury. The Tourist Information Office was closed, but, after hours, they often posted available accommodations on the door. Wayne ran to check while I huddled with the luggage in a stone arch out of the rain.

The longer I stood there, the more aware I was of sensations similar to the ones at Stonehenge. This time, the "electrical currents" came up from the sidewalk, through my feet and all the way up to tingle my scalp. "This is too weird. I must be really tired."

…Trudging up Wearyall Hill toward our B & B, lugging heavy bags on our backs, we commented on the appropriateness of its name.

Glastonbury is allegedly one of the most powerful "acupuncture" points on earth, on the "ley line" (meridian) that runs, point to point, directly through the Great Pyramid in Egypt. The Abbey is said to be situated where several ley lines intersect, and to possess extremely powerful energy.

...Legend has it that when Jesus was a boy he traveled here with his mother's uncle, Joseph of Arimathea, a wealthy tin merchant. After Jesus' crucifixion, Joseph returned to Glastonbury, then an island in the sea, bringing with him the Silver Chalice used at the Last Supper. This Holy Grail was supposedly buried for safekeeping near a natural spring -- the Chalice Well. Many believe it is still there.

On Wearyall Hill, a few yards from our B & B, is a thorn tree said to have sprouted from Joseph of Arimathea's staff, which he stuck in the ground where he first set foot on land.

...Glastonbury is steeped in Arthurian legends as well: Camelot is very near Glastonbury. In the 5th century, when Arthur was mortally wounded, he was taken by rowboat to the mythic Isle of Avalon, his burial place. In the 12th century, his tomb was uncovered just outside Glastonbury Cathedral. In the tomb lay a lead cross inscribed in Latin, "Here lies interred, in the Isle of Avalon, the renowned King Arthur." The skeletons of a man over 6' tall and a small flaxen-haired woman -- his Guinevere -- were dug up, then reburied at the cathedral's altar. Both the early and later burial sites are marked.

...Glastonbury Abbey was among the first to include articles of art and beauty. The Abbot in power believed spirituality may be enhanced through art; an edifice built for the purpose of glorifying God should be a beauteous thing. Though censured, he insisted that paintings, sculpture, mosaics, stained-glass, etc., be in this temple. When it was built, in the Dark Ages, it was believed such things would distract worshippers.

We walked through all sections of the Abbey -- the large chambers and the main altar. Then we stepped into a small plain room. There, a tingling sensation such as I felt the previous evening began again. We were in "St. Mary's Chapel", which is the site of the daub-and-wattle church built by Joesph of Arimathea and the 12 men who came with him from Jerusalem. When we went out, the tingling stopped, only to resume when we returned.

Leaving the Abbey grounds, I recognized this place. This was where I'd stood the night before to keep out of the rain. It was the main entrance to the Abbey. I've since learned that this whole area gives off such high energy that sensations like the ones I experienced are quite commonplace.

...The Glastonbury Abbey is in ruins only because in 1539, when the pope denied King Henry VIII permission to divorce his first wife, Catherine of Aragon,

Henry issued an edict that all English churches sever their ties with Rome. The Abbot of Glastonbury refused. This so enraged King Henry that he ordered the Abbot hung, drawn and quartered. He then sold the Abbey to the highest bidder, a man who cared nothing for history or religion. The new owner used it as a quarry, selling it off, stone by stone. Throughout the city, bits and pieces of the old cathedral can be seen in homes, shops, and gardens.

...A pattern was emerging in our travels. Most places we went, I wanted to settle in and get the feel of the place, relax and enjoy it. Wayne, however, would get to a place, look around, and say, "Well, we were going to stay here XXX days, but we can see everything in XX -- or maybe even X days."

Wherever we were, his head was already in the next place as he studied its guidebook. Before leaving home he promised not to be like the father, played by Chevy Chase, in the National Lampoon movie, "Vacation": after great difficulties and multiple delays, the family arrives at the Grand Canyon, takes a 3-second look, piles back in the car and drives off. This was what was happening. We'd spend great gobs of time, effort and money to get somewhere, only to have a "3-second look" and move on to the next place.

We left Glastonbury before I was ready.

Findhorn

Findhorn, which from the beginning had a strongly spiritual basis, first became known for its unorthodox gardening methods. It has since become a center for spiritual and holistic education. The Findhorn brochure states:

> We have no formal doctrine or creed. The Foundation is based on the idea that humanity is involved in an evolutionary expansion of consciousness which will, in turn, create new patterns of civilisation for all of society and promote a planetary culture infused with spiritual values.
>
> Our educational programmes aim to nourish this step by helping participants discover their own inner spirit and wisdom.
>
> Life itself is seen as the classroom, and living in the community is our main educational experience, because it provides a supportive setting for our work of raising consciousness and embodying spiritual qualities in our daily lives.
>
> Communal living is our "common unity." It forms the living laboratory in which spiritual ideals presented in workshops and courses are actually tested out in our daily lives.

This was my kind of place, my kind of spirituality.

...Half of every day was spent working. Hatha yoga. Wayne wanted to cook. I chose the garden. ...Business executives scrubbed toilets; a terrified schoolteacher scraped paint high atop a wobbly ladder; a scientist tended trees in the nursery; a pre-school teacher sanded walls; and a nurse, an electronics engineer, and I pulled weeds in the garden.

..."Findhorn runs on tea." Those of us in the garden spent most of our time getting into and out of our "Wellies" (Wellington rubber boots) and rain gear. With all the tea breaks, it's a miracle anything ever got done.

The other half of the day was spent as a group: "attuning", sharing, meditating, and dancing sacred dances from many cultures. We played games that teach cooperation, trust, and unity rather than competition and separation. All the growth-oriented exercises and activities were aimed at expansion of consciousness.

...We bought a few books. One included this poem by one of Findhorn's founding members, Eileen Caddy.

> Wake up and live.
> Set your sights high, the higher the better.
> Expect the most wonderful things to happen,
>   not in the future but right now.
> Realize that nothing is too good.
> Allow absolutely nothing to hamper you
>   or hold you up in any way.
> Be enthusiastic about life;
>   it is a wonderful life.
> Make it so by your enthusiasm.

...For me, the high point of the week was a field trip to a forest glen on the Findhorn River for a morning of meditation and quietude. The forest was beautiful -- green, soothing, healing, so serene -- with the swift Findhorn River running through it, forcible and black.[18]

I made my way down to the river's edge and walked until I found a rocky outcropping jutting out over the surging river above an eddy. I contemplated the swooshing, swishing, swirling black water; the rushing, whirling, dizzying vortex. Drawn out of myself, I was lured through its spiraling maelström, deeper

18. The water runs through peat bogs before reaching the Findhorn River, turning it black.

and deeper into some mysterious space beyond.

...On Friday night we had a farewell party, with songs and laughter, music and dancing, wine and snacks. Since we'd leave at 5 a.m., we said our good-byes that night. In the party atmosphere, Wayne's secondary addiction reared its ugly head. He poured himself glass after glass after glass of red wine from a gallon jug (until someone snatched it up and put it away), transforming from a congenial chap to a belligerent, insulting misanthrope, wiping out the goodwill he'd built up over a week of camaraderie and communal living.

Glasgow

...In Glasgow we had to change trains and train stations, necessitating a jog through the center of town. From quite a distance, approaching the square in the city center, we heard bagpipes. Quickening our steps, we thought excitedly, "We'll get to see a band of *real* Scottish pipers *in* Scotland."

There it was as we rounded the corner, its members dressed in tartan kilts and sashes, tasseled knee-high stockings and small plaid hats, marching through the square, with the leader high-stepping and thrusting his baton skyward. We were thrilled to see actual Scotsmen marching and playing the screechy music of the bagpipe, the drummer marking time on the big bass drum.

Finally close enough to see the print on the drum, we read, "The Capitol City Highlanders Pipe Band of Austin, Texas." *Çest la vie.*

Paris & Chartres

...We felt like dancing in the streets. So we did. "Our hearts were young and gay." We felt 20. Being in Paris is like drinking champagne. We were in the world's most fantastic city.

But even here, Wayne took one look around and said, "We can do this town in three days." Our original plan was six. I put my foot down; six days it was. I was learning.

The setting on the Seine and the architecture of Paris makes it the most beautiful city in the world. Walking through the city, we were continually awestruck.

...Paris, "The City of Lights." The whole world seemed to be abroad that evening. Everyone was simply *toujours gai.* Sidewalk cafés did a lively business, serving wines and liqueurs while street musicians strolled and entertained. The streets were filled with lovers, young and not so young, walking arm-in-arm, laughing, snuggling.

I'd always heard that Parisians were arrogant and unfriendly. The opposite was true for us. The Parisians we met couldn't have been nicer or more helpful. On our last night we went to a little neighborhood café where we struck up a conversation with one of the other patrons. He ran down the street to his home and brought back a small signed oil painting of the Notre Dame, which he gave us. "*Souvenir de Paris.*"

Parisian exuberance is infectious. We couldn't help but catch the French virus -- this *Joie de Vivre* -- and hoped we'd never be cured.

…We rode the train to Chartres, an hour-and-a-half from Paris, to see for ourselves what was so special about its Gothic cathedral. Begun in 1194 AD, it was completed in only 27 years by the same group of builders, as opposed to the several generations of workers it took to complete the *Notre Dame de Paris* in over 300 years.

…Built on the highest spot in the area, its two dissimilar spires were visible long before we reached the station. On entering its cool candlelit chamber we were overwhelmed.

Its stained glass windows may be the most exquisite anywhere. The enormous circular one high in the front wall, elegant and ethereal, with countless tiny pieces of glass in shades of blue, took my breath away. The cathedral provided a three-dimensional "picture book" for the illiterate populace in the middle ages. Statues and carvings in all parts of the edifice, inside and out, depict religious life and history as well as secular life in that time.

…Our last night in Paris, walking through this city of romance, we set out to drink in the champagne that is Paris. We celebrated *Joie de Vivre! Au Revoir, Paris.*

…We were wearing down. We drove ourselves hard, making every minute count. We may never pass this way again, so we had to do it all now.

Traveling is exhausting. Getting from place to place can be grueling, requiring long hours in uncomfortable situations. Then you're on the go. You have to learn everything you can, experience it fully, and move on to the next place. There are no days off; every day is as fatiguing as every other.

"Travel," I remembered, is derived from "travail": *painfully difficult or burdensome work, toil; pain, anguish, suffering resulting from mental or physical hardship; torment; agony.* Too true. At times, this all seemed masochistic.

On the other hand, there were rewards. When asked why he climbed Mt. Everest, Sir Edmund Hillary answered, "Because it's there." What he didn't say was that the struggle to the top, while difficult and exhausting, is also exhilarating, and that the spectacular view from the peak makes it worthwhile.

Switzerland

…There's nothing subtle about Switzerland, it's always stunning, always surprising, always breathtaking.

The terrain changed quickly as we entered Switzerland. Suddenly we were out of the gentle hills of France and into steep mountains with dramatic vistas. The snow-covered peaks looked over valleys so deep and green and peaceful, where coke-bottle-green glacial rivers followed their ancient courses, and lapis-lazuli lakes mirrored the sky.

For the first time we were traveling by car and therefore able to get to places inaccessible by public transportation. Since we were their passengers, just along for the ride, our German friends, Wolfgang and Niels,[19] set the tone and the pace, which was relaxed and playful. No 3-second stops for them.

…We'd never heard of Schweibenalp or the "All Religions Conference", so we had no expectations except that we'd be the only Americans at this remote Hindu community high in the Alps.

Since Wayne and I had no sleeping bags, it was reassuring to learn that beds with linens and blankets were provided. Simple vegetarian meals were included, and various activities scheduled for the next four days. No one knew how many people were expected, but it didn't seem to matter.

After conferring with Niels and Wolfgang, we registered for only two nights in case it was awful. We paid our fee ($10 per day per person) and were shown to our rooms. Wall-to-wall mattresses carpeted the small room. We'd sleep on the floor with eight other people. The communal bathroom, with stall showers and toilets, was down the hall. I doubted there'd be sufficient hot water for everyone. Meals would be served outdoors in the open space in front of the hotel.

---

19. We'd met Wolfgang at Findhorn and arranged to hook up with him and Niels, for travel through Eastern France and Switzerland.

...Twenty-two people from Marin County, just half-an-hour from home, were there. They had planned their trip for over a year and couldn't believe we'd just heard of this the day before and dropped in because we were in the neighborhood.

This annual conference was sponsored by the Schweibenalp "Center of Unity" Siddhashram. These European Hindus, mostly Swiss and German, who followed the teachings of Sri Babaji, were barefoot and dressed in cotton sarongs -- appropriate to India, but not the Swiss Alps. Many young women had shaved heads, and all smeared red or yellow paint across their foreheads.

...Nearly 400 people overflowed the facility designed for 70.

There were Hindus, Buddhists, Sufis, Muslims, Christians, Spiritualists, and several other sects, all in friendly competition. The aim was to foster tolerance and forgiveness, respect for the philosophies and practices of others, and in so doing, enhance our humanity as one human family. *Cool.*

...I needn't have worried about hot showers. Cleanliness and purity are important elements of Hinduism, so enormous water heaters had been installed.

...We stayed the full four days, participating in all the groups' activities. We sang with Hindus, chanted with Muslims, danced with Sufis, meditated with Buddhists, and prayed with Christians. For the next several months we sang and hummed snatches of songs and chants from various groups. The Hindu chant, *OM Namaha Shivaya,* stayed in our heads the rest of the trip and even now pops up at odd times.

...The Marinites had the usual American irreverence and poked fun at everything. One said, "The Cha Room[20] reminds me of the Inter-Galactic Bar scene in Star Wars." He was right. People in exotic costumes, headdresses and hairstyles -- and no-hair -- had tea and cakes together as if it were the most natural thing in the world. No one would have blinked if C3P0 and a couple of Wookies walked in, sat down and ordered cha and cake.

By Sunday, five members of the Marin group needed a change of menu. They invited us to join them for Sunday brunch at one of the nearby mountaintop ski resorts. We selected the one with the most spectacular vista.

A stupendous gourmet buffet was laid out. ...Thinking it would be a good idea to walk off our meal, we started hoofing it down the mountain. The altitude

---

20. A dimly-lit tea room open nightly after scheduled activities.

went to our heads. In the midst of towering peaks and verdant valleys, with fluffy clouds drifting across the sapphire sky, we posed with milk-chocolate-colored cows for each other's cameras. We crossed bridges over rushing streams. Wildflowers created a kaleidoscope of colors on the hillsides. It was such a beautiful day. In high spirits, we couldn't resist.

Spontaneously whirling, with arms outstretched, we burst into song. "The hills are alive with the sound of music." Skipping down the road we sang; "Doe, a deer, a female deer; Ray, a drop of golden sun; Mi, a name I call myself; Fa, a long long way to run," and as we started up a rise, "Climb every mountain, Ford every stream, Follow every rainbow, 'Til you find your dream," laughing and dancing with joyful abandon. On that day, in that setting, it was just right.

…While attending religious activities of the different groups, I felt intensely uncomfortable. I guess I'm resistant to dogma and ritual … in any religion. What does it mean to live a spiritual life? How does religion relate to it?

Had we been led to this gathering of ecumenical tolerance and understanding? Perhaps my lesson was in this quotation from Sri Babaji:

> …Being a human being is the most
> important element in life.
> It is the only valid religion:
> being an example of tolerance and forgiveness.

It struck a resonant chord. It reminded me of this short poem by Ella Wheeler Wilcox which hung in my kitchen in Santa Rosa:

> So many gods, so many creeds,
> So many paths that wind and wind,
> While just the art of being kind,
> Is all this sad world needs.

…The Marin group invited Wayne and me to go with them to Assisi, Italy. They believed they were together in another lifetime, with Saint Francis in his hometown. They wanted me to do a group past-life regression there so they could "re-experience the events of that life and their relationship to Saint Francis and one another."

It would have been fun. We had to make a difficult choice and give up one desired experience for another. We were headed in the opposite direction. *Çest la vie.*

Wayne and I, with Wolfgang and Niels, piled back into the Citroën and drove through the Swiss and Bavarian Alps. I'd spent nearly thirty years trying to get back to Germany and my dear friend, Annelore. The last time we saw each other I'd just celebrated my 21st birthday -- and now I was turning 50.

Within 24 hours I'd be back in the house where I'd lived as a teenaged bride, in the small village where I felt so at home, and see my dear friend again. I couldn't wait!

Jugenheim a.d. Bergstrasse

I didn't even try to fight nostalgia as we drove down the winding cobblestone streets of the medieval village at the edge of the Odenwald (Forest). Through tears I found the house at *Seeheimerstr. 22* on the first try.

Across the years Annelore and I had corresponded sporadically and sent the occasional photo. Her son had visited us in Santa Rosa and my nephews visited her in Jugenheim. But thirty years had passed since we'd seen each other. I stood before that well-remembered door, breathing deeply to capture the familiar fragrances: linden trees along the street, roses, ripe pears and gooseberries from the garden, *Apfelkuchen* and strong *Kaffee* from the kitchen.

I recalled the first time, nearly thirty-two years earlier when I was a fresh-faced kid with a sun-bleached ponytail. After my long trip by ocean liner and train all the way from central California, I was excited and anxious in anticipation of the wonderful unknown. Annelore and her family's warm friendliness assured me everything was going to be all right.

Now, all those years later, I stood on that exact spot, once again excited and nervous. My hair was now silver-streaked and my face etched with crows' feet and laugh lines. My once-slim body had blossomed and, like the sands of time, shifted downward. I wondered if she'd recognize me. Reaching up to turn the bell-knob, my hand quivered.

The door swung open. Annelore clasped her hands and exclaimed, "Our little Carol, our little Carol! Still looking just the same."

And you know, in my eyes, she was as she had been all those years ago, too, still blonde and beautiful, still effervescent and ebullient. Maybe our vision was blurred by tears, or maybe we saw with our hearts rather than our eyes.

I settled in to enjoy my reunion with Annelore, whose 70th birthday we'd missed by a few days, and show Wayne points of interest, while renewing my acquaintance with this place so fondly remembered.

Luckily, her grandson, Garrelt Gaetcke, was visiting his *Omi*. "Gary" had lived in England since age-nine and spoke perfect English. Wayne and Annelore discovered that their ancestors were from the same part of East Prussia, so he was accepted as family, too. The meals she cooked especially for him reminded him of his grandma's kitchen in Chicago.

...I wanted to spend an entire day with Annelore, so Wayne went sightseeing while she and I visited and shopped in the village. She walked with a limp and moved slowly, slowly.

...There is now a "supermarket" for one-stop shopping. A tiny grocery store, it sold a variety of food and sundries. The passing years had produced a number of changes. The greengrocer's on the corner, where I'd shopped regularly then pedaled home with a bulging string bag hanging from the handlebars, was now a video store. My favorite *Bäckerei,* run by the smiling, rosy-cheeked Frau Vogel, who often held a loaf of braided *Eibrot* (egg bread) for me, and the *Metzgerei* (butcher shop), the proprietor of which was the rotund, florid-faced Herr Metzger -- all gone, with nothing of interest to replace them. The *Strassenbahn,* which used to look like the Toonerville Trolley, now boasted sleek, modern cars, and went all the way to Benzheim, where one could catch another to Heidelberg.

Over the next few days we stopped by the exquisite Russian Orthodox chapel built for Nicholas' Czarina, Alexandra, to pray in when visiting her home in the state of Hesse. We went to Heidelberg, and visited *viele Biergärten und Gasthäuser* (lots of beer gardens and eateries). En route to Darmstadt, I pointed out *Schloss Frankenstein* (Frankenstein's Castle), on a hilltop above *der Bergstrasse.* The inspiration for Mary Shelley's Gothic novel, *Frankenstein,* its rocky ruins are now a *Biergarten.*

Although I'd spoken nary a word of German in thirty years, I was amazed that the appropriate words and phrases popped out of my mouth. I didn't have to think about it.

...My dear friend's poor health influenced our decision for an early departure. After tearful assurances that we would meet again before another thirty years, we took our leave.[21]

Venice

To get into Venice you must take a "water-taxi", which is nothing like a

---

21. Two years later, Annelore died of pneumonia following hip replacement surgery. I'm so grateful we had that time together.

taxi. …Our destination was a *penzione* (small hotel) within a stone's throw of *Piazza San Marco*. Along the way we passed under bridges familiar from photographs and paintings, and passed medieval buildings whose walls rose straight up from the canals, their paint and plaster crumbling, with pointy-topped windows, wrought iron balconies strewn with pots of flowers and laundry blowing in the wind.

Traffic was as busy as on any city's main street. Rowboats darted this way and that, motorboats buzzed by, freight boats delivered goods, and water-taxis *putt-putted* along. In the midst of it all, graceful gondolas glided, lending the charm for which Venice is beloved. There were even traffic jams, with Italian boatmen vigorously suggesting, with indecent gestures, how to clear the jam.

We had stopped at the railroad station to get Italian *Lire* and arrange for lodging. When we came out our pockets bulged. The exchange rate that day was 1,930 *Lire* to the dollar. It seemed like Monopoly money. Multicolored and fancifully decorated, Italian currency makes up in artistry what it lacks in value. But you're dealing in such enormous sums you feel rich. As you peel off 20,000 *Lire* here, 50,000 there, and 150,000 somewhere else, you feel rich as Onassis.

…We quickly found our *penzione* and stowed our luggage so we could hurry out to enjoy the Venetian sunset. We settled ourselves at a table on *Piazza San Marco* near a grand piano from which came strains of music-to-watch-sunsets-by. In sight of *San Marco Basilica* that balmy twilight, beneath a cotton-candy sunset, we felt like elegant, sophisticated characters in an Epic Romance.

…The proprietors of our *penzione* spoke no English, and with *Buon Giorno, Buona Sera,* and *Marcello Mastroiani,* my Italian was exhausted. This small hotel's entry, just a doorway with shops on each side, was marked at street level by an unobtrusive sign above a nondescript door. The hotel was on the second, third and fourth floors. The office and breakfast room were on the second floor, our pee-in-the-sink room on the third (bathroom down the hall), and more rooms on the fourth level. Our window table in the second floor breakfast room jutted out over the street.

Each morning at breakfast, small birds landed on the stone window ledge and hopped onto our table. As the city came to life on the street below, we fed them crumbs and listened to their tweets and chirps.

…Gondoliers in straw hats, striped shirts, and tight black pants serenaded as they poled their crafts through the canals. Gondola romance doesn't come cheap, though. We'd forgo that voyage through Venice's liquid streets.

Everywhere you turn, Venice looks like a picture postcard or painting. In fact, we often stumbled upon painters, their easels set up in a small square or beside a canal, capturing its magic on canvas.

…Returning from the glass factory at Murano, we passed the island that is Venice's cemetery, encountering a Venetian-style funeral procession. The hearse was a dignified black-lacquered, gold-leafed barge carrying the flower-laden casket. The mourners followed: First, the limousine-boat, richly lacquered and gold-trimmed like the hearse, taking the priest and grieving family members, then a convoy of boats of every shape, color, and condition, in a long line, conveying the rest of the mourners to the island burial site. Only in Venice.

One early evening, at a table in San Marco Square, sipping *Pinot Grigio* and watching people, pigeons, the orange and lavender post-sunset sky, the following scenario unfolded:

At the next table sat a middle-aged Mediterranean couple -- Spanish? Italian? Greek? -- enjoying the panoply on the *piazza* when a low-flying pigeon "dumped" on the man's head. The man shot up out of his chair, practically knocking the table over, shouting, shaking his fist and finger-gesturing at the bird, swearing and stomping, his face turned a blotchy magenta. He and his lady hurriedly left the *piazza.* Their fun evening was over.

Coincidentally, a few minutes later, another pigeon scored a direct hit on the head of an English woman a few tables away. She just said, "Oh my," and reached into her bag for a tissue with which she wiped it off. Chuckling, her husband dipped his handkerchief in his drink and finished the clean-up job. They calmly finished their drinks and continued enjoying the moment.

If you can imagine that Mediterranean man and that English woman *married* you have a pretty good picture of John's and my marriage. Cultural differences!

…Truly an exquisite, exotic, exciting, extravagant city, Venice was pure pleasure, and a real indulgence. Our budget was blown to smithereens, even though we bought nothing except meager meals and four glass (Murano) buttons for the sweater I finished knitting as we pulled into Venice.

…Throughout the trip Wayne kept a record of our expenses, noting every *florin, shilling, pfennig, franc, lire,* etc. He thought it would be interesting to know where we spent the most, where the least; what percentage on what, *et cetera.* Of course, the real benefit was to have a true picture of our expenses relative to our daily budget and the overall trip budget.

There was a problem, though. He began to see himself as "Guardian Of The Money". He loved to be in charge.

…We had to move on. We had agreed to meet our friend "Annette" on or around September 26 in Athens.

…Wayne's depressive mode hit a new low. He bewailed the fact that his life had no purpose. "We're just wasting time. I don't know my purpose. I'm nothing." *Et cetera, ad infinitum. Ad nauseum.*

"Oh for pity's sake, Wayne, we're living everyone's dream! People are living vicariously through us. We owe it to them to enjoy it. Why can't that be purpose enough?"

At home he'd whined about his lack of purpose. People kept telling him, "Just pick a worthwhile project and do it." He held onto the notion that somehow his purpose and his passion would magically appear. God would present something grand and glorious on a silver platter. Then he'd be happy.

Naïvely I thought our fabulous adventure might make him happy. Clearly, I didn't fully understand Bi-Polar Disorder.

He had moments, even days, when he was okay and fun to be with, but then he got miserable again, moaning, weeping, lamenting. As time went on, his depressive moods deepened and lengthened while the space between them shrunk.

It was about then that I became aware of my own unconscious agenda -- my 50th birthday. It became important that we get to Nepal so I could celebrate turning 50 by taking a Himalayan trek.

Yugoslavia

…On the train from Trieste in Italy to Rijke, Yugoslavia, where we'd board a ship to the island of Hvar in the Adriatic Sea, we struck up a conversation with a Yugoslavian couple. They told us that this train trip actually takes longer now than it did in 1900. The reason: Communist red tape.

The gentleman told us about their country. He said "Yugoslavia" translates as "United Slavs", composed as it is of six highly individual ethnic groups, with four different languages (Slovenian, Croatian, Serbian and Macedonian); two distinct alphabets (Cyrillic and Roman); and three religions (Eastern Orthodox, Roman Catholic, and Muslim). "It is a very schizophrenic country; we are all confused all the time," he laughed. "Even those who speak the same language can't read the same newspapers. It produces some difficulties." An understatement, no doubt.

...At 5 p.m., we boarded the ship on which we'd cruise the Adriatic Sea. It was sparkling white and looked like any other cruise liner. But its cleanliness was a fleeting thing. All housekeeping was done at the ship's ultimate destinations at opposite ends of the Adriatic. By midmorning the first day out, the bathrooms had no toilet paper, wastebaskets overflowed, floors were littered, the wash basins and toilets were filthy and stinky. In the ship's common rooms, tables were littered with cups, crumpled napkins, apple cores, and butt-filled ashtrays, the floors in need of a good swabbing. We wondered how it would look (and smell) by the time the ship got to Greece three days later.

It was not our problem. We'd be getting off soon.

Hvar

The city of Hvar, crowned by a Napoleonic fortress on a hilltop, looked inviting. The hilly city of wheat-colored stone buildings with red-tiled roofs and marble-smooth streets surrounds a small blue bay. Pretty.

Fending off the determined dock-side innkeepers, we found the Office of Tourism. Inside, a young woman who spoke some German but no English waited on us. She and I were doing fine, but when we showed our American passports, a formidable older woman shoved her aside. This heavyset, dark-eyed, olive-skinned, no-nonsense woman demanded, "You stay *my* house! First Class." It was clearly an order, not an invitation. This woman -- apparently of the Yugoslavian Maffia -- was not to be trifled with. Trying to appear as if the decision was ours, we agreed to stay at her house.

...We were happy to be out of the cold, wet, miserable summer in expensive northern Europe. We tried various open-air restaurants and cafés, all excellent. In Hvar our small budget covered full meals, rather than the snacks we had in Venice.

...Toward dusk one day as we headed into the outdoor market, a man spotted Wayne's *California Does Have Its Faults* tee shirt. "Oh," he exclaimed, "you must be from California."

As I looked him full in the face I recognized him. "I know you!" I exclaimed. "You live at Monan's Rill!"[22]

His jaw dropped. "You know Monan's Rill? Who are you? How do you know me?"

"We met at the YWCA Awards Dinner in April," I said. (I could have called him and his wife by name -- Russ and Mary Jorgensen -- and told what they were wearing when we met.) "We live in Santa Rosa. Melissa and Virginia (Monan's Rillers) are good friends of mine."

"Mary! Mary! Come here!" he shouted to his wife who was exiting the market's stone gate. "These folks are from Santa Rosa! And they know Melissa and Virginia. And Monan's Rill!" Whoops of surprise and hugs followed.

It was about dinner time, so we moved to a bayfront restaurant to dine and gossip and retrace our connections. We were flabbergasted that here on a tiny, remote island off the coast of Yugoslavia, we'd bumped into people from home.

…We traded our Newsweek for their Herald Tribune -- standard procedure. Whenever we met English-speakers, we shared and traded magazines and newspapers and passed along books. Sometimes, having been out of touch for awhile, we also asked what day of the week or date it was. Such it is with world travelers.

Dubrovnik

…George Bernard Shaw wrote, "Those who seek Earthly Paradise should come and see Dubrovnik."

The gracefully curving city walls enclose the city's narrow stone streets, many consisting only of stone steps up steep hills. Its houses and shops, churches, cathedrals, monasteries, museums, offices, restaurants, grand hotels and halls are crammed together within the walls of the old city.

Walking through the sparkling streets, washed daily with soapy water and scrub brushes, we peeked through open doors into people's living rooms just a wall's thickness away. Often we stopped to admire the handiwork of women wearing the traditional black skirt, lace-edged white blouse, and starched white cap, sitting in the shade of their doorway embroidering. They would be happy

---

22. An intentional community of Friends (Quakers) in the hills between Santa Rosa and St. Helena.

to sell us their needlework but we couldn't take their picture.

The city is chock-a-block with churches -- from tiny personal chapels to grand cathedrals -- all of which are art galleries and museums, with splendid collections. Conquering Normans, Venetians, and French all left their mark on the city.

Prices in Yugoslavia were very reasonable. In Dubrovnik's most popular tourist area we had Chateaubriand for two, with all the trimmings, and a liter of excellent local wine for $9 U.S.

Considering the low prices, visitors were disappointed that there was no variety or selection in the stores -- nor were there many stores. We went to the new part of town to the department store. But inside were mostly empty shelves.

The most interesting feature of the government-operated department store was its tavern, situated just inside the door. If you can't find anything to buy, at least you can drink.

…We lugged our belongings to the bus stop and when the city bus pulled up, we scrambled to get our gear on, dig for the correct change, find seats and settle all our stuff around us. Through a long circuitous route it eventually made its way to the terminal where we'd catch a second bus, to the airport.

Half-an-hour later, as we stepped off the first bus, Wayne asked, "Have you got the camera bag?"

"No," I replied. "You do."

"No, I don't. Oh my God! … Okay, let's not panic. Let's double check. You absolutely don't have it?"

"Yes. I absolutely don't have it."

"Crap! It's got all the camera equipment in it!" Hysteria crept into his voice. "And my hearing aid! And our address book. And your glasses!" He sucked air. "Okay, let's stay calm. Where's the last place you remember seeing it? Did we have it on the bus?"

"I don't remember seeing it," I began, shaking my head. "No. Did we have it at the bus stop? Maybe we left it at Zora's B & B. No, I'm sure we had it at the bus stop. Yeah, I remember seeing it on the bench."

"Yeah, so do I. Shit! … Well … that's it, then. It's gone."

"Probably. But we have to try."

"I know it won't be there, but you're right. You wait with the bags. I'll take a cab. I'll be back before the bus leaves. If it's gone, it's gone, but we have to know."

Certain it was futile, Wayne hailed a cab and, speaking only English to a driver who spoke only Croatian or Serbian, tried to make him understand. He didn't know street names. All he knew was, it was down the hill from Zora's B & B near the south gate of *Stari Grad*. Miscommunication, confusion and hysteria resulted in multiple detours and delays. At least thirty minutes later they arrived at the bus stop on the busy street. To his amazement, the green canvas shoulder bag was on the bench, right where we'd left it a full hour earlier.

Nothing was missing -- one of the benefits of visiting a country with a repressive totalitarian government. People are too scared to steal.

...To avoid a 14-hour bus ride, we'd fly Yugoslav Airlines to Skopje -- a 45-minute flight, scheduled to leave at 7 p.m. -- which would get us to Skopje in time for the 10:30 p.m. train to Greece. It was delayed and *finally* left at 12:30 a.m.

Two girls, 19 or 20 years old, from New England, the only other English-speakers on the flight, found us; we hung out with them playing Rummy and Go Fish. We'd missed our train and it was too late to get a hotel. We hiked the several blocks to the Skopje railroad station, where the girls and I were the only females. The bar, riotous with drunken soldiers, was the only place to sit down. And the next train to Thessalonika wasn't until 9:30 the next morning.

We sat in the tavern. The soldiers ogled and taunted the girls, who clung to us like Velcro. Though uncomfortable, we could last out the night in the station's saloon. Except that at 3 a.m. it closed and they put us out. This was going to be a very long night.

But the girls had sleeping bags. Searching out a place where we could clear the floor, we unzipped and spread them out. With our ponchos for cover, we four went to sleep. On that cement floor, with lights glaring, loudspeakers announcing arrivals and departures, and trains roaring through the station all night, we actually slept.

At 6 a.m., we were awakened by a tapping on our feet and a Slavic station worker singing, *"Vake op, leetle Suzee. Vake op"!*

Greece

Athens

Before Annette's arrival in Athens, Wayne and I took a three-day holiday on the beaches of Thessalonika on the Aegean Sea. Finally.

Before we left home, Annette, recently single, asked if she could meet us in Athens and travel with us for four weeks. We had qualms about it -- Wayne initially said, "No way!" But after getting basic agreements, we acquiesced:

- We are not going to be "Siamese triplets." If one of us wants to do something the others don't, he or she can go off and do it.
- We are on a low-budget trip. We'll be staying in reasonably priced B & Bs and One-Star hotels, and eating where we can afford to.
- You're newly single and might want to go to singles hangouts. We're an old married couple. If you want to do the singles' scene, you should travel with a single girlfriend or by yourself.
- Each of us is responsible for his/her own belongings.

Annette agreed. She *had* to travel with us -- not someone else, and definitely not alone. She declared our rules "reasonable".

Okay, so long as she understands and agrees.

Annette would arrive at Athens International within the hour. This would be a big change for us. We had become accustomed to traveling as a couple. Although unaware of it, we'd developed our own culture on this trip. We had a rhythm. As a result of carrying our heavy bags and walking many miles a day, we were strong and robust, and didn't dilly-dally. We were on a low-budget trip and had adapted to that lifestyle. We were globetrotters.

As Wayne and I made our way from our small one-star hotel to the Airport-Bus stop, he stopped in his tracks and grabbed my arm.

"We have to make a pact," he declared.

"Huh? What?"

"We have to make a pact," he repeated. "We're not going to carry Annette's stuff. She's going to carry her own bags."

"Off course Annette's going to carry her own bags. You carry yours, I carry mine, Annette carries hers."

"Make a pact!" he insisted. "We are *not* going to carry her bags."

"Oh, all right. It's a pact." *How dumb. She knows the rules. We talked about all that before we left home.* But there on the sidewalk in Athens, we shook hands on our pact.

When we met Annette at the airport and escorted her to the baggage carousel, she started grabbing bags. Not one. Not two. Not three. But four(!) bags. They weren't terribly large or heavy, but there were four of them. If she strapped one on her back and carried one in each hand, one was left over, unless she planned to balance it on her head. She didn't. That meant that wherever she went, someone had to carry one of her bags.

But it wasn't going to be us. We had a pact. Wayne looked at me, his eyebrows raised and lips pursed, as if to say, "What did I tell you?"

He told Annette, "We'll help you out today because you're tired after your long flight. *And* because *our* bags are already at the hotel. But after this, you're responsible for your stuff. All of it."

When we got to our hotel, clean but simple, and checked her into her room, her first statement was, "You expect me to stay in this flea-bag hotel?"

"Hey, you can go to the Hilton if you want," I said. "But we're staying here."

Reluctantly unpacking in her "flea-bag" room, she said, "I didn't bring an iron 'cause I knew you had one."

"We weren't using it so we got rid of it."

"Well, I *care* how I look," she declared self-righteously.

"Oh don't worry." I chuckled. "You'll get over that in a hurry."

If looks could kill. . . . . This was going to be interesting.

Our first foray into the streets of Athens was to the Agora -- the ancient marketplace which is still in use today. At one of the shops, Annette purchased a bunch of touristy items for her kids, paying full price. I selected a lavender scarf -- I forgot to bring one -- and took it to the proprietor, offering half the price marked.

He shrugged. "Okay."

Indignant, Annette said, "Wait a minute! I didn't know you could do that!" She ripped her purchases out of her bag and threw them on the counter. "I don't want this. Here, take it back."

The guy shook his head and looked at her like, *You gotta be kidding!*

"But she only paid half-price!" she pointed out.

He shrugged.

"Annette," I said, "once you make a bargain, that's it. You've paid for it. It's a done deal.

"But I didn't know . . . "

...A day or two later (September 27), Annette announced, "I'm going to rent a car and drive to Delphi tomorrow. If you want to come along, you're welcome. I'm going anyway. Besides, it's your birthday, Wayne. Why don't you let me take you guys as your birthday present?"

"We'd love to. Thanks."

...After the rental car was delivered to our hotel, we stopped at the agency to drop off the delivery guy and Annette went in to sign the contract.

...In Greece people drive like maniacs. I don't know which was scarier: being a pedestrian, a passenger, or a driver. People drive on the sidewalk, swerve in and out in no discernible pattern, and race along at breakneck speeds with screeching whiplash stops.

...Lunch was in a small restaurant in a wide-spot-in-the-road-town near Delphi where villagers gathered for coffee, ouzo, and gossip. The proprietor couldn't do enough for us. Since we had no common language he took us into the kitchen to make up plates and bowls from pots and pans on the stove.

Tourists generally whizz past in huge tour buses, which we would have done if not for Annette's generous offer.

The Temple of Apollo is high up in the mountains with a panoramic view over the valleys to the sea below. Early Greeks considered Delphi the Center of the Earth. In mythology, Zeus released two eagles, one from the east, the other from the west. They flew toward the center. The point at which they met was where they built Delphi. The exact spot is marked by a stone, known as the *omphalos* (bellybutton), in the temple.

Even today, two eagles often circle above the sacred site. As luck would have it, they flew overhead the day we were there. A blessing and an omen.

...We drove back to Athens and stopped at the car rental agency where Annette went in to settle up. Moments later she emerged, reeling from shock. The tiny print on the contract said, in both Greek and English, that there were mileage fees. Instead of the $20 she thought she agreed to, she was charged more than $80.

We had a wonderful day, and Wayne a great birthday. But no more rental cars.

...We were leaving for the Greek Isles the next day for two-and-a -half weeks of rest, sun and fun on the fabulous islands. Our plan was to sail to a different island every four or five days, exploring and enjoying the uniqueness of each.

Mykonos

... At the port of Mykonos we were greeted by a scruffy pelican strutting as if he owned the place. He had been there for years, we learned, and was the island's mascot. He was on the pier, among the beached boats on the shore, wandering in and out of waterfront shops and cafes, every day. Fed and petted by islanders and tourists alike, he seemed to take his privileged status for granted.

...It's always "party-time" on Mykonos, which is known as "The Anything Goes Island". Residents tolerate whatever tourists come to spend their money. It's become a vacation haven for the world's gay population, as well as honeymooners. Other than these two specific groups, anyone interested in cutting loose and having fun is welcome on Mykonos. The *tavernas* are lively and noisy into the night, with tourists drinking, singing, "Zorba dancing", and getting crazy.

Mykonos was a delight on many levels -- not the least of which was the availability of English-language books. We found several secondhand bookstores, so we bought as many book as we could stuff in our packs and carry.

...Strong winds blew without letup, day after day and through the night. We now understood why Mykonos was dotted with windmills. They were not in operation while we were there, however; it was too windy! Each day the TV newscasters assured us gullible tourists "The wind will lay down tomorrow".

We photographed the island's white buildings with colorful doors and shutters, brilliantly contrasted with hot-pink bougainvilleas and electric-blue morning glories; its donkeys with deep baskets astride, often topped with a bouquet of flowers; its distinctive churches with full-bearded, black-robed priests blessing villagers; its windmills topping the hills and lining the shores; its elegant shops displaying jewels and furs in the hot Ægean sun; its sidewalks lined with baskets of sea-sponges; and babushka'd women gossiping along the docks.

Each day we believed the TV weatherman's promise that the wind would stop. "We'll go to the beach tomorrow, it's too windy today. Let's shop and take some more pictures today." After four days we'd done more than enough shopping, and had plenty of white-on-white pictures: white buildings and white dogs, cats and birds.

The wind howled day and night. Sand was in our hair, our ears, our noses, our eyes, between our teeth, and even under our fingernails. Our skin felt sandblasted. Only the large ferries to and from Athens were running in these heavy seas, so island hopping was impossible.

Finally, Wayne went to the Greek equivalent of the Coast Guard for an honest answer. They said, "It might keep up this way until April!"

…I was in favor of going back to the beach on Thessalonika. We deserved a vacation after all our hard traveling. But Wayne, with his let's-get-going, push-push-push tendency, and Annette, fresh from home, felt differently.

…We'd fly to Istanbul the following morning for whatever adventures awaited there.

Istanbul

…To save time, Annette and I went to the Tourist Office to arrange for a hotel while Wayne went to the money-changer in the next booth. Just as he got to the head of his line, Annette realized she would need Turkish money too. She rushed over and set $150 beside his elbow, asking him to change it for her. Without waiting for an answer, she rushed back to the Tourist Office.

Meanwhile, Wayne was busy calculating the exchange rate, going from window to window dealing with bureaucratic red tape, and finally, counting the unfamiliar money.

Having taken care of business, we caught the bus from the international airport to the domestic airport, where we'd catch a second bus into Istanbul. As the bus pulled away, Annette asked for her money.

Wayne looked blank. "What money?"

"I put $150 on the counter and asked you to change it for me."

"I didn't see any money. I didn't hear you. … Driver! Stop! Stop the bus! We have to go back," Wayne shouted.

…As the bus pulled away we hiked back to the terminal. Wayne hopped on another bus back to the International Airport while Annette and I waited. It was cash, American money, unmarked bills, there for the taking. Once again, knowing it was a waste of time and effort, Wayne returned to the scene. In a state of upset, turmoil, anger and despair, we tried to remain calm.

…Here he came. He didn't look distraught or angry. Could it be? Yes, he had the money.

…Hesitatingly, he had asked, "Um, did you find some American money on the counter? 150 dollars? Cash."

The man behind the counter replied, "Yes. We've been waiting for you. We didn't know who left it, but we knew someone would come back for it."

Another miracle, this one truly unbelievable. The day was saved. The trip was saved. What wonderful people the Turks are.

The rule about personal belongings was reiterated: "Annette, you take care of your stuff and we take care of ours. Period. No exceptions."

…Wherever we went in Turkey we had at least one "guide" -- always male -- who wanted only to enhance visitors' enjoyment of his city and practice his English.

…Wayne and I charged along at our usual pace. Panting and running to keep up, Annette shouted, "Do you two have to *march* everywhere? Can't you just walk? Like normal people!" We thought we *were* walking like normal people.

…Wayne enjoyed traveling with two women in this Islamic country. Men asked, "You have two wives?" Sometimes he'd say Yes, and watch their reaction. But mostly he said No, and watched their reaction. They always seemed pleased that Annette was the unattached one. Attractive and vivacious, with emerald eyes, luxuriant ash blond hair, and a slim willowy figure, she was greatly admired and, no doubt, stirred their fantasies.

As a matter of fact, she quickly found a male escort in virtually every city we visited. So we were not Siamese triplets, after all.

That was fine with us, except that the morning we were to leave Istanbul, our bags were packed, we checked out of the hotel and waited at the front door, ready to leave for the airport. At 7 a.m., she still hadn't returned. Getting no answer at her door, we had the hotel manager open it so we could check on her. No Annette.

We didn't know where to look. We didn't know her date's name or where they'd planned to go. What were we to do? Leave without her? Reschedule our flight? Call the police? But what would we tell them?

Worried and furious, we pounced on her when she sashayed in like *LaDeeDa*. According to her, we had no right to worry. She was an adult and could do as she pleased. How dare we fret! She was just fine, thank you.

"We didn't know that! For all we knew, you'd been kidnapped! Or worse! How were we supposed to feel?"

She was angry we didn't trust her to get back in time. Our relationship had become one of Overbearing Parents and an Acting-out Teen.

…Everywhere we went, Annette got someone to carry her extra bag by looking pitiful and batting her eyelashes. Eventually she consolidated a couple of bags into one with little wobbly wheels that veered off in different directions, making it impossible to pull in a straight line. Yanking and tugging it along, she continued to look helpless and elicit offers of help.

…Turkish tea was the first real steeped tea we'd had since leaving home. Here in Turkey they make a true pot of tea with honest-to-goodness tea leaves. It is served in glasses on trays with a curved handle over the top. It seems always to be Tea Time. Men scurry down the street at all hours of the day, balancing trays of tea glasses, rushing to deliver them steaming hot to shops and offices.

…The first item on our Istanbul To-Do List was a Turkish bath. The one we chose, an enormous circular marble building, dates back to the 16th century. Annette and I entered the women's chamber. A raised marble platform stood in the center. In the high dome over the enormous spa were small windows of colored glass in a circular pattern, creating a dance of colored lights on the walls, floors, and bathers below. Everyone, including the masseuses, was nude.

…Annette's attendant was a muscular middle-aged woman. Mine looked a hundred years old, toothless and emaciated, with wrinkled skin and flat, pruney breasts. I was amazed, then, at the tremendous strength and vigor of her massage. But first she washed my body with a scratchy washcloth, lathering me up and scrubbing as you'd scrub a filthy child. Every inch of me tingled.

Then came the shampoo. … My masseuse did a job on my head too, leaving my scalp smarting from the pressure of her bony fingers. Then came the massage. Where that ancient Turk got the strength in that decrepit little body I'll never know, but she laid into me and unkinked every muscle, using fingers, hands, elbows, shoulders, and knees. When our massages were finished, Annette and I lay like limp noodles on luxuriously warm marble slabs.

…Istanbul's ancient bazaar covers two million square feet and houses 4000 shops. It is divided into categories, with coffee shops and restaurants scattered throughout.

…Throughout Istanbul are magnificent domed mosques, each flanked by four slender minarets from which the faithful are called to prayer over a loudspeaker five times a day. Silhouetted against the evening sky, the domed temples and elegant minarets are stunningly beautiful. After dark, the major mosques are illuminated. Gorgeous.

...Saint Sofia (Ayasofya), once the world's largest and most splendid Christian cathedral, combines aspects of Christianity and Islam, having been converted to a mosque following the Ottoman conquest by Suleiman the Magnificent in 1453.

...Topkapi Palace -- the Sultan's palace, complete with harem -- must be seen to be believed. What is reportedly the world's largest, richest collection of jewels and treasures is in this palace museum. There are solid gold thrones and chairs, liberally encrusted with jewels; a solid-gold cradle, set with dazzling gemstones; emeralds as big as a man's fist; pearls the size of kumquats; jewel-encrusted swords, pistols and rifles; the famed Topkapi dagger. We came away dazed and bedazzled.

...Interested in seeing a real Turkish belly-dancer, we asked our "guides" -- a couple of 20-something Turks -- about it. "The real belly-dancers are in private clubs and don't perform until after midnight. The skinny ones in tourist nightclubs are no good," he told us authoritatively. "Real belly-dancers are fat and middle-aged."

The older Young Turk had lived in New York and knew American slang from that era. "But good golly, we never pay to see a belly-dancer. We just have a party and give the girls a lot of drinks. Then some of them belly-dance for us," he laughed. "They stick the eraser-end of a pencil in their belly-button. The one who can make the best Figure-8 on the tablet held in front of her is the champion belly-dancer of the evening."

"These girls are students at the university?" I asked.

"Yes, coeds," he nodded, smiling broadly.

"What would you do if you walked into a party and saw your sister with a pencil in her bellybutton, making Figure-8s?"

He pretended not to hear me.

Egypt

Cairo

Egypt is the land of Pyramids, the Valley of the Kings, the holy cities of Luxor and Karnak . . . . and Baksheesh. Wherever you go in Egypt, day or night, you always have a "new best friend". Child or adult, this "new best friend" ingratiates himself to you, does "favors" you don't want, sticks to you like Crazy-Glue, and will not leave until you pay him. That's Baksheesh. Even though you tell them 'No, No, No!" and "Get Lost!" they won't quit until you pay them. They even follow you to your hotel, right up to your room, or climb into your taxi with you. After the first couple of days we wouldn't look anyone in the face, because at the instant of eye-contact he'd become our "new best friend" and demand Baksheesh.

...We had come to Cairo to see the pyramids and go inside the largest, Cheops. As luck would have it, we arrived at noon when the bus loads of tour groups were at lunch, so we had the world's most popular tourist attraction all to ourselves. Dry, airless and still, with only a candle for light, the dark tomb took on an eerie, ghostly quality.

"Carol, go lie down in the sarcophagus," Annette insisted. "I want to take your picture."

I remembered stories of the mummy's curse. "Nope," I shook my head. "I saw that movie. I'm not gettin' in that thing."

Annette cajoled. I declined. This girl's not tempting fate.

...Pyramid means "Fire in the Center". The pyramid is said to receive and accumulate intensified energy from the cosmos, with the very apex of intense energy reception in the inner chamber, right where we were.

...Here, in the King's Pyramid, dissected by the ley lines that go through Chartres, Glastonbury and Stonehenge, I expected to feel something like what I'd felt there: vibrations, euphoria, excitement, energetic surges. Something. In those places, where I'd expected nothing, I got something. Here, where I eagerly anticipated something, there was nothing. *Watch your expectations.*

...Out in the glaring light of day, I wanted a picture of Wayne and me on a camel with the Great Pyramid in the background. Plenty of camels were for hire. One, with multi-colored tassels on head, body and saddle, was situated against the pyramid where the light was just right.

"How much just to take a picture on it? No ride," we asked its owner.

"Whatever you wish," he answered.

Okay. We'd give him a couple of bucks and have our picture for posterity. Before I got on the camel Annette took a photo of me with her camera (Page 355), and would take another -- once we got on the camel -- with ours. I handed it over as we headed for the tasseled "ship of the desert".

The camel driver brought the animal to its knees. I climbed aboard and Wayne got on behind me. Annette *click-click-clicked* with our camera. When the camel rose to its feet we smiled and waved. The animal quickly returned to its knees while we rocked perilously on its back. Clumsily, we stepped off. The whole thing took less than forty-five seconds. Wayne handed the man two Egyptian £'s (about $2).

The Arab was enraged. "No! 10£!"

"But you said, 'Whatever you wish.' You didn't say 10£."

"It's 10£!" he raged throwing the two £ notes in Wayne's face.

"I'm not paying 10£ for that! You said, 'Whatever you wish,' and I *wish* to pay 2£."

Wayne was getting heated. I added my two cents. The Arab raged and cursed, shaking his fist. The two men nearly came to blows. Finally, Wayne threw 4£ at his feet, shouting over his shoulder, "Take it or leave it!" We stalked away. To Annette's delight, she had the entire episode on film.

The posterity photos? I had unknowingly pushed the button under the camera preventing the film from advancing. We don't have a single picture.

This was a "teaching moment": Don't touch that little button under the camera; And don't believe it when someone says, "Whatever you wish." Get a firm price before proceeding.

…In Egypt it seemed as if every male over fourteen carried an automatic submachine gun like a toy. Young boys walked the streets or crowded market-places with gun-butts under their arms and fingers on the trigger. Scary!

…To save a night's hotel and meal bills, we took the sleeper train to Luxor. Departing Cairo at 6 p.m., we'd arrive twelve hours later, at 6 a.m.

The French train was new and sleek, clean and elegant. A conductor in a starched white jacket came through taking dinner orders as we whizzed through Cairo, then past the countryside: palm trees, vegetable gardens, and humble clay houses along the Nile, with the inevitable donkey tied outside.

On a small fold-down table, dinner was served on a linen-covered tray with a yellow rose in a bud vase. As we sped through the evening, our waiter uncorked the linen-wrapped wine bottle with a flourish and filled the crystal goblets. Annette joined us for dinner. Both the meal and the moment were delicious.

…As darkness descended we closed the blinds and wound down. The gentle motion of the train lulled us to sleep. The next thing we knew we were awakened for breakfast, which we finished just as the train pulled into the Luxor station.

Luxor & Karnak

...Our hotel, at the edge of a dusty marketplace, sat a block from the Nile, a quarter-mile from the temple of Luxor and, in the opposite direction, about two miles from the temples at Karnak.

A wide promenade, the Avenue of the Ram-Headed Sphinxes, leads to the Luxor temple. Although many of the Sphinxes are missing or damaged, enough remained for us to imagine its splendor with Sphinxes guarding and inspiring the priests and pharaohs as they walked between the temples.

… The following day a horse-drawn hansom cab took us to Karnak. We were unprepared for it. Covering 400 acres, it is made up of many temples, each built by a different pharaoh and dedicated to a different god.

...The next morning we met our Arab guide at 7 a.m. We'd ride donkeys to the Valleys of the Kings and Queens. The dry desert air was already hot. We slathered on sunblock and I carried a bright blue umbrella for shade.

Crossing the Nile by ferry, we were greeted by our donkeys, who knew the way by heart. As we started off across the desert, mine took the lead. We went through villages right out of the Bible. People still dressed in burnooses as they did then; their mud homes had no electricity or plumbing; farming methods were equally antiquated.

Modern tour buses go directly from Luxor to the Valley of the Kings; then, in just minutes, over to the Valley of the Queens, and back to Luxor. We felt sorry for their passengers. We were having much more fun bouncing across the desert on our asses.

Mine had an ego problem. He had to be in the lead. If anyone tried to get ahead of us we'd be off, galloping across the desert to regain our lead. "Hi Ho, Silver!" There was no holding him back. Actually, it was kind of fun -- except when someone got ahead of us on the side of a hill, with no passing lane. More than once, as we passed on the outside curve of the narrow trail, my mount's feet slipped, sending rocks tumbling down the steep side of the mountain, with no assurance that donkey and rider would not follow. But he was a pro. I now knew what it meant to "covet my neighbor's ass". I'd have traded him off in a heartbeat.

Bottled water is a necessity in the desert. We were appalled at the mountains of discarded plastic bottles, which will probably lie there forever. If people can carry them out onto the desert full, why can't they bring them back empty?

Around 9:30 a.m. we reached the area where the pharaohs' burial chambers lay deep in the ground. Although empty of all contents, they were exciting. The walls of the tombs are covered -- every inch -- with hieroglyphics and paintings depicting the life and times of that pharaoh, including inventories of crops and supplies. The amazing thing is that the 5000-year-old paint is still as vibrant as the day it was applied.

"No Photographs" signs were posted. Annette seemed determined to take pictures of every single prohibited thing. Here in the cave, she directed, "You stand outside and let me know if someone's coming."

"You can't take pictures in here. The flash damages the paint."

"A couple of little flashes aren't going to hurt anything."

"What if everyone did that?"

"But everyone doesn't. And I won't get caught. It's all right. Just let me know if someone's coming."

"Wait a minute," I began. "Let me understand this. You're saying, if you don't get caught you haven't done anything wrong?"

"Well, ye-ah." She took her pictures. And she didn't get caught.

In Athens she took photos of a trained bear on a busy street. The bear rode a bicycle and did tricks while its owner collected money from bystanders, charging them for the right to photograph it. "Annette! You can't just take pictures. That's how he makes his living!"

"For taking pictures of a bear?! On a public street?"

"Yes!"

"Well, he can't stop me. What's he going to do, sic the bear on me? Ha ha." *Click, click.*

In Turkey, through the window of a speeding bus she took photos of a Turkish military base, disobeying signs all along its fence. I told her, "It's not allowed. You could get arrested as a spy!"

"They won't catch me."

"Fine. But if you get arrested, we'll go on with our trip and leave you here to rot. You're on your own."

She continued photographing everything she could on that Army base.

...One evening as we passed through the busy marketplace in Luxor, Egyptians crowded around a TV sitting on the dirt walkway. At least a dozen Egyptians gathered 'round. An enraged President Mubarek ranted and railed, castigating the United States and President Reagan again and again. We didn't understand anything else, but those two names came through loud and clear. He sounded furious.

We were in the middle of an international incident. On October 7, four heavily-armed PLO terrorists had hijacked the Italian cruise ship *Achille Lauro* in Egyptian waters. They'd shot and killed a disabled American, throwing him overboard, still in his wheelchair. US Navy F-14 fighter jets had intercepted the Egypt Airlines plane that was flying the hijackers to freedom in Tunisia. It was forced to land in Sicily, where the hijackers were arrested. The Egyptian president was mighty displeased with the U.S. military's actions.

...At the end of each day we looked forward to sunset on the Nile. Luxor is on the eastern shore of the river, so, looking across, we were treated to a sunset-spectacular every evening. Graceful *foluccas* (sailboats) glided by, framed by the huge fiery ball -- the sun god RA -- setting on the horizon.

...From the minute she got off the plane in Athens, Annette and Wayne had reacted to one another like vinegar and baking soda. By this time, they exchanged mostly animosities. As they carped at one another I was out of the line of fire, but it was uncomfortable and it wasn't fun.

...Boarding the plane back to Cairo, a Boeing 737, Annette looked around and declared, "I'm not flying in this dinky little airplane!"

Had I heard right? A 737 is dinky? Little?

"Get me out of here!" she said, panicking. "I'm not going anywhere in this puny little thing!"

"Okay," I said. "Take your bags and find another way back to Cairo. See ya there."

Wayne looked like he wanted to throttle her but kept his cool. "It's not a Piper Cub," he said, shoving his bag into the overhead compartment. "It's only a 45-minute flight. 747s are for transoceanic or transcontinental flights." He settled into his seat.

With no one to coddle her, she huffed and puffed, but got into her seat and fumed all the way to Cairo.

...Back in Cairo we visited the Museum of Egyptian Antiquities, where treasures from Tuthankanon's tomb were on display. I'd seen the King Tut Exhibit in San Francisco. But it meant even more now that we'd actually been to the Valley of the Kings.

...There was a bus from Cairo to Tel Aviv. Should we worry about going from Egypt to Israel? Just that week, four tourists had been shot and killed on the Gaza Strip. We might never be this close to Israel again. We'd always known some risks were involved. And we really wanted to visit Israel.

...The journey from Cairo to Tel Aviv, which took Moses forty years, took us just eight hours in an air-conditioned bus outfitted with a lavatory. We brought bread, cheese, fruit, bottled water and juices for sustenance. The only stop would be at the Egypt/Israel border.

...Due to the week's international tensions there were only seven passengers: we three and four others.

Our bus crossed the Suez Canal on a barge, then drove through the monochromatic beige desert. The land was barren and impoverished... just dry desert dotted with distantly spaced oases.

Israel

A chain-link fence. The border between Egypt and Israel was just a chain-link fence. It seemed as if the two countries were separated by a universe -- and millenea. On one side lay desert wasteland, on the other, lush farmland. On one side, dirt and poverty, on the other, cleanliness and abundance. On one side, people were apathetic and lethargic (except in the pursuit of Baksheesh), on the other, energetic and enterprising. One side was modern, its people moving into the future, the other seemed mired in the past. Such dichotomy in the space of a chain-link fence!

...Tel Aviv reminded us of Santa Cruz. Traffic hummed along its clean paved streets in predictable patterns. Beach-front restaurants served pizza, steaks, fish 'n' chips, hamburgers & fries. People were upbeat and lively -- and comical. And nobody was hustling us. It felt like home and, at the same time, an exciting new place.

The next day (October 15) we took the one-hour bus trip to Jerusalem. Our guidebook listed a low-cost hotel in an "interesting neighborhood," which turned out to be a Hasidic enclave. Signs warned that modest attire was required: No shorts, mini-skirts, or bare arms. Our hotel's manager said the Hasidim sometimes throw rocks at anyone improperly dressed in their neighborhood.

We were close to the old walled city -- a small area jam-packed with historical and religious significance. For about an hour Wayne and I wandered through modern Jerusalem: shopping malls and office buildings, luxury hotels, fabulous bakeries and restaurants; ever-present armed soldiers of both genders. (Wayne loved the shapely machine gun-toting female soldiers with dangly earrings and long lacquered nails.) People were generally categorized by religion (Orthodox Jews, Hasidim, Reform Jews, Christians, and Arabs). We expected overt religious tensions, but everyone seemed to live, work, shop, and worship peacefully, side by side.

...The Tourist Information office had closed for the day, so we set off without a map, just to get the feel and flavor of the old city, inside high stone walls. Followers of Judaism, Christianity, and Islam, as well as secular tourists, arrive by the thousands every day.

...Meandering aimlessly, we were greeted by an adolescent Arab boy who told us, "I know where you're going. I'll take you there. We'll go the back way and avoid the crowds." This could be interesting. He knew where we were going even if we didn't.

He led us up a flight of stone stairs and over the city's rooftops. Each place along the way was viewed with interest. *Is this it? Is this where we're going?* We peered into a Catholic monastery and a convent. Our "new best friend" led us onward to a narrow staircase leading down four or five stairs to a closed door. Through it was a tiny chapel where an old priest prayed. "New best friend" whispered and pointed the way through, then extended his hand. Once paid, he disappeared. We were *there*, but had no idea where *there* was.

Quietly, so as not to disturb the supplicant, we made our way through a small sanctuary, opened the door and stepped into a cavernous building with a high domed ceiling, cool marble floors and columns. Religious paintings and relics, incense, and a lot of Westerners made it obvious we were in an Christian church of huge proportions.

The instant we stepped inside I felt a sense of loss. After a few minutes I said, "There's a terrible sadness here."

We continued on toward the center of the cathedral, past altars and slabs, through hordes of people.

The sadness deepened. Although there was no apparent reason for it, tremendous sorrow overwhelmed me.

"There's no joy here, no joy at all; only terrible sadness," I observed.

After awhile I told Wayne, "I'm going to find a place to sit awhile. You go along. I'll catch up with you later."

I found an out-of-the-way stone bench. Within seconds, dozens of people showed up and milled about, though. As I sat, tears flowed. I felt foolish. I didn't want to attract notice. I didn't want to weep but couldn't help myself. After several minutes I told myself, *C'mon now, Carol, pull yourself together.* I wiped my eyes, blew my nose, and made my way toward the exit.

I soon found Wayne. By this time I felt more-or-less okay. But as I approached him, I lost it. He spread his arms and I collapsed, sobbing, against him.

"What is it, Carol?" he asked. "What's the matter?"

"I don't know!" I wailed. "I feel such despair. Such total despair!" Consoled, I regained my composure. We went outside into the bright sunlight and continued wandering. This was the most intense experience of my life. So much so that I couldn't even talk about it for nearly a year, and then, not without profound emotion.

The following day we stopped by the Tourist Office and picked up maps. Wandering through the old city, we arrived at the Church of the Holy Sepulchre, the most sacred place in Christendom. It encompasses the site of Jesus' crucifixion. Once inside I realized this was the same building that produced my great despair the day before. This time we'd entered through the front door.

I was astounded. Could it be that over the course of this trip I had become so attuned that I could feel the site's 2000-year-old sorrow?

This time I visited the Church of the Holy Sepulchre as any other tourist would, i.e., without emotion. But it was interesting to learn that the bench where I'd sat weeping was just a few feet from the spot where the cross stood -- where Jesus was crucified.

...During the three and a half centuries of Roman occupation, starting in 63 AD, Jews and Christians were banished from Jerusalem, the city was razed, and a new city -- Ælia Capitolina -- built on its ruins.

More than 300 years later, Helena, mother of Constantine the Great, the first Christian emperor of Rome and Byzantium, visited Israel to search for relics with which to document Christian history, including the site of the crucifixion. Emperor Constantine then erected Christian shrines, the most important being the Church of the Holy Sepulchre, and restored the name Jerusalem to the city.

I think it's important that each of us trust our own experience and find our own relationship with whatever we call God. As for myself, here in Jerusalem I felt close to the essence of Christianity; close, also, to the essence of Judaism and Islam, without their iconoclastic trappings. It seems to me that the *core* of all religions is the same: love of Spirit, love of our fellow humans, and love of life itself.

Judging from my reactions at the Church of the Holy Sepulchre, Helena was correct about the site of the crucifixion. But, inasmuch as I felt not one iota of joy or hope there, I'm quite certain no resurrection occurred, at least not within that particular area.[23]

Over the next few days, we visited the Garden of Gethsemane, the Mount of Olives, Masada, the Wailing Wall, the Dome of the Rock, the Dead Sea, Jericho, Tiberias, Safed, Bethlehem, and spent an afternoon at the Holocaust Museum, which was both moving and horrifying.

…We were aware that Sabbath begins at sundown on Friday. We knew Jewish businesses close from sundown Friday until sundown Saturday. But there were plenty of Christian and Arab businesses in the city, so we weren't concerned.

Late Friday afternoon, as we ambled back to our hotel, the streets were full of cars, buses, trucks, taxis, and people scurrying about, coming and going, hustling and bustling. Within seconds, we were the only sign of life. The city had imploded. It was quiet as a tomb; the streets completely devoid of human activity. It was eerily apocalyptic, as if we were the only people left on earth.

Our hotel had a kitchen we could have used, but we had no food. We hadn't stocked up. We didn't imagine we had to.

In our "interesting neighborhood" the streets were blocked off so no vehicular traffic violated the Sabbath. It was spooky-quiet.

Later, after Sabbath services, children came out to play. Dressed in their Sabbath best, they laughed and shrieked, playing hopscotch, jump rope and tag in the street. Mothers pushed baby carriages. Whole families strolled and

23. Catholics and Greek/Russian Orthodox believe the resurrection took place within these walls. Protestants believe it was near the Church of Mary Magdalene, some distance away. I felt nothing there either, though.

visited with their neighbors in the festive atmosphere.

Picture-taking on the Sabbath is forbidden in Hasidic neighborhoods. So we have only mental images. The men were elegant in black cashmere, white prayer shawls, and enormous round hats of mink. The women wore nice dresses and scarves, but could not compete with the men.

We hoped some shops or grocery stores would open, or better yet, a restaurant, at sundown on Saturday. Having gone from lunchtime on Friday to Saturday evening without so much as a cracker or a cup of tea, we were starving. After an exhaustive search we found a little burger joint and paid a fortune for a really awful hamburger. But we were grateful for it.

Before leaving Jerusalem we asked for a recommendation of a good Jewish deli. Our hotel manager laughed. "Oh, you have to go to New York City to find a good Jewish deli!"

Back in Athens, we said farewell to Annette.

Our plan for the next few months, after Rome and Florence, was to stop in New Delhi for an "appetizer" taste of India and pick up our mail at American Express. We'd fly to Nepal, where we'd spend three or four weeks, go on a trek, then back to India where we'd buy bicycles and roam the country by train and bike for three months, on to Sri Lanka for a week with our friends the Burkes, then return to southern India to resume the flight path of our Around-the-World tickets before going on to Singapore.

Rome & Florence

We tried to get India visas before leaving home, again in London, in Athens, and now in Rome. It was unbelievably difficult and, after waiting and waiting for a response, we decided to go directly to Kathmandu and apply there, since we'd be spending four weeks in Nepal, which should allow enough time, even for the Indian government.

No one sang in the streets of Rome anymore. It seemed kind of dull without wannabe Luciano Pavarrotis and Frank Sinatras serenading. But it was still beautiful -- an amazing city of history and romance.

To guarantee our return we threw coins in Trevi Fountain. We climbed the Spanish Steps, stood in the Colosseum.

Built in the first century AD, the Colosseum seated more than 50,000 spectators. Roman aristocracy and commoners alike gathered to watch circuses, plays and sporting events, the most popular being Lions vs. Christians. After the fall of Rome, the Colosseum fell into disuse. Much of it, including nearly all its marble façade, was raided and turned up in Renaissance churches and palaces, as well as Roman homes and businesses. To save it, the Pope sanctified the Colosseum, making it a shrine to the Christians martyred there. So what was left of it was preserved.

We walked the length of the Forum where Roman Senators debated and legislated. Several mansions of Rome's leaders were on these grounds, too. Since there was no reason to make this complex into a Christian monument, most of these grand buildings were sacked. The remaining remnants spoke volumes of the scope, might and brilliance of the Roman Empire.

We visited *Citta del Vaticano* -- Vatican City, a separate country in the middle of Rome. Its 108 acres are separated from Rome by a thick, high wall. 1,000 people live inside, publishing their own newspaper, issuing their own stamps, printing their own money. It has its own flag, print shops, power plant, radio station, glass-making factory, observatory, post office, and barracks for the Swiss Guards, who have protected it since the late 15th century.

Approaching St. Peter's on the *Via della Conciliazione* gave us time to become get used to the enormity of the square and basilica. *Piazza del San Pietro*, completed in 1667, is a Bernini masterpiece. Surrounded by a pair of quadruple colonades, it reaches out like welcoming arms to embrace the faithful. Up to 400,000 have stood in this *piazza* at one time. Emperor Constantine built the basilica over the tomb of St. Peter.

In 1508, Pope Julius commissioned Michelangelo to paint a fresco on the 10,000 square foot ceiling. Its completion took four years.

We then entered the massive marble temple dedicated to St. Peter. It dwarfs all other Christian churches. All is hushed and cool in this expanse of gold and polished marble. In the first chapel on the right, rests Michelangelo's *Pieta*, sculpted by the 22-year-old Michelangelo.

Here in this building, I had another inexplicable experience -- an emotional reaction as unexpected and nearly as powerful as the one in Jerusalem. However, rather than the sorrow I felt there, here, inside St. Peter's, I felt anger, to the point of rage. I told Wayne, "Look, you stay if you want to, but I gotta get out of here. There's so much anger in this building I can't stand it."[24]

24. I had a similar experience visiting St. Peter's in 1955, but to a lesser

He was ready to leave. As we walked down the steps of St. Peter's, the anger dissolved. I have no idea where it came from. I'm sure it wasn't me.

…Florence is glorious. We set out to find the *Galleria dell' Accademia* and Michelangelo's David. With our map we found the building that covered a city block, and searched for the entrance. After circling three of its four sides we turned a corner. The entrance had to be here. We were running out of sides. We walked up to the first door, on which was a hand-lettered sign (in English): DAVID'S NOT HERE --with an arrow pointing to the correct door, farther along. Underneath, someone had pencilled in: WHERE'S GOLIATH? Graffiti humor, even in Italy.

As we entered the museum we stopped cold. David is magnificent. Alone in the large room and showcased on a pedestal, the marble figure is illuminated by spotlights from both floor and ceiling, allowing the viewer to see it from every angle. The sculpture is startling in its perfection. Our senses feasted on this visual banquet for some time before we forced ourselves to pull away. It alone was worth the trip, not only to Florence, but even to Italy.

In Florence, art is everywhere. This is the city of art and artists. There are more galleries, museums and palaces than we could do justice to in a month, much less a day. We wanted to do it all. If the Air India tickets weren't such a difficulty, and if we hadn't already reserved flights to Kathmandu, and if I weren't determined to spend my birthday in the Himalayas, we'd have extended our Florentine stay.

New Delhi

The Rome-to-New Delhi flight was delayed and we missed our connecting flight to Kathmandu, the last one of the day. We'd have to overnight in New Delhi. But, despite repeated attempts, we still had no Indian visas. After a great deal of upheaval and upset, immigration officials declared we could not stay the night in India without them. We'd have to return to Rome or go straight to Singapore. After a lot of international wrangling we got permission to stay in the airport until boarding our Royal Nepal Airline flight the next morning.

It wasn't a wonderful solution, but it was better than nothing. And we would arrive in Nepal on my 50th birthday. We were taken to a room in a distant corner

---

degree. At that time I also had a powerful reaction to the Colosseum, which wasn't repeated this time, though.

of the airport -- a holding cell for visa-less travelers. Several others were there; a couple from England, a fellow from New Zealand, and another American, all busy phoning their embassies, pulling strings to get sprung.

It never occurred to us to call our embassy. We didn't figure we were important enough to get any strings pulled. We were just relieved we didn't have to go back to Rome or on to Singapore. It was going to be a long wait, so Wayne went around meeting the others in this ridiculous situation while I got out my stitchery. Later, Wayne came to get me and I went over to meet the other prisoners.

The English woman told me, "It's so quieting, seeing you sitting there embroidering, ever so serenely. It's like having Mum here with her sewing, calm in the face of calamity, letting us know everything will be all right. It's quite a comfort."

That was a benefit of my stitching that hadn't occurred to me. It calmed me, but I had never thought of it having that effect on others.

By nightfall, the New Zealander, the American, and the British couple had secured their release. Our guards, standing by with automatic submachine guns, never left our sides. When their shift ended with the changing of the guard, the ones who'd been with us for the last several hours let us know they expected a gratuity. That's rich. Not only were we held prisoner, we had to give our wardens a tip.

Even the turbanned guy from the Immigration counter, who had interceded on our behalf, came to us at the end of his shift. Without a hint of embarrassment, he stated, "I want to buy perfume for my girlfriend in the duty-free shop. I need $20 U.S." (Short pause.) "It closes in ten minutes."

So, this is how it's done. We wondered then what might have happened if we'd slipped the Immigration guy a twenty in our passports.

Air India bought our dinner. Wayne sensibly chose something familiar -- western-style chicken. Ever the adventurer, I ordered an exotic native dish. After a long wait our meals arrived. I don't know what mine was, but it was so highly spiced that with the first bite my mouth was on fire, then my throat, and all the way to my stomach. Within seconds, my nose was running, my eyes watering. I'd have killed for a bottle of potable water, but none was available. And I had to eat what I'd ordered. I didn't know when, where, or what my next meal would be.

Wayne had spotted rats scurrying about, so we lined up chairs to make "beds" up off the floor, raided our suitcases for clothes for covers, and bedded down. At least rats weren't running over us.

When we awoke the following morning, after a sleepless night on hard wooden chairs, it was my 50ᵗʰ birthday. Every bit of me ached. I felt 100 and was grateful there were no mirrors. I was more exhausted than I could ever remember being. But we'd soon be on our way to Nepal and everything would be fine.

One guard escorted Wayne to purchase our tickets from Royal Nepal Airline while another stood over me, his machine gun at the ready in case I tried to make a break for it. After further difficulties too tedious to discuss, we boarded the plane to Kathmandu.

As it rose into the sky, my spirits lifted too. The plane soared over the Himalayas. The morning sun cast a crimson glow on jagged snowy peaks. I felt my heart would burst. This was the most beautiful, perfect, fantastic birthday present possible.

Kathmandu

…We treated ourselves to the best offerings of an upscale Chinese restaurant near our hotel. Soft lights from filigreed lanterns enhanced its red and gold interior, heady aromas of pungent spices and tantalizing flavors quickened our hunger pangs. The young Chinese *mâitre'd* showed us to our table, presenting the Chinese/English menus with pomp and ceremony, as if aware this was a special occasion. A pot of steaming tea materialized almost instantly; we sipped delicate jasmine tea while perusing the menu.

When our soup arrived we breathed deeply of the savory steam, which seemed the breath of life to these weary souls. It was like nothing we'd ever tasted. It warmed, soothed, and stimulated the senses. One dish after another was presented, each more exquisite and delicious than the last. This sumptuous meal, served with traditional Chinese hospitality, did a great deal to bring us back to life.

From the far reaches of my mind (high school Latin class): "restaurant" derives from *restaurāre* -- "to restore". The word is from an era when travel was torturous; eateries along the way were hostels in which weary travelers were restored, enabling them to continue on. After our ghastly experiences of the past few days, we felt the term appropriate in this palace of restoration.

"Well sweetheart, we made it!" said Wayne. "You're in Nepal for your birthday, after all. It wasn't easy, but we did it."

"Now that we're here, I still want to slow the trip down. A two-week trek will be a good start. Do you think you'll be able to mellow out?"

"I'll try, I really will. Now, back to your birthday, how does it feel to be half-a-century old?"

"Actually, it feels pretty good. Trekking the Himalayas will be a great start to my second half-century. I know the second half of life is going to be even more exciting than the first."

There was a heart-tug because my sons weren't there to help me celebrate my big Five-O. Wayne toasted me on their behalf, bringing them into our presence 15,000 miles from home.

The chilly mountain air revitalized us on our stroll back to the hotel. The full moon hung low in the sky, an incandescent ball. In the magic of moonlight, the mountains looming over the city lent enchantment to the evening. Grateful for this perfect gift, we wended our way back to the Snow Lion Hotel and climbed the three flights to our room. By morning, fully restored, we were back among the human race.

…Trekking companies abounded in this Himalayan city. Treks of all sorts were available: three-days to two-months, bare-bones-basic to luxurious. We set up a nine-day trek to start on November 4. Hiking boots and down jackets as well as sleeping bags, tents, food, a cook, a guide, and sherpas were provided. Since the boots our guide brought fit neither Wayne's size 15 feet or my size 5½ feet, we were assured his Nikes and my Reeboks would do fine.

I couldn't remember being this excited, ever. The rest of the trip had been in preparation for this. I was in better shape than ever. Over the past three-and-a-half months, hiking five-to-eight hours nearly every day, frequently lugging a 35-pound pack, I was lean and mean. Man, I was ready!

Postcards bragging about trekking in Nepal went out to everyone we knew. It would be the high point of the whole trip, both literally and figuratively.

This was the start of the exotic portion of the trip. Kathmandu teemed with people, holy cows, temples, open-air curio shops, rugs, orange-dyed goat heads, tee shirts, *et cetera*. Street entrepreneurs, including children, conversant in several languages, dealt with tourists of every description. Their ingenuity was impressive. One adolescent boy offered, for a few rupees, to clean the wax out of our ears.

A younger boy, one of many shoeshine kids, had a special offering as well. "I give you shoe shine, lady," after passing over Wayne who wore Birkenstocks.

I shook my head. "No, thank you." I continued on, my once-white leather tennies kicking up street dust.

He walked alongside, cute as could be. "Where you from?"

"California," I answered.

"Oh California. Disneyland!"

"Yes. Disneyland."

He walked beside us. "I give you very nice shoe shine."

"No, thank you. I don't need one."

He didn't agree. We tramped on. His face lit up and he announced enthusiastically, "Hey! I got a great idea!"

"Okay," I bit. "Let's hear it. What's your great idea?"

"I'll use *white* shoe polish!"

"Oh," I smiled. "That *is* a great idea." Who could resist?

Nepalese are small, dark and beautiful, with delicate features. The women wear flowing sarees (the plural of sari), black kohl around their eyes, and a red dot over the "third eye" in the center of their foreheads. (Most now wear a peel-off, stick-on dot.) The men wear sarongs with tees or button-front shirts. Both males and females sprinkle yellow or orange marigold petals over their obsidian hair.

Occasionally, we came upon a small temple in the center of a hub, with several streets radiating from it. These temples are thousands of years old. Worshippers leave fresh flowers, caress the sacred statues, and pray among the hustle and bustle of shoppers and tourists. In the center of the city is a large square bordered by several temples, some of which have enormous almond eyes painted on them, monitoring one's approach.

Everywhere, Nepalese and Tibetans twirl prayer wheels, which consist of a small metal drum on a stick, with a tasseled counterweight. Their prayer, *Om Mani Padme Hum*,[25] written on rice paper, is placed inside. Each revolution of the wheel is a repetition of the prayer.

I tried the *Om Mani Padme Hum* mantra myself, sans prayer wheel, and was instantly transported into an altered state, one of peace and euphoria. It's powerful!

25. It is said that all the teachings of the Buddha are contained in this mantra. *Om Mani Padme Hum* cannot be translated into a simple phrase.

One thing we learned about shopping in Kathmandu: if you see something you want, buy it immediately because you'll never find that shop again. The streets are laid out in such a way as to guarantee chaos and confusion. Several times, when we returned to get something at a shop whose the location we were sure we knew, it wasn't there. We were lost.

…Kathmandu suffered an influx of Hippies in the 1960s and '70s -- dropouts from Western culture seeking instant enlightenment and cheap hashish. "Freak Street" was so named because it was littered with stoned-out-of-their-mind "freaks". A marvelous legacy from those days, however, is the grand array of wonderful European bakeries and American pie shops. In the '60s and '70s, the youth of America and Europe, so far from home, must have hankered for Mom's apple pie or *Mutti's Apfelstrudel*. While there we learned that an intense craving for sweets accompanies a hashish high.

Kathmandu was full of excellent restaurants of every ethnicity. The cost of living in this country was low, so restaurant prices were very reasonable.

…After brief exuberance at arriving in Nepal, Wayne again plunged into despondency. His few short "ups" were mere blips between his long, deep "downs". His life had no purpose. It was meaningless. He was wasting his life. When was God going to notice his special-ness and give him the happiness he deserved?

I was not going to let his "downs" spoil my birthday trek.

…Early the morning we left for our Himalayan adventure we walked the few blocks to the bus terminal, shivering in the cold mountain air. Our guide escorted us to a battered red and white bus festooned with more tinsel and glitter than Woolworth's at Christmas. We climbed aboard and made for seats in the back. The guide intercepted us, taking us to the front section. First Class. We settled in, Wayne and I on the bench next to the driver, inches from the windshield, our guide behind us. The door between us and the rear passenger section slammed shut.

Our adventure had begun. I tingled with excitement and couldn't stop grinning.

En route to Pokhara -- the town at base camp -- the road had huge potholes, washouts, landslides. Just outside Kathmandu it narrowed to one lane. There were few cars in Nepal but plenty of buses and trucks. Nepal is similar to Switzerland with deep, deep valleys, glacial-green rivers and majestic mountains. Many world travelers call it the most beautiful place on earth.

The further we got from the Kathmandu valley, the more beautiful the scenery. Cool morning mists lent a mystical air. The near mountains, terraced and planted with crops from bottom to top, were overspread by a vertical green and gold patchwork quilt. Beyond lay snow-covered 28,000' peaks reflecting the apricot and raspberry hues of the sunrise. This panorama was astonishingly, spectacularly beautiful.

We passed tiny villages and isolated farmhouses perched on precipitous mountainsides. In icy mountain streams families bathed, brushed their teeth, washed breakfast dishes.

…The entire trip was on a one-lane road carved into the side of an alpine mountain, our bus going hell-bent uphill, with trucks and buses coming hell-bent downhill. This road is the only place local residents can walk, so, along with their animals, they use the middle of the road, moving aside only at a horn-blast.

…After waiting several hours for a landslide to be cleared, we stopped in a village at 3:30 p.m. for lunch. The driver left through the door next to his seat. The other passengers headed for the many "Cold Drinks" shacks, and the fields beyond. When we tried to enter the main part of the bus, the door wouldn't open. The belongings of the passengers had been piled against it. It would not budge, even when Wayne and our guide shoved with all their might. We were forced to exit through the driver's door next to his seat.

The bus was on an incline, its right side higher than the left. Our exit was on the high side, next to a creek lined with large flagstones. Our guide jumped. Wayne jumped. It was my turn. I hesitated. Coaxed by Wayne and the guide, I eventually leapt across the creek.

When I hit the ground a terrific pain shot through my left foot. It had landed on one of the stones lining the stream. I saw stars … really. "I think I broke something."

Wayne supported me as I hopped to the creek where I plunged my foot into its icy water. A couple of toothless old villagers hobbled over to offer counsel. Cackling, they pantomimed that what I needed was hashish. I nodded enthusiastically, but none was produced.

Other travelers told us there was an excellent fracture clinic at Pokhara. I encouraged Wayne to go ahead on the trek since it was paid for and our sherpas awaited. "I'll stay behind in Pokhara. I'll make new friends. Undoubtedly, there'll be books and magazines. I'll be fine. Really. Go ahead. Please."

He decided not to. We'd return to Kathmandu and go to the Seventh-Day Adventist hospital, as advised.

...By the time the return bus came I had emptied a small bottle of brandy. With the bus in sight, I sent Wayne running for another to see me through the long trip, and maybe the night. I wrapped my lavender scarf, soaked in icy stream water, around my swollen foot. Wayne lifted me through the rear door onto the overcrowded bus, where room was cleared on the bench seat.

...It might be necessary to begin conserving my "anæsthetic". Wayne consumed a bit from time to time to alleviate *his* stress. At one point, feeling effusive, he passed it around the bus. The bottle came back empty. So much for it getting me through the night. But Wayne won the "Mr. Congeniality" title.

...Our itinerary had changed. We would not trek the Himalayas. We would not bicycle through India. It was unlikely we would do much of anything for awhile. Should we go home? I voted no. The E.R. doctor who "plastered" my foot said it was a minor break and the plaster could come off in three weeks. (Although we instructed our guide to take us to the Seventh-Day Adventist hospital, we ended up at Pataan General Hospital. We found out much later that the doctor didn't know how to read X-Rays. It was *not* a minor break.)

We phoned our friends, Tom and Kathy Burke, in Colombo, Sri Lanka. "Come on down," they said. We gave Tom our arrival date and time.

...Finally, Wayne had a purpose -- taking care of me. He had to be my hero. I didn't have crutches, so anywhere I couldn't go in an airport wheelchair, he had to carry me, including on and off airplanes. I was completely dependent.

...Our trip from Kathmandu to New Delhi to Bombay to Madras to Colombo -- four flights over four days -- was mercifully shortened to two. Every time we arrived in a new city we were put on an earlier flight. One flight was eliminated altogether; we flew directly from Bombay (Mumbai) to Colombo, bypassing Madras.

Wayne tried to call Tom to tell him about our earlier arrival. Continuously from 6 a.m. until 4 p.m., the operator in the Bombay airport worked on completing the call. Wayne kept checking with him. Finally, after our flight was announced and we were boarding the plane, the operator ran up, shouting,

"Sir! Sir! I have your connection!"

Knowing it might be tenuous, Wayne shouted into the phone, "We're coming tonight. 6:45." It went dead.

My wheelchair was pushed out to the plane for pre-boarding. When Wayne tried to come with me they shoved him back and slammed the door in his face. A member of the Air India staff, wearing a dark blue uniform with brass buttons, greeted me on the steamy tarmac that blistering afternoon.

"I am here to assist you in boarding the plane," he singsonged.

"Oh good. Thank you."

He looked at my plastered foot. "Are you able to walk at all?"

I shook my head. "No."

He looked at me, at the aluminum stairs, then back at me, perplexed. He scratched his chin, looking back and forth between me and the steps, stood first on one foot, then the other. Finally, in frustration and bewilderment, he blurted, "But then . . . how are you going to get up all those stairs?!"

Taking a moment to recover, I countered with, "Well, my husband *was* going to carry me onto the plane, but your people kept him inside the terminal. So I don't know how I am going to do it."

It was obvious *he* wasn't going to carry me onto the plane. He stood there scratching his chin, repeating, "I'm here to assist you."

Finally, I said, "Just get me over to the stairs. I'll get up them somehow."

He pushed my wheelchair to the foot of the portable stairway. I stood on my good foot. Standing beside me, he held my elbow. I thought I could grasp the handrails and hop, one-footed, from step to step, up into the plane. To say that didn't work is an understatement. As I stood on the metal staircase, trying to figure it out, my "assistant" smiled and nodded encouragement, grasping my elbow for support.

All I could think of was to crawl on my hands and knees up the stairs. So that's what I did, my progress impeded by my "assistant's" firm grip on my right elbow. Once on the plane, I stopped, thinking someone there would come to my aid. No one did. From my knees-and-elbows position, I held my ticket, which I'd held in my teeth, up to the flight attendant. The plane, which started in London with stops in Rome and New Delhi, was full of passengers. I crawled to my seat, smiling self-consciously at fellow passengers as I passed by. At least my "assistant" didn't accompany me through the plane.

We hoped and prayed Tom had heard our message.

Sri Lanka

Colombo

Sri Lankans are some of the world's handsomest people, with large dark eyes, fringed with long black lashes, jet-black hair in smooth silky waves, satiny Hershey-Chocolate-hued skin and gleaming white smiles.

We were delirious to be there. Wayne was burned out. All he wanted was to find Tom and get settled, free of the responsibility of carting a crippled wife and two backpacks through the world, making travel arrangements, searching out meals, *et cetera*.

He chose to view my broken foot as nothing but bad luck, rather than a chance to serve, i.e., a purpose. It's possible that over the years he'd been presented with any number of "purposes" which had passed by unrecognized. Perhaps, like this one, they hadn't seemed grand enough.

…Thank God, Tom stood at the curb beside his idling car. We greeted him like the savior he was. Wayne lifted me from the wheelchair into the backseat.

…Kathy welcomed us at their door. I hopped into the house and sank into her arms. This was our oasis, our refuge. It happened to be her birthday and their anniversary. November 9. A celebratory dinner was ready. Tom and Kathy are both gourmands and gourmet cooks. Obviously, we'd come to the right place.

Their house had four bedroom suites, each with a full bath. In addition, it had a formal dining room and a living room furnished in rattan and glass, ceiling fans in every room, a fully-equipped kitchen, a beautifully land-scaped patio shaded by a palm tree with a huge purple orchid on its trunk, and servant-quarters for Mary, their full-time maid.

Tom, employed by an American construction firm, supervised a crew of Americans and Sri Lankans. Kathy was president of the American Women's Association in Sri Lanka. Activities in the ex-pat community were planned for every evening and weekend. It sounded exhausting, but it would be a new experience.

We explained that in three weeks I'd be back on my feet and we'd be on our way. We didn't want to put them out so we said we'd find an apartment nearby.

They wouldn't hear of it.

"We've got this big house and you're more than welcome to stay with us. You'll be here for Thanksgiving. And we really want you to stay for Christmas. You can tour the island if you want to, or settle into ex-pat life here in Colombo, or both."

…Armed with purloined X-Rays and the medical report from Pataan General Hospital, we went to a local doctor. Although not a orthopædist, "Dr. Sue" had received her medical training in the U.S.; that was good enough for us.

"Why didn't you call the American Embassy?" she chastised. "The best orthopædic surgeon in the Orient is in Kathmandu!"

"But we didn't get back to Kathmandu until well after midnight."

"You *always* call the American Embassy. There's someone on the switch-board 24 hours a day."

Again, we hadn't called our embassy when we should have. Would we ever learn?

She promised to get me crutches. … The next day, she met us in the hospital parking lot with non-adjustable wooden crutches built for a six-footer. The underarm piece fanned the breeze *above* my shoulders. They were better than nothing, but not much.

"Take them for now," said Dr. Sue. "I'll try to find you a more suitable pair."

A couple of days later she got aluminum crutches adjustable to my size. From there on, I was relatively independent.

Stairs presented a real challenge, though. Since our suite was upstairs, I had to figure out something. Through trial and error I devised the best method: sling the crutches ahead and scoot up or down on my bottom. Until I mastered stairs -- at least three weeks later, I simply scooted, even in public buildings. Undignified as it was, it did the job.

…Being a typical middle-class American, I had difficulty adjusting to having servants. My first day on proper crutches I ventured into the kitchen to fix myself lunch. The crutches required the use of both hands, so moving food from the refrigerator to the counter, six feet away, was clumsy. Just short of my goal I lost my balance and toppled over backwards, tossing bowls of food onto the counter, just as Mary came through the door. She rushed in, trying to break my fall, but I was too far gone.

"I'm okay!" I assured her. A look at the counter let her know what I was up to.

Looking worried, she cried, "Madam, why didn't you ask for help?"

"I didn't want to bother you," I replied.

"But, madam!" she cried, exasperated. "That's what I'm here for!"

...Tom and Kathy were to go about their normal lives. To maintain our independence and allow them theirs, Kathy arranged for us to hire a tri-shaw -- motorized tricycle rickshaw -- whose driver was known to be reliable. Wayne joined the Colombo Swimming Club so he could swim daily, resuming his normal routine. The tri-shaw picked him up every morning and dropped him off, returning an hour later to fetch him.

...My foot was not mending as predicted. I needed more time before hitting the road again. Concerned about overstaying our welcome, we looked for alternatives to hanging around the Burkes' house.

Since the beginning of this trip I vowed to slow it down somehow before we were through. Well, I'd certainly done that, hadn't I? *Be careful what you wish for.*

We had collected literature about Kanduboda, a Buddhist Vipassana Meditation training retreat, surrounded by a coconut plantation on a plateau. We would check in for the 21-day training. That would get us back in time for the Burkes' Christmas Tree Trimming Party. We'd spend Christmas with them, after all, then take off for a week of sightseeing in central and southern Sri Lanka, return to Colombo for the big New Years Eve party at the swimming club, and be on our way again on January 3. This would allow extra healing time for my foot while giving Tom and Kathy a respite from house guests.

Before committing to three weeks in Kanduboda we went for an interview and inspection of it. We were led to a small building inside the compound. Wayne was asked to remove his shoes before entering. I could wear my Berkies due to my handicapped status. We were to speak with the priest who interviewed prospective guest-meditators. This elderly priest with kind eyes wore an ochre robe with one shoulder bare and an ochre shawl over the other. His head was shaved, his feet bare. Tufts of gray hair emerged from his ears.

"I'm afraid I shan't be able to spend a great deal of time with you," he apologized. "Your visit was unexpected. I am scheduled to be in a meeting with the other priests right now."

He spoke of the Buddhist theory of relativity. "Nothing in the world is absolute. Everything is conditional, relative, and interdependent. The perspective view of a thing gives it its relative beauty. For example, to someone in grief, a rose can bring sadness, whereas, to someone in love, it can bring joy. So are our thoughts relative and conditional, as well. We empower our thoughts and allow them to rule us. But through meditation we learn to control them and become mindful.

"Excuse me," he quietly interrupted himself. "I'm feeling very warm. Would you mind opening the window?"

Wayne opened the windows nearest the priest while I opened the one behind me.

"Thank you." He went on. "In Buddhism, the four Sublime States are: Extending unlimited *Universal love and good will* to all living beings without discrimination; *Compassion* for all living things who are suffering, in trouble or afflicted; *Sympathetic joy* in others' successes, welfare and happiness; and . . . "

Once again he stopped. "You're going to have to excuse me. I'm feeling quite unwell." He rose and bowed.

We stood and bowed to him, palms together, fingertips under our chins. "We look forward to seeing you when we return."

Very slowly and carefully he made his way down the steps. At the front office we arranged for our 21-day retreat, which would begin the day after Thanksgiving.

...Most of the day after Thanksgiving was spent in doctors' offices. Dr. Sue gave us Vitamin B-12 and hepatitis shots. An orthopædic surgeon cut the plaster cast off. I'd still need crutches, though. He charged more for the Ace-bandage he wrapped around my foot than for his professional services. When I commented on it, he replied with a twinkle, "Oh, but you see, the bandage is imported. I am not."

We were ready to go. Wearing borrowed white cotton clothes, we left behind the camera, all reading material, and anything else that might be distracting, and arrived at the meditation retreat center at twilight.

Kanduboda

...Smiling serenely, the administrator welcomed us warmly, then quickly changed the subject. "Do you remember the old priest who gave you the orientation the last time you were here?"

"Yes, of course."

He smiled radiantly. "Well, within minutes after he left you, he died." He beamed as if he were giving us a most glorious gift.

I didn't know how to react. "It was a great honor for us to have been with him," I mumbled uncertainly, " . . . in his final hour."

He nodded, glowing. "Yes. He died teaching *The Truth*. While he was with you he had a heart attack. And before you were off the grounds he expired."

Over the next few days many people greeted us as if we were honored guests, which, it turned out, we were. When a Buddhist dies teaching *The Truth*, his or her soul is greatly elevated and exalted. By making it possible for the old priest to die teaching *The Truth*, we likewise were elevated and exalted.

Because of this, we were accorded unusual privileges. And because we were so "elevated and exalted" it was, apparently, unnecessary to inform us of the rules of Kanduboda, much less of Buddhism, about which we knew next to nothing. Wayne and I would have our daily lessons together, which was unheard of. Because I was on crutches, I was granted further privileges, such as having Wayne fetch me at the women's compound to escort me to our lessons. In addition, I was excused from small chores like raking the yard every morning and cleaning the common area, and from wearing a shawl over my left shoulder. Someone carried my dishes to and from the dining hall.

My room was a spare cubicle with a narrow bed, a nightstand and a straight-backed chair on a concrete floor. Down the hall were two bathrooms, each with a flush toilet. This building, I learned, was only for Westerners. Asian meditators' quarters were far less luxurious.

...The other guests in my quarters were a WASB (White Anglo-Saxon Buddhist) from Berkeley, California, who had joined the monastery "for life", a woman from Australia, and two teenagers -- Jane, from New Zealand, and Diedre, from Sydney -- on a cross-cultural student exchange. In charge of this dorm was Sita, a beautiful middle-aged Sri Lankan.

...The girls were happy to have a break in the routine and a new person not yet involved in meditation who would talk with them. We whispered.

"During meals you can't speak. And they keep putting food on your plate until you give them the signal to stop." They showed me the stop sign.

"We carry our plates and cups, covered with a white serviette.[26] Did you

26. Dinner napkin.

bring a serviette?"

"No," I answered. "No one told me to."

"Oh, dear. You *must* have a serviette to cover your dish. Do you have anything that's small and white?"

I did a quick mental inventory and shook my head. "The only thing I have that's small and white is my underpants. Do you suppose they'll do?"

The girls smothered their giggles as they pictured me entering the dining hall with my panties over my plate. Obviously, there's little comic relief at Kanduboda Meditation Retreat.

…"No food is allowed in the rooms, and we're not supposed to eat anything after Noon. But we sneak bananas or sweets under our serviettes for later."

…"The Sri Lankan women in charge are very sweet and nice, but that American woman… " They shuddered and grimaced.

"That American woman" had offered to get me tea and a book. When she delivered them (the book was *What The Buddha Taught*), the girls fell silent. Although not a nun, her head was shaved in devotion to the Buddha. (Some heads are meant to be covered with hair. Hers was one of them. Before long I nicknamed her "Berkeley Baldy".)

Since I arrived shortly before the evening meditation and hadn't yet had a lesson, she gave me a basic meditation to repeat like a mantra:

The Metta Meditation

I am happy. I am well. I am at peace.
I am free of hatred, anger, pain, suspicion, fear, negativity.
I radiate this sense of well-being outward to my
loved ones, my family, friends, associates,
acquaintances . . . and to my enemies.
Just as a pebble dropped into a pond produces
ever-widening ripples, this well-being radiates
outward in ever-widening circles -- ever expanding,
but never lessening in strength, force or energy.

Over the next couple of days, the girls quietly eased my entry into monastic life, for which I was very grateful. When they left a few days later I missed them.

…Each day a different Sri Lankan village brings food fit for a wedding feast. It's a great privilege to do so. At mealtime, they watch the meditators eat. At first, it seemed to me like feeding time at the zoo. And I was one of the animals. Over my three weeks there, I got used to it, though. They also brought gifts for the meditators; bath soap the most common. Men were given the same gifts as the women, and others besides, including a mildly narcotic betel nut daily.

...Rural Sri Lankans eat with their fingers, mooshing the food around, scooping it up with their fingers and delivering it into their mouths with great finesse. This is a lot more difficult than it looks. I never mastered it. Food always landed on my shirt or dribbled down my chin and forearm.

...We were to meet with the priest for our meditation training daily at 3:00 o'clock. Based upon his intuition about our readiness, he put each of us on a schedule to learn the Vipassana Mindfulness Meditation technique. Wayne was to start at the basic beginner level while I started at a higher one. I was to concentrate on my upper lip, just beneath the nostrils, as I breathed in and out, in and out, in and out, the entire meditation time. It's not as easy as it sounds. Nothing in this meditating business is. It took a couple of days of constant effort before I could do it.

I occasionally read *What the Buddha Taught*. Once, Berkeley Baldy caught me at it and chastised me. "You must not read!" she lectured. "You must empty your mind. Reading interferes with meditation, so you must put it aside."

If they don't want us to read why do they have a library?

Berkeley Baldy's scolding sent me underground. Every time I sneaked to read *What the Buddha Taught* I felt like a naughty kid reading by flashlight under the covers.

...To sum up, I advanced in my meditation. Wayne did not. He asked the priest how this could be, and why I had been put on a more advanced course since I was not spiritual in any sense of the word. He'd worked long and hard at meditating while I hadn't. He'd read and studied, and I hadn't. He felt cheated and unacknowledged.

The priest replied, "Ah, yes. But your wife has worked very hard in previous lives."

This sort of thing kept happening. I received special treatment in the retreat center. I was invited to the ordination of a new priest, a very rare and special occasion. Wayne was not included, which hurt and enraged him. One day, in meditation, I had a transcendent experience.[27] When I described it to the

___

27. In the pure-clear-mind meditation, I felt (or saw) purple-tinged gold light streaming into the top of my head, all through my being; radiant energy flowing

priest he was beside himself. He announced ecstatically, "You have achieved *Samadhi!*" According to him, it's a high state of enlightenment.

On our way back to the women's compound, Wayne exploded. "It's not fair! I've worked so hard, and you don't even give a shit!"

Within a couple of days, he had a total meltdown. When he came to fetch for me for our lesson, he arrived early. We sat beneath a tree. His body shook with sobs; I put my arms around him to comfort him, unwittingly committing a *faux pas* which turned us into "Ugly Americans".

Word of our transgression quickly reached the priest's ears. He seemed mystified by, uncomfortable with, and gravely disapproving of Wayne's display of emotions. In that culture, men don't cry. Ever. But even worse, we'd touched. Sri Lankan men and women never touch except for sex, so our touching was construed as sexual. And we'd done it right out in the open, scandalizing everyone.

By our age, sex was to be set aside in favor of spiritual devotion. He was adamant about this. He then spent the next hour lecturing us, "You absolutely must not think about sex!"

It was pointless to tell him that when I comforted Wayne in his distress, sex was the farthest thing from our minds.

Our earlier sins had been overlooked because of our "special relationship" with the old priest. It was becoming apparent that we were quite ordinary humans. Their tolerance wore thin. Each of us was given a talking-to, at the same time. Separate but equal.

Now, finally, in week-three, we were given some guidelines. I tried to be good. I kept myself from looking up or around, and moved slowly . . . slowly . . . slowly. I closed down all thoughts and sensations. And I felt like a zombie.

When I tried to re-achieve *Samadhi*, I was unable to. After Wayne's emotional breakdown, I think I, being The Placator, The Caregiver, The Consummate Codependent, The *Wife*, simply shut down. Subconsciously, not wanting to be the cause of his pain, I quit the program. His gigantic, yet oh-so fragile ego had taken a beating, so I did the only thing I knew to alleviate his suffering. I went back to not giving a shit.

About that same time, one evening just at dusk, I sat in quiet meditation

---

through me. I became that radiant energy, that gold and purple light, bodiless -- weightless, formless, transparent; floating and luminescent. It was ecstasy, euphoria; serenity, aliveness -- unity and oneness with Spirit.

I've never done drugs, but I can't imagine they'd be any better than that.

when startled by a noise. I looked up. A foreign object appeared over the 10-foot-high wall just outside my door. I jumped up to give it a closer look. Just then, WASB-Berkeley Baldy walked by and demanded, "What are you doing?"

"I saw something come over the wall. It looked like someone was pushing something over it. But it was just a cat."

"I'd like to tell you a story. May I?"

"Sure," I answered, thinking she might begin to be a little more human.

"May I sit with you?" She told this story.

> Once, there was a priest who had gone to a cave to sit in meditation, undisturbed by the world. He sat in his cave, day after day, month after month, year after year, in solitary meditation. After fifteen years in this cave, he had a visitor. The visitor paid him proper homage, then looked around, exclaiming, 'What magnificent paintings there are on the walls of this cave!'
> The priest looked up in astonishment and said, 'Why, so there are. I never noticed.'

"That," continued Berkeley Baldy, "is how each of us should be. No matter what happens, we must stay single-minded in our meditation and not notice what goes on around us."[28]

I allowed myself this fantasy:

> This same priest who sat 15+ years in a cave without noticing his surroundings arrives in Heaven/Nirvana and is greeted by God, who says, "Did you enjoy the welcome I prepared for you? The glorious colors of the light show and the celestial music and the fragrance-perfumed breezes . . . "
> The priest righteously replies, "Oh no! I never notice things like that. I direct my attention inward and heavenward. I never notice worldly things!"
> In dismay, God instructs, "Then you must go back to earth to learn to appreciate the gifts I have given you, the beautiful sunsets, the brilliant flowers, the tranquil lakes and healing waterfalls, the beauty of the animals of the land and the fish of the sea, the miracle in a grain of rice."
> And the priest has to go back in another incarnation.

I felt like Maria in *The Sound of Music* -- always in trouble. Our days of being in everyone's good graces were over. At that point my rebellious nature

28. I didn't think to ask why she didn't do that herself? Why she was always on the lookout for others' infractions.

took over. I would follow all the rules that could be policed: I would keep my eyes lowered; I would move slowly; I would not wear flowers in my hair; I would not read; I would not throw banana peels over the wall; I would keep to their schedule; I would not touch Wayne. But they could not control my mind, which got very busy.

…It seemed to me that the Buddhism I read about in *What the Buddha Taught* bore little resemblance to that practiced at Kanduboda. As with every sect I've ever investigated, I like what the Master taught but not what is practiced. It has been corrupted by his followers, oft'times to suit their own purposes.

I particularly liked what the Buddha taught about questioning:

> Believe nothing on the faith of traditions, even though they have
> been held in honor for many generations and in diverse places.
> Do not believe a thing because many people speak of it.
> Do not believe on the faith of the sages of the past.
> Do not believe what you yourself have imagined, persuading
> yourself that a god inspires you.
> Believe nothing on the sole authority of your masters or priests.
> After examination, believe what you yourself have tested and
> found to be reasonable, and conform your conduct thereto.

That's what the Buddha did, what Jesus did, what Lao Tzu did, what Muhammad did, what Confucius did, what all the great thinkers and doers did. They questioned the ideas their forefathers and peers blindly accepted and clung to. They discovered their own truth and shared it with others. They were all simple people living simple lives, experiencing simple truths. The rules and rituals came later from those who interpreted -- and misinterpreted -- the Master's words and deeds.

Here's another quotation from the Buddha that I like:

> Rituals have little to do with the Real Path; they satisfy the needs of
> those less advanced in helping them gradually along the Path.

That makes sense to me. The rituals and ceremonial trappings of religion, the rules and regulations, the special robes and hats or shaved heads, amulets, rings, etc., are there for those who need them, those who are impressed by them or feel insecure without them. But they are just reminders, not the essence or meaning of the teachings.

It is my observation that in the world's religions, the rituals and ceremonies, rules and regulations, and food and clothing restrictions are often substituted for the "real path", obfuscating that which they were meant to illuminate.

Singapore

What a beautiful city Singapore is. Especially after months in third-world countries. It's billed as the cleanest city in the world, and I don't doubt it. It sparkles. It has real highways landscaped with lawns, flowers, trees and shrubs, and it has street lights. And you can drink the water.

At American Express we picked up our mail, which included a letter from my sister telling me my aunt and guardian -- my beloved Aunt Bill -- had died. I had visited her just days before starting off on this trip, certain it would be the last time I saw her. Her death, though not unexpected, hit harder than I thought it would.

All through the day, as we went about our business, my former sister-in-law -- John's sister, Frances, and her husband, Fred -- were on my mind. I hadn't been in touch with them for several years. I knew they were living in Seoul, South Korea, but beyond that, nothing. I *felt* their presence to the extent that I searched through crowds and looked back over my shoulder all day, expecting to see them any minute. It was a full day of banking, shopping, making travel arrangements, enjoying being in a world-class city.

I wanted to go to Raffles Hotel and have a Singapore Sling, which Wayne resisted. "Gawd Carol, that's so touristy," he said. But I insisted. It was a longtime dream of mine. We planned to be there at 4 p.m., but my still bruised, swollen, painful foot slowed me down causing us to miss a couple of buses. By the time we got there it was closer to 5. Raffles is magnificent. Built in 1887 in the colonial style, it's like being in a time machine. We passed through the hotel's elegant lobby, then walked the length of the Long Bar and found a table. Wayne made me order; it was so touristy he'd be embarrassed. Okay by me.

I looked around this fabled place. The long bar was polished wood, probably mahogany. Plantation rattan tables and chairs, and cushions in a tropical print. The bartenders and waiters were elegant in white jackets. From the grand piano came "I'll See You Again".

It was like a dream. Who could have imagined that Carol Petersen, a farm kid from Fresno, California, would ever be in this glamorous setting in far-off, exotic Singapore?

The Long Bar, inspired by a Malayan plantation, is a very large room. At cocktail time it was crowded. My gaze drifted over it when, what to my wondering eyes should appear, but Frances and Fred Gurr sipping Singapore Slings. We'd passed them on our way in. I got up and, with the assistance of my carved ebony and ivory cane, hurried over, leaving Wayne scratching his shiny bald head. I presented myself before my former relatives. "Hi!"

I was greeted with blank expressions.

"It's me!" I announced. "Carol!"

"Oh my god!" Hugs all around. Wayne came over to meet them.

"What are you doing here?" they asked, stunned. "We didn't recognize you because we didn't expect to see you here. How did you recognize us?"

I shrugged. "I've been looking for you all day."

"Why? How did you know we were here?"

"I didn't. But I *felt* you. The only thing I can think of is, I knew you lived in Korea . . . . so you're in the neighborhood."

Fred laughed. "Some neighborhood! We flew seven hours by jet plane to get here."

Frances asked, "Did you know about this place? I'd never even heard of Raffles until two days ago. A friend of mine in Seoul said, 'If you're going to Singapore, you *have* to go to Raffles Hotel. And you *have* to have a Singapore Sling.' I'd never heard of them either. But she said we had to, so here we are."

They were in Singapore for an aeronautical engineers' conference. We spent as much time with them as possible over the next three days. (Photo - page 355.)

As Fred said, "You know, the timing on that had to be perfect. Ten minutes in either direction we'd have missed each other."

It was as if it had been choreographed.

No one, least of all me, understood how I "knew" they were in Singapore, and why I'd looked for them. All this ESP stuff was new to me . . . and really weird.

BALI

Aussies sure know how to party. It was cheaper, including airfare, for them to holiday in Bali than in Australia, and the joint was jumpin'. With their boomboxes cranked up full volume, a 24/7 raucous ruckus was in progress.

But middle-aged and travel-weary, we weren't ready to rumble. Wanting serenity and beauty, such as is promoted on Bali's travel posters, we scooted over to the Tourist Office.

"We want a place that's like Bali *before* all the tourists," I told the man behind the counter. "Quiet, peaceful, beautiful. We don't want a fancy hotel, just a quiet cottage on the beach. That kind of thing."

After trying to phone a special place but getting no answer, he gave us directions to it: Take two or three jitney buses, then walk down this road, you'll see a small hand-lettered sign that reads *Pura Candidasa, et cetera.* We arrived at a lovely place on the beach, with individual hand-hewn cottages among the palm trees, a covered outdoor dining room, green lawns, a sleepy lagoon. It was quiet, beautiful, and peaceful; just what we ordered. A diminutive Balinese woman in her 60s came out. "I can't talk with you right now. Can you wait?"

We waited 45 minutes. Then she interviewed us for at least an hour. "Who sent you here?"

"The Tourist Office," I replied.

"No. The Tourist Office never sends people here," she stated. "They send people to hotels. This is an ashram -- an ecumenical ashram. It's not for tourists."

We didn't know why he sent us there, but he did. And, clearly, we were in the right place. We explained the "comparative religions" ecumenical aspect of our trip: Stonehenge, Chartres, the All-Religions Conference at Scheibenalp, The Great Pyramid and Luxor/Karnak, St. Sophia's Cathedral, Istanbul's mosques, St. Peter's Cathedral, a week at Findhorn, and three weeks in meditation in Kanduboda. She let us stay.

This was the culmination of our trip -- the tying together of our experiences over the past several months. *Ibu* (Mother) Gedong,[29] devotee of Mahatma Gandhi and peace worker, had established this ashram to teach its members the Gandhian philosophies of non-violence, simplicity, self-sufficiency, and service to the community; to keep traditional Balinese arts alive; and to welcome peace-workers and spiritual-seekers from around the world.

On an idyllic site next to Candidasa Beach on Bali's east coast, a spring-fed lagoon runs into the Indian Ocean. Thatched roofed cottages built the ancient way, hand-carved, perfectly fitted together without nails or screws. Each of the larger buildings in the ashram was inscribed with a Ghandi quotation, such as, "Let us live simply so others may live," and "He who eats but does not

---

29. Ibu Gedong Oka was most impressive: Mother of six sons, University professor (of English Lit), Member of Parliament, Founding member and, eventually, president of the World Council for Religion and Peace, Board member of several international and domestic social organizations. In 1994 she received the Gandhi Peace Award. In addition, she visited the White House of two or three U.S. presidents, spoke multiple times at the UN, and hosted President Franklin D. and Eleanor Roosevelt at her home on Bali.

work eats stolen food."

In the seawall on ashram property, symbols representing the world's major religions were embedded.

A strict disciplinarian, she ran classes for ashram members. But we guests were on holiday, with only a few in attendance at any time. We ate in the outdoor dining room, cementing friendships with people of all backgrounds from all over the world. Ashram guests' commonality was devotion to and striving for world peace and/or spiritual growth. (Photo - page 355.)

Candidasa had no televisions, radios, or newspapers, so we were out of touch with the rest of the world. On January 29, Wayne and I took a series of jitney buses to Ubud, an up-island city of artists.

In shock and dismay, tourists we met there told us about the spaceship *Challenger,* which had broken apart immediately after lift-off, disintegrating into the ocean and killing all seven astronauts aboard. We brought this terrible news back to the ashram.

At Candidasa Ashram Wayne got his mojo back. He talked the talk. He played the role. He pronounced his spirituality to the skies. *Ibu* Gedong and some of the other guests bought it. His ego, deflated in Kanduboda, got pumped back up on Bali. His shoulders squared and a smile returned to his face. Ever so pleased with himself, he strutted like a popinjay.

Mr. Spiritual was back.

Home Again

Our trip of a lifetime was certainly that. No matter what else happened, neither of us would ever regret taking it. We learned a lot about the world, and, in the process, ourselves.

To our surprise, upon re-entering our own country we experienced culture-shock. Everyone seemed hung up on trivialities. Dinner party conversations seemed so superficial. It took several months before we felt "at home" again.

Once back on my native soil, I never experienced the "energy" of a place again, nor have I had any premonitions such as the one in Singapore. I still don't understand it, but in any case, it's gone. As quickly and unexpectedly as it came upon me, it vanished.

I resumed my therapy practice, wrote a couple of novels, taught seminars and workshops in various areas of personal growth, led women's retreats at the seashore and weekly meditation groups in our living room.

Wayne continued down the slippery slope of despondency and despair. His self-aggrandizement turned people off, which puzzled him and exacerbated his depressed mental state. Over the next four years, he spiraled down, down, down, still refusing to consider medical or psychological help.

After awhile I started getting phone calls from friends, imploring, "Carol, can't you leave him?"

I didn't feel as if I could.

They said things like, "He's sucked all the life out of you. There's no 'Carol' left."

Due to his superior attitude and insulting behaviors he was banned from the homes of several of our friends. "Carol, you're welcome in our home anytime, but Wayne can never come here again."

I still couldn't leave him. As is true of most therapists, it was much easier to see and "fix" other people's problems than my own.

Wayne developed Meniere's Disease, an imbalance of the inner ear which causes vertigo, nausea, weakness, *et cetera*. For this he did see a doctor and get a diagnosis, but there was no treatment.

And he still wanted to live the lifestyle of the rich and famous. When he told me for at least the thousandth time, "I wish you'd hurry up and get your act together so you can support me in the manner to which I'd like to become accustomed," I replied, "That's not funny, Wayne."

"Oh, you can't think I'm serious, Carol. I'm joking!"

"No, Wayne. You've said it way too often for it to be a joke. You're more serious about that than anything else you've ever said."

All that "Be all you can be" and "Live up to your highest potential" was for his benefit, not mine -- so I could provide for him as he'd like me to. How about him living up to *his* highest potential and being all *he* could be? How about *him* getting *his* act together?

That's the day it dawned on me that his primary addictions were: *Sympathy* -- He set up his life in such a way that people would feel sorry for him. Since I was joined to him, my life was seriously affected. I didn't need or want that; and *Sloth and dependency* -- As his spouse, I was responsible for his needs. Considering everything, I didn't need or want that either.

I doubt that his ploys for sympathy were conscious. But they were there and they were very real.

The subconscious mind is an amazing thing. It does what's necessary to give us what we believe we need. In the end, in addition to Bi-Polar Disorder, it created Meniere's Disease so he would get the sympathy he craved. What a wonderful thing.

When we finally separated, he immediately went to a doctor who recommended SSI Disability. He wouldn't have to work. Ever. If I wouldn't support him, he'd get the government to. Not in the manner to which he'd like to become accustomed, but he took it.

This leaves me with some questions about me. Why had I chosen the men I had, both of whom believed deep in their hearts that I was put on this earth solely to serve them?

I'd had red flags with John, but I was young and naïve (as was he) . . . and so alone.

Why did I believe I deserved to be treated poorly?

In the years between my two marriages, men had shown an interest in me. I'd even had proposals. Why did I pick Wayne?

I guess I was doing the pendulum-swing thing. I married John believing he was opposite Tracey. Then I married Wayne believing he was totally unlike John.

In some ways they were opposite. John was in contrast to Tracey in that he was college educated, had a conscience, and wasn't rude, crude and lewd. Wayne was dissimilar to John in that he encouraged me to have a career, be gregarious, and not be overly modest.

But both were self-sabotaging: John was self-defeatingly humble; Wayne self-defeatingly egoistic.

One of my highly intuitive acquaintances told me I'd married the same man twice -- different sides of the same coin. I suppose that's possible. They were polar opposites, but the end result was the same. When I left John I promised myself that from then on I would be in control of my life. I believed I was healed by leaving him, which, by the way, took more courage than anything else I've ever done. I didn't know if I could make it on my own, and truly believed his brainwashing that no other man would ever want me and I'd be alone forever.

Fifteen years later -- five as a single woman and ten married to Wayne -- I believed I'd healed myself by leaving him. It's not that easy.

My childhood wounds and relationship imprints were strong and deep too. I'd thought that because Tracey wasn't part of our family (it was Mom, Pat and me), and because I made a point of ignoring him as much as possible, his impact was minimal. Not so. It was huge.

I figured out that I needed to stop falling for men at the outer edges of the pendulum swing. I needed a mid-point kind of guy, if such a man existed. I needed a man who wasn't seriously wounded, who could have a healthy relationship in which respect and kindness were key.

I've often said, "All I ever wanted was a man who would be kind to me."

Short of that, I'd have to be content to have relationships with my family, my women friends, platonic guy friends, and myself.

All of life's experiences present opportunities to learn. And we are all each others' teachers.

I wasn't healed. I still had one more to go. And this one was a real doozie. The only saving grace was that I wouldn't end up with a broken heart that time. It was strictly business. It resulted in broken finances, but my heart remained intact. Once again I allowed myself to be mistreated and misused by a male. But I'm getting ahead of myself.

The day I *got* that Wayne's major addictions were sympathy and sloth was the day I said "I don't want to be married anymore." However, that didn't happen until after the next mini-memoir, "A Fun Day".

Although it was written for a Creative Writing class (at SRJC the summer of 1990), every word of "A Fun Day" is true. The writing of it was a turning point. With each rewrite, each tweak, I grew furiouser and furiouser.

I finally saw that my husband was treating me like "a piece of mooseshit" and had been all along. This story shows pretty much how our whole trip around the world went -- how our marriage was, for that matter. This little story is a microcosm -- a hologram -- of our life together.

And yes, I know I was as responsible as he. I should have been less co-dependent, less concerned with placating and nurturing him and more about self-nurturing and assertiveness.

With its writing I climbed out of the deep ditch of denial. I allowed myself to see things as they were, not as I wished they were. I permitted myself to stop suppressing my authentic feelings. I made big strides in becoming non-codependent.

Ah, the benefits of a Creative Writing class!

Several things came together at once, ripping the blindfold of denial off my eyes.

A Fun Day

We are going to have such a fun day today!" says Wayne, lookin' like a little kid on his way to Disneyland.

I check to make sure the cats have their Science Diet and water, squirt industrial-strength cleanser on the stove where the cream of broccoli soup boiled over and crusted on the night before, and turn the answering machine on.

"We'll go to Chinatown for Dim Sum and Oo-long tea," says Wayne with that look he gets when he's gettin' things all lined up and organized ahead of time -- you know, kinda manic. "And there's this bookstore I want to check out on Grant Avenue. And we can poke around in those little shops down there. Then we'll go walk around Golden Gate Park and visit whatever exhibits they've got going there. After that, we'll go for pie and coffee at that little pie café on Union Street. Then we'll get half-price tickets at the stall on Union Square and go to a play. How does that sound, hon?"

"Okay," I say. I'd really like to leave a little room for spontaneity but keep my lips zipped.

"Would you mind driving, sweets? I've been really stressed out. I feel like I'm on the verge of an attack, but I don't want to just stay home and do nothing. I want to go have some fun."

I have to admit, he looks a little shaky. But if he thinks he can handle it, I'm game. I'm looking forward to a day away from clients. I need a day of relaxation and fun, too. "No, I don't mind driving," I tell him. "Be sure to take your magic potions. Just in case."

Wayne won't go to doctors, but he heard about these little bottles of herbs. And you don't even have to open them. Swear to God. You don't swallow anything, sniff anything, or rub anything on. All you do is hold the bottles with the tips of your fingers. That's all, just hold the tops of these little bottles, with their bottoms in water. Sounds crazy, like witchcraft or voodoo. It's something about electromagnetic fields and subtle energies and . . . like that. It's kind of embarrassing, but hey, at this point it's whatever works.

Well, damned if the silly things don't work. That is, they work better than anything else. For a whole week after he started using them he didn't have a single attack, after three in four days. And then, whenever he felt one coming on (you know, real dizzy, off balance, pukin' and all), he'd do the bottles and the symptoms would go away. More or less. But more-or-less is a helluva lot better than anything else he's tried. So, anymore, I don't let him leave home without 'em.

So we start off for our fun day in San Francisco with me at the wheel and him holding onto a little brown bottle in a burnt-orange Tupperware bowl on his lap. We're in his Volvo so the radio's set to one of those talk shows he likes. You know, the ones where the host tells what he thinks about a subject and then he asks people to call in and tell what they think and then they discuss it for awhile.

I *detest* those programs. Oh, I don't mind Larry King Live. He usually has a somewhat interesting guest who brings a degree of expertise, and the topics are fairly interesting. But most of these guys just wing it by themselves. It must be a real cheap kind of program because all the stations have 'em. Anyway, these guys talk about something they have strong opinions on but don't really know all that much about, and then people who are equally opinionated and equally uninformed call in, and everything that can possibly be said about it by uninformed, opinionated people gets said in the first ten minutes but there's a whole hour to fill so they talk on and on repeating themselves over and over -- one inanity after another 'til I think I'll go nuts! I mean, these folks should get a life!

But Wayne likes this twaddle, and he's stressed out, so I don't say anything. I let him listen.

" . . . Thanks for calling, Herb. I respect your opinion. I don't agree with it, but I respect it and I'll fight to the death for your right to say it. Next . . . Melba in San Mateo. What do you think about car phones, Melba?"

"Well, I have a cousin who has one and he says . . ." Blah, blah, blah.

Blah, blah, blah, . . . "Thanks for calling, Melba. That was real interesting. Next . . . Dudley from Concord. You're on, Dud."

"I'm calling on my cellular phone from the MacArthur Freeway, currently goin' 70 mph, and I'm here to tell ya . . ." Blah, blah, blah.

"Hey, I'm on your side, buddy. Keep phonin' in . . . on your car phone!" Heh, heh, heh. "We have to break for a commercial. Keep those calls comin' in, folks, at K-GAG Talk Radio, 555-K-G-A-G. This is Rod Elwin on 'Keep Talking.'"

I never thought I'd be grateful for a commercial. I look over at Wayne and there he is with his hand around a little brown bottle in the plastic bowl, his eyes closed, lookin' for all the world like he's asleep. I reach over and change the station. There's gotta be something better than this.

"I was enjoying that!" barks Wayne, real affronted-like.

Okay, he's stressed out and I don't want to stress him out more, so I switch back to K-GAG Talk Radio, Rod Elwin, "Keep Talking," wondering how an otherwise intelligent person can listen to such claptrap, and gettin' madder every time someone opens his mouth on this stupid talk show and says something so incredibly witless that I want to punch their teeth down their throat.

We go on, with him listening to his goddam talk show, twiddlin' his goddam little bottle, with his goddam eyes closed.

We cross the bridge and there's a traffic tie-up, something about roadwork on the San Francisco side, so we sit one car back from the tollbooth and the tollbooth guy and the driver in front of me are gabbin' like old friends while the road maintenance crew go back and forth, doin' God-knows-what, and Rod Elwin is sayin', "This *is* the nineties. Car phones are a necessity of modern day living, and I'll argue with anyone who says different. Next caller."

Right, Rod, I'm thinkin', tappin' the steering wheel, waitin' to get goin' again. *This is a truly earth-shaking issue that deserves a whole hour of my time? Friggin' idiot!*

Finally, the traffic starts to move and we drive down to the Marina. Wayne's eyes are open now and he's switched to a different little brown bottle. I sorta get caught up in bein' pissed-off at Rod Elwin and his stupid car phones and miss the turn. Oh well, no biggee. I can turn any place. It's a nice day for a drive.

"Where ya goin?" Wayne growls.

"Chinatown," I say, all innocence.

"Why didn't you turn on Stockton like we always do?"

Quite reasonably I respond, "It doesn't make any difference. We'll get there."

"You got some new map that says Chinatown's over here now?" he snarls.

"We'll get there, okay?" I'm tryin' to stay calm 'cause he's stressed out, but *my* blood pressure's startin' to spike, too.

Well, we're drivin' up Pacific, which is about as wide as two rickshaws need to pass each other, lookin' for a place to park. I'm right on the tail end of a big smelly Muni bus fartin' fumes up my nose when Wayne shouts, "Hey! There was one back there!"

I look back and sure enough, half a block behind there's a parking place I missed. The street is clear so I back up all the way and go to parallel-park when Wayne squints at the meter and declares, "It's only an hour."

I step on the brake and look at him like, *You want me to park there or not?* and when he doesn't say anything I start to back in.

"Well, goddam!" he says, real agitated. "Any idiot would know better than that! We're gonna be here for more than an hour, for chrissake! You put your brain on hold today, or what?!"

Well, he's stressed, right? So I bite my tongue and go catch up to the Muni bus, lookin' right and left for a parking place. We go past Hong Kong Garden, which is where we're headed for Dim Sum and Oo-long, and drive on up the hill. I, bein' in the driver's seat and all, make a unilateral decision to turn right and look for a space off Pacific. I get in the left lane and the street I turned onto is the one where if you're in the left lane you have to turn left and it goes directly into the Broadway tunnel which takes you out of Chinatown.

Damn! That's not what I wanted to do.

"Go right!" Wayne screams in my ear. "Go around the tunnel!"

I can tell, his stress level is up around the top of the TransAmerica Pyramid. I swerve right, like he says, avoid the tunnel and go on lookin'. I make another turn. Wayne goes *Tccch* with his tongue on the back of his teeth. Still no parking spaces, but at least we're in the two-hour parking meter zone now. I make another turn and Wayne goes *Tccch* again, so I make another turn, trying to correct whatever I did wrong, and he snarls, "Why'dja go that way?!"

"One street's as good as another, isn't it?" I say sweetly, tryin' hard to stay calm and pacify him at the same time. I'm drivin' real slow, lookin' everywhere for a parking space, but all of 'em I think I find turn out to be goddam drive-ways or fire hydrants.

Wayne puts the little brown bottle back in its neon-blue zippered nylon case, covers the Tupperware bowl and burps it. He sits up straight and gets super-alert. I turn left onto a street several blocks from Hong Kong Garden and have to brake for this antique Chinaman who's crossin' the street like an arthritic snail. Wayne says, like it's my fault this old guy is in the street in front of us, "Let me drive, dammit! I'm more used to driving in the city than you are!"

Okay, fi-ine! I don't know what he's so mad about, but by then I'm a little ticked myself. I mean, maybe we drive different, but that doesn't make me wrong. I mean, when he's driving, I don't rag on him all the time 'cause he does some things different than I would, and I don't think he should get pissed-off at me all the time because I don't do everything exactly like he'd do it. I do just fine, thank you, when he's not around. And I am too used to driving in the city. What he's used to is bein' an asshole!

I crank the wheel hard, swerve into the next driveway and get out. Wayne gets out, too, and stomps around the car. We stomp right past each other but I don't even look at him. If I open my mouth I'm sure to say somethin' that'll up his stress level. My chest is heaving, I'm breathing like a horse after a race. My eyes are little-bitty slits, my forehead's all bunched up, my lips are pucker-clinched, and my shoulders are hunched real tight. I get in on the passenger side and slam the door as hard as I can. The car rocks.

I sit down and kind'a zone out, trying to calm myself. Eventually Wayne finds a parking place and we get out.

So here's the deal: we're walkin' down the hill toward Hong Kong Garden. Wayne wraps his arm around me, looks down at me and flashes a smile, all sweetness and light. He gives a little squeeze and says, "You're beautiful, sweets! We are going to have such a fun day!"

This is too much! *This* I cannot believe! If he thinks he can treat me like a major piece of mooseshit, and then, like flippin' a switch, everything's all hunky-dory with a smile and a squeeze, he's got another think coming.

By this time I've had it, so without even thinking, I shove him in front of the first speeding truck that comes by and go off and have a fun day all by myself.

. . . .

Okay, okay, I confess, that last bit is a fantasy. It's what I woulda done if I coulda, but the reality is, I'm a puny 5'2", 110 pounds, whereas he is 6' tall, 200 pounds of solid muscle. And the further reality of it is that there are no speeding trucks in Chinatown. So, even if I could manage the shove, which I can't, it wouldn't accomplish what I set out to do. He might get a little discombobulated, but he'd still be among the living. And you gotta know, he'd be 'way madder at me than he was before.

No, it'd definitely cause more problems than it would solve.

So, we just go ahead and do the "fun day" Wayne planned, but there sure as hell isn't any fun in it.

I Want You to Leave

I don't want to be married anymore.
Yeah, that's right, I don't.
I want you to leave. Now. Go!

You look stunned. You're hurt. You're angry.
You're feeling rejected and unloved.
You're confused.

Well, turnabout's fair play, for
right after the "I do's"
you started with the "I don't's."

"I don't love you."
"I don't want to make love to you."
"I don't care about your needs."

I was stunned. *I* was hurt. *I* was angry.
I felt rejected and unloved.
And, boy, was I confused.

Why did you marry me
and bind my life to yours,
only to use me and abuse me?

I thought, *If only I can be perfect*
-- sweet and sexy and fun --
then surely he will love me.

So I jumped through hoops to please you,
knocked myself out day-by-day.
You never tried to please me.

No, you ravaged me with rage,
rejection and rebuke, you
raped my soul with bogus love.

Since day-one I've been your yo-yo.
You distance, discard me.
When you need me you retrieve me.

Hmmmm . . . Now you say you love me,
you cannot live without me.
That's not love. That's selfish fear.

Love is connection and caring,
support, growth and sharing.
I doubt you know how to love.

You do know how to destroy,
to disparage, diminish, disdain.
My heart is dead . . . and with it, love.

So I don't want to be married anymore.
Yeah that's right, I don't.
I want you to leave. Now. Go.

Now I'm not angry or hurt or confused.
I'm just weary, done in, burnt out.
Now it's time to take care of me.

I'm going to need to rebuild myself,
to revive the parts that died.
I must relearn to love myself.

So I don't want to be married anymore.
Yeah, that's right, I don't.
I just want you to leave. . . . Now.

Part V
On My Own

Manitou Springs

E very time I convince myself it was just a figment of my imagination something happens to jar me out of my complacency.

The first inkling I had of it was when my friend, Jo Madrid -- a professional psychic in northern California -- came for a brief visit. As we drove up the mountain, past the old stone castle, to my little house on the side of Pikes Peak, she shivered. "Ooooh, I don't like this place at all. Look at my arms – the hairs are standing up. The back of my neck prickles."

"What is it, Jo?" I asked.

"I'm not sure. All I know is, I'm glad I'm only staying three days. I'll do some meditating while I'm here and see what I can find out."

I'd lived in Manitou Springs, Colorado just a few months. I loved my little house, which I was upgrading little by little.

My first project was replacing the drafty old single pane living room windows which looked out over a canyon. As I sat at my computer in front of them, frigid wind blew through the closed windows, ruffling my hair, chilling the air. They had to go. I got new ones put in. To save money I painted the back of the house myself so the new asbestos shingles would match the old ones and city officials wouldn't catch on that I'd "remodeled" without a permit.

Newly single and determined I could go it alone, I stood atop the wobbly 30′ extension ladder, holding the paint can in one hand and stretching full length on tiptoes to brush paint on with the other. The ladder's bottom sat on a steep slope; its top leaning precariously against the house. Miraculously, it didn't topple, but I shiver when I think about it.

Next, I gave the fireplace and hearth a new façade in matte tile -- the palest mauve -- then painted the living room to match. Just those little changes made my heart sing. This would be my "forever house". I'd sold my house in Santa Rosa and paid cash for this little cottage on Pilot Knob Avenue. I'd moved, along with my cats, Sam and Squirrel, to Manitou Springs. The only way I'd move out of this house was in a pine box.

I was delighted to find Manitou Springs, a charming Victorian town midway between spectacular Garden of the Gods and the top of Pikes Peak. My house was at approximately 7000'. (Pikes Peak's summit is 14,115'.) The Manitou Springs area, with gorgeous views and mineral springs, was regarded as sacred by the various Native American tribes who traversed the area. Manitou means "Spirit" or "Great Spirit."

White settlers were no doubt unaware of its spiritual nature and, more than likely, didn't know about native lore that bad luck will befall anyone who defaces a sacred place. (Building on it or using it for anything other than sacred activities qualifies as defacing.) Obviously, some of the settlers had prospered. Perhaps it was the town itself on which misfortune would be visited.

Wayne and I separated in November of 1990, right after my 55th birthday, making every effort to part amicably. He came with me to house-hunt. Since he was a Realtor® he might able to help. Then, when I actually moved, he offered to drive the U-Haul moving van the 1500 miles over mountains and plains, pulling my 1979 Plymouth Champ behind, and help me move in. Intimidated at the thought of driving it myself, I accepted. We weren't 20 miles down the road before I realized I could have done it. *Whatever.*

Both cats yowled all the way past Sacramento, protesting the move.

Wayne still thought that if we spent enough time together and he was really nice to me he could change my mind. But we'd been through all that before. He vowed he'd change.

"Fine. If you can maintain the changes for five years, we'll talk."

His pained expression said it all. "Five years is a long time."

That told me that any changes he was willing to make would be short-term. Very short-term. Which I already knew. His previous changes lasted 3-to-4 days, maximum.

When we arrived in Manitou Springs and got my furniture and boxes in the house, he started issuing orders. "Put the armoire here. The bed has to face that way. This tree has to be cut down." *Et cetera.*

"Wait a minute," I wanted to shout. "This is not your house. It has nothing to do with you. You don't get to say what goes on in my house."

My friend Judith Daley, who lives in Colorado Springs and came to help me settle in, said, "He's pissing in all the corners." Translation: He's marking his territory.

But he was leaving soon so I didn't make a fuss. He was still certain he'd be living there with me, certain I'd beg him to come back.

A couple of weeks before I moved to Manitou Springs, Steve, my eldest son, his wife Jill, and Hannah, their nearly 3-year-old daughter, moved to Colorado Springs from Anchorage, Alaska. The distance between our two houses was exactly five miles. We'd be each other's support system.

Wayne went on his way. I settled in and started my new life. But I was lonely and homesick. Every time I saw a TV commercial showing beautiful Sonoma County I felt a pang of remorse. My loneliness made me want, at times, to retreat into the familiar misery of marriage. To keep from calling him I posted a list next to the phone where I couldn't miss it: *REASONS I LEFT WAYNE.*

This was the first time I'd ever lived alone. The part I loved about it was that I could do whatever I wanted. It was my house. I didn't have to consider anyone else's tastes or preferences. I didn't have to ask permission to make changes. And if I made a mistake, so what? There was nobody to yell at me and tell me how stupid I was.

I purchased some wallpaper for my bedroom. Three matching patterns. On the way home I questioned my decisions. *I spent too much. What if it looks awful? What if I hate it?* Then I reminded myself, *So what? If it doesn't turn out as well as I think it will, I'll just take it down and do something different. It's only money.* I laughed out loud in my car, suddenly feeling empowered and okay with myself. (It turned out great.)

Colorado was in an economic slump and a number of Californians were relocating there. Coloradans' animosity toward Californians is legendary. And there in my driveway, right out in the open, sat a car with the despised California plates.

From day one, my neighbors on Pilot Knob Avenue were not only not friendly, they were downright *un*friendly. Not one of them ever made eye-contact, much less spoke to me. If I said "Hello" to one, she or he would mumble something without looking up and hurry on. One day I knocked on my next door neighbor's door to introduce myself. She was inside but didn't answer the door. God forbid I should ever need a cup of sugar or a battery jump.

I'd no sooner gotten moved in when I started traveling, which may have made it seem to my neighbors that I was a California gadfly who had little interest in their community. Not true. But, *Maybe that's why they don't like me.* Only four weeks after moving in, I left with Judith to "babysit" a Buddhist retreat center with natural hot springs in Jemez, New Mexico while its regular caretaker took the month of December off. Then, practically as soon as I got back from Jemez, I left for Boston because my son Alex had been mugged and was hospitalized. I was gone two weeks that time. (Story - page 296.)

Once, I came home a day or two early from a trip. A DHL truck showed up with a package addressed to me. "I didn't order anything," I declared, preparing to refuse the package.

"According to this slip, you called yesterday wanting to know why it hadn't arrived, since it was to be sent 'Express,'" the delivery man said. "There was a blizzard back east and all the planes were grounded. We got it here as fast as we could. The dispatcher wrote, 'Customer very upset!'" He showed it to me.

"I didn't call. I was in New Mexico. I just got home. And I didn't order anything."

He put in a call to his office. "This your name? This your address? This the last four digits of your credit card?"

"Yes," I answered. "All of the above. But I didn't order anything."

"What do you want me to do with it?"

"I'll take it," I answered. "Obviously, somebody's using my identity. And they were in a big hurry to get this stuff before I got back. Has to be a neighbor."

I cancelled my American Express card, then took the box to the police station. They held it for evidence and called American Express to inform them of the fraud. They were pretty sure they knew who did it -- my next door neighbor, a *strange* woman. It had to be a female who lived close enough that she could watch for the truck, then run out and sign for the package. The box contained expensive software for a MAC computer. I found out later, my *strange* neighbor's computer was identical to mine. She must have taken my credit card bill out of my mailbox which stood next to hers at the road, and gotten my information before resealing and returning it.

As the months wore on, I started seeing therapy clients in my home, as I had in Santa Rosa. And I had a job that twice weekly took me to Denver, where I met "Will". I knew it was unwise to start dating so soon, but jumped right in, on the rebound. I wasn't even close to being over the Wayne-thing. I transferred all the emotion from that breakup to Will. Bad idea.

A number of people visited me in my new location. My honorary brother, "Hal," drove out from California. Martin, my middle son, came to stay awhile. My local son, Steve, dropped by from time to time. A couple of former clients came from California to visit. I had real estate agents in both Colorado Springs and Denver, helping in my search for investment properties. And carpenters and handymen came and went with some frequency. So a lot of men were in and out of my house. All very innocent though; my relationship with Will was 100% monogamous.

And Jo came to visit. Before leaving three days later, she was adamant. "You have to get out of this house. The energy here is very bad."

"I would have felt it if it was that bad," I said, recalling my experiences on the 'round the world trip.

"This town is full of witches," Jo went on, "and they're after you. There are three covens[30] right around you – two that are very powerful; the third is less so, but it's becoming more powerful all the time."

"Witches?!" I said, disbelieving. "Don't be ridiculous. I don't believe in witches."

"Well, you better, because they're here. And they don't like you at all. They don't want you here and they're working their witchcraft on you."

"You mean like, casting *evil spells* on me?" I snickered, raising my eyebrows. "*Wooooo.*"

"Exactly! They're doing it." She was dead serious.

"But Jo, you know I believe in the power of love. It's much stronger than the power of hate. Or fear. So they can't hurt me," I said confidently.

"Maybe. But remember, there's only one of you. There are thirty-six of

---

30. Groups consisting of 12 witches each.

them. Maybe more. And they're combining all their dark power; they're using all their satanic rituals and witchy stuff against you. That makes them very powerful. If it were me, I'd put a FOR SALE sign up on the house so fast it'd make your head spin."

"But why me?" I asked, still a nonbeliever but playing along. "What did I ever do to them?"

"I don't know. Maybe it's because you're so powerful on the opposite side – the light side. Quite a few people regard you as their spiritual teacher -- their guru. You teach about light and love and positive energy. Maybe the witches feel threatened by you. They can feel your light energy, you know."

She went on, insisting, "You have to protect yourself against them."

"How?"

"Surround yourself with white light -- a beam of white light that goes out to the heavens. Lock it in. Do this every day. Smudge your house with sage smoke, inside and out. Burn herbal incense every day."

That's where we left it, except that, once back in California she called at least once a week imploring, "Sell that house. Get out of it, now." Every time she called I answered with some variation of, "Don't worry, Jo. The power of love is stronger than the power of hate. I'll just keep beaming love at them. I'll love 'em to death!"

As I went about my life in the Rocky Mountains, I began hearing hints and rumors of witches and devil-worshippers' goings-on in Manitou Springs. All quite fanciful, in my opinion. There were stories about homeless people who simply disappeared; of infant and animal sacrifices; of a "secret tunnel" between the public park in Manitou Springs and Miramont Castle on the mountain, allegedly the means of spiriting people away to torturous, ritualistic, satanic deaths.

Back in the '60s and '70s, the Colorado Springs Gazette ran articles about the witches, warlocks and Satan worshippers practicing their evil *magick* in Manitou Springs.

But all this was news to me. The Chamber of Commerce didn't mention this aspect of their fair city. Nor did the Realtor who sold me my house.

During this time I was shopping for investment properties – commercial buildings and multi-unit rentals. More than once I stumbled upon an apartment painted all black, including ceilings and woodwork, with black furniture and drapes, its generously tattooed occupant black-clad from head to foot, and weird items such as a black candle, and a crystal ball imbedded in a skull, set on black velvet. I became familiar with the term "warlock" – a male witch. I was learning about the dark forces.

But I also learned about white witches – "Wicca" – who worship nature and are quite benign. Quite a few Wiccans lived in Manitou too. Most of the residents of Manitou Springs seemed unaffected by the town's dark culture. They went about their business in that quaint little town as if it was Mayberry, looking as apple-pie-normal as Andy, Barney, and Aunt Bea.

But then, witches don't wear identifying badges, do they? Any of the town's residents might have been witches or warlocks: the mayor, the banker, the waitress at Adam's Café, the cute young policeman, the gas station attendant, the minister/priest, the art store's owner, the maid at Pikes Peak Inn, my next door neighbor -- any of them. Or none of them.

I held out. I still didn't believe in witches and witchcraft. And even if they did exist in my adopted hometown, even if they were targeting me, surely I could combat them. Couldn't I?

. . . .

Current excerpts from newspapers posted on the internet when I wrote this piece -- January 4, 2010:

While we all know Manitou Springs is home and haven to witches, wizards, dragons and hippies, it also harbors a lesser known contingency of the population: potters. -- Colorado Springs Independent, January 4, 2010

Launching a church in a city that was a well-known haven for witches and followers of the occult, Burton began a prayer event called "Pray Manitou Springs. ... People made it clear to me that they didn't want us there," Burton said. -- Christian Newswire, October 27, 2009.

Manitou Springs - Continued

O f course, none of it can be proved. It all may have been mere coincidence. People have told me, "That's life. Like the bumper sticker says,
'Shit Happens' ...... to everyone." So I've stopped talking about
witches. I guess I'll never know for sure.

Thinking back over the eighteen months I lived on Pilot Knob Avenue, it
seems as if first one area of my life went bad, then another. I could have marked
it off on the calendar – if I'd been more aware at the time. In retrospect, the
witches -- or the fates – seem to have been playing with me....... Or maybe they
weren't playing at all. Maybe they were dead serious. And maybe I had someone
looking after me, protecting me somewhat. Here's how I envision it:

It was a dark and stormy night.......

Three covens of witches dressed in black with pointy hats, sat in
a circle in someone's dark living room – or maybe all three covens
converged in a dark room at the castle or church basement – hovering
over a large cauldron – whispering incantations and chanting spells as
they tossed in evil charms, like *magick* gemstones, frogs' toenails and
newts' boogers.

"Let's screw up her finances this moon cycle," says one. The rest nod
and cackle.

So for awhile, bills and checks sent to me from the west coast or even
Colorado Springs were routed by way of New Jersey or Hawaii. Some never
arrived at all. My ability to pay my bills was severely affected.

Then it was, "Okay, now, let's attack her transportation." I can just
see them chortling, rubbing their hands in glee.

In one two-week period, in the exact same spot, I was front-ended twice.
The first time, I'd just turned off Ruxton Avenue, heading uphill toward the

castle which I had to pass to get to my house, and came to a halt behind a pickup that had stopped in the middle of the street, in the middle of the block. Next thing I knew, that pickup backed up and banged into my Plymouth Champ, crunching its front end. The driver climbed out and came over. "Oh, I'm sorry. I didn't see you there."

Huh? You have a rearview mirror, don't you?

He was totally apologetic. "I can't imagine how I could not have seen you. I swear I looked before I backed up."

There wasn't a lot of damage, but the repairs cost several hundred dollars. I had it repaired immediately, at his expense, of course.

Less than two weeks later I was heading down the hill in front of the castle and stopped one car back from Ruxton Avenue. (Same place as before, going in the opposite direction, on the other side of the road.) This car was stopped before making a left turn when, all of a sudden, it backed up, smack into my car. *Why would someone who was preparing to turn left onto Ruxton Avenue suddenly change his mind and back up? Without looking behind him?* Again, the driver got out and came over to me, shaking his head.

"Sonovagun!" he exclaimed. "Where did you come from? I sure didn't see you back here."

I replied, "I've been sitting here awhile waiting for you to turn left."

Again, minor damage to the car. And none to me personally.

Is it possible that the witches had rendered my car invisible in this particular spot? It certainly seemed so. I started using the alternate route.

In retrospect, it seems that my special angel, my "spirit guide", Jamal, may have run interference for me. I'd like to believe his protectiveness diminished the power of the witches' spells, keeping me safe. He didn't keep me from doing dumb things and hurting myself, but he could, and did, keep me safe from damage inflicted by others. And maybe he even has, on occasion, protected me from myself, if what I was doing was dumb enough to kill or seriously injure myself.

Who knows? Maybe he steadied the ladder the day I painted the back of the house, for it should have gone over. If it had, it would have killed me.

As a matter of fact, I never felt in physical danger from these folk, which is strange. But no stranger, I suppose, than the fact that I've never in my life feared physical danger, which has enabled me to plunge into situations where others bigger and stronger, and, no doubt smarter, feared to tread. And I've always come out okay. I think I felt Jamal's protective shield around me even before I learned of his existence.

But I digress.

Next, my dark-forces neighbors went after my relationship. I imagine they really enjoyed this one.

There they sat, in the dark of night, plotting how to do the greatest damage to my love life.

If they could read my mind and emotions, they knew of my attraction to Will. Our chemistry astonished both of us. Neither of us had ever experienced anything like it. But we were absolutely wrong for each other. He was a Born-Again Christian; I'm an Agnostic with New-Age leanings. He was a rigid conservative; I'm a loosey-goosey liberal. Each one's religious and political beliefs were anathematic to the other.

But he was terribly attractive. And extremely attentive and loving.

Who knows, maybe by the time I met Will the witches of Manitou were already playing with me (and him), pulling our strings and drawing us together.

About this time, almost every night – every night I was alone, that is -- I started getting middle-of-the-night phone calls. Phone calls with nobody on the other end. That was unnerving, to say the least. It continued until I moved away and got a new unlisted number.

One day I came home to find a printed flyer on my front steps -- an invitation to a block party. On its top stuck a piece of tape which had been affixed somewhere before it sailed over to my doorstep. It had come loose and blown over to my house. On it was handwritten: "L___ (next door neighbor's name), You did a great job on this flyer."

The flyer itself said, in part, *NEWCOMERS ARE NOT INVITED.* It invited participants to bring stories -- anything they knew about their neighbors -- and photos, if possible.

Paranoia set in. I imagined my neighbors in the bushes, snapping pictures of me and my guests, and inventing lurid stories to tell at the party.

But mostly, this was just another example of my neighbors not wanting to have anything to do with me, something I'd never experienced before. I couldn't imagine what they thought of me, or why they were so unfriendly.

Another day, Will was coming over. But one of my therapy clients, a handsome guy with a snazzy red sports car, called to say he was in crisis and needed an appointment, ". . . right now". I called Will. "Got a therapy emergency. I'll be tied up for awhile. If a red sports car is out front when you get here, please wait." When the therapy appointment ended, I sent the "handsome guy with a snazzy red sports car" on his way and Will came in with this story.

He'd hung around out front, leaning on my mailbox, which, remember, was adjacent to L___'s. She ran out screaming, "What are you doing at my mailbox?"

Stepping back, he answered, "Nothing. I'm here to see Carol. I'm just waitin' my turn."

Her sourpuss went even sourer as she huffed and went back inside, mumbling, "Stay away from my mailbox."

"She does know what you do, doesn't she? She knows you're a therapist?"

I shook my head. "No. I don't think so."

Beset, he offered to go to her house and explain. I said, "No. Leave it alone. She wouldn't believe you anyway. She wouldn't even answer the door."

He'd unwittingly given my neighbors ammunition to use against me. It was probably the topic of their next party's neighbor-bashing.

One day, on a visit to my house, my friend Charlotte spotted something under the rear bumper of my car in the driveway. It sparkled in the sunlight, so she leaned over to give it a closer look. It was a piece of rose quartz or pink glass with the letter "C" carved in it. Thinking, "Oh, how nice. It's got Carol's initial in it. Mine too," she picked it up and brought it inside. I thought nothing of it and set it on my desk beside my computer.

A few days later, I hired a carpet cleaner. I visited with this guy -- tall, thin, sparse stringy hair -- awhile, discussing what I needed done, when he got up and walked to the window. Looking down at my desk he saw the pink thing with the "C" in it. "Where did you get that?"

I told him.

He said, "That's the kind of thing witches use in spells. You need to get rid of it right away. If it were me, I'd take it clear across Colorado Springs and throw it as hard as I could to the far side of the county dump." He was so vehement that I paid attention.

Then he gave me a tutorial on the witches of Manitou Springs, ending with, "If they went to all the trouble to put your initial in that thing, they're really serious about doing you harm. You need to look all around your house, all around your property, all around your car, for anything else they might have put there. They've put a curse on you."

"What kind of thing?" I asked, totally naïve.

"Feathers, stones, crossed sticks, chicken bones. Lots of things."

"But those things could just be there naturally. If I find anything like that, how will I know they're part of an evil spell?"

"Maybe you can't, but I'd pick them up and take them to the dump too. And then I'd go down to the Catholic Church and get some holy water to sprinkle all around your property. I'm telling you, they're out to get you."

Well, I did as he said. And I don't know if it did any good . . . or if any of the things I found all around my house were witchy.

One night, I was in bed when my cat, Squirrel, started gagging. I grabbed her and threw her out the front door, but not before she'd vomited all over my bedroom, dining room, and hall. I cleaned it up and went back to bed. She didn't show up the next morning. Or the next. Or the next. I searched everywhere, and found her body under some bushes down the mountain behind my house. (Yes, I felt guilty that I had callously tossed her out into the night.)

She'd been poisoned. I surmised that someone put poison in a piece of meat and placed it where my cats would find it. Sam, a vegetarian cat, was not tempted and so was saved. (I know, "vegetarian cat" is an oxymoron, but he really was one.)

I kept telling myself, "I'm not going to let them win. I'm not going to let them win. This is my house. I'm not going to let them chase me out of my own house."

A couple of times friends who drove up to Pilot Knob Avenue couldn't force themselves to get out of their car, but drove back down the mountain. "The energy was so evil I had to get away."

Why hadn't I felt it? As I traveled around the world I'd felt the energy of every place we visited, good and bad. Why not here? If it's that intense, why don't I feel it?

Jim, my Denver Real Estate agent who had become a friend, came to visit. Knowing about his well-developed intuition, I asked, "Do you feel anything weird about my house? Or about this neighborhood? Or anything?"

"Yeah. But I never said anything 'cause I didn't want to scare you."

"What do you feel?"

"Bad. It feels bad. It feels like you need to get out of here A-SAP. You're surrounded by evil people who don't want you here. If I could, I'd pick you up and move you out of here tonight. But I can't. If I were you, I'd sure as hell put it up for sale first thing tomorrow."

"But what about not selling it, just renting it out?" I loved my little house.

"No. As long as you own this house they'll be after you."

As soon as he left that evening, I called my old friend, Evelyn, in Santa Rosa. Evelyn was extremely psychic but did not use her abilities professionally. (I seem to attract psychics. I have no idea why.) I asked, "Evelyn, what do you feel about my house here in Colorado?"

"Oh, thank God!" she breathed. "You have no idea how many times since you moved there that I've reached for the phone to tell you to get out of that house. But I couldn't until you asked." She validated what Jo Madrid, and then Jim, had told me. Then added, "Wayne's energy is all over that house too. That's not good for you either. You need to get rid of it."

That was all a bit overwhelming. But by that time I was more open to the idea that witches existed and were after me. I called a local Realtor the next day and put my wonderful little house up for sale.

Since I couldn't move out until it sold, my son Steve brought 3″ screws and secured all the ground-level windows, which included those in my bedroom. I told him I didn't think it was necessary. I really didn't think anyone would personally harm me. He absolutely didn't believe in anything hinting of the supernatural, so the only way he could protect me was to screw my house shut.

(To this day, I've never told him, or anyone else, about Jamal.)

I started doing a visualization and affirmation as I fell asleep every night. I pictured a large SOLD sign on my front lawn, while repeating over and over, "My house sells quickly and easily. The people who buy it may have looked at a hundred houses, but mine is the only one they really love and want. The sale of my house is in the best interests of all concerned."

I had opened a counseling center in Colorado Springs, so was gone most of the day. (I'd concluded it wasn't a good idea to see clients in my home.) A number of Realtors' cards showed up on my kitchen counter. I did the visualization and affirmation several times a day and as I fell asleep at night. Before leaving for work I turned the oven on low and set frozen cinnamon rolls in it so the house would be filled with welcoming, homey aromas.

A young couple bought it. I hoped their experience of ownership would be better than mine. Before I moved out, the buyers brought their parents to see their new house. The girl's mother "Ooohed" and "Aaahed" and exclaimed, "This little house just oozes charm. Most of them you look at are just houses. This one is a home."

Her daughter, the new owner, said, "You know, I bet we looked at a hundred houses, but this is the only one that we really loved and wanted."

I almost dropped my teeth as the exact words of my affirmation came out of her mouth.

I do believe. I do believe. I do believe.

Life After Manitou Springs

aybe there were witches and maybe there weren't. Maybe they were after me and maybe they weren't. I honestly don't know. Life went on. Soon, when Steve, Jill and Hannah went to live in New Guinea, I moved into their house where I knew and trusted the neighbors.

I can't say things were all good, but they weren't all bad either. The more time that passed since moving out of the Pilot Knob house, the more I convinced myself that all that weirdness had never happened. There was nothing that couldn't be explained by coincidence.

It was during that time that I started teaching memoir writing classes, which I absolutely loved, through Colorado Springs Parks & Recreation. I loved hearing everyone's stories – personal stories – stories from the heart. I already considered myself a writer. I'd written all my life, and now had written two novels. But this opened up a whole new career path.

I had some other difficulties. "Shit happens". I ran into financial difficulties, asset-rich but cash-poor. I suffered an estrangement from my three sons, who decided I needed a keeper. When I let them know that, at 58, I wasn't ready for a conservator, I shut the door on our relationship for awhile.

One of the classes I proposed to Parks & Rec was a workshop on *The Celestine Prophesy*. It was advertised in their bulletin, which sent the city's religious nuts into orbit. A *Letters to the Editor* campaign denounced Colorado Springs for allowing a "New Age, Anti-Christian"[31] program to be offered through the city. That was wonderful. They did all my advertising for me. The class had to

---

31. It may be New Age, but it's hardly Anti-Christian.

be moved to larger quarters twice to accommodate the crowd.

Nearly a hundred people showed up for the class. I divided them into groups of four, which would be their small group through the ten weeks of the class. One small group had only three, so I became its fourth. This first small group meeting was for getting acquainted before returning to the larger group.

We introduced ourselves and chatted a bit. One member of our little group mentioned the witches in Manitou Springs and their terrible goings-on.

Another said, "Oh, I don't think it's as bad as all that."

Quietly I said, "That wasn't my experience."

Their gaze shifted in my direction. Their faces held question marks. I repeated, "That wasn't my experience. I lived there a year and a half, and . . . . well, that wasn't my experience."

One of them gasped. "It's you!" she said. "You're the one! I wondered why your name was so familiar!"

"What are you talking about? Why is my name familiar?" I was baffled.

"You were under psychic attack by the dark forces in Manitou," she declared. "Right?"

"Um . . . yes. I guess so. Maybe. But how did you know?"

"Everyone in the spiritual community – the Wiccans and other New Agers -- in The Springs (Manitou and Colorado) knew about it. We were all praying for you and sending you positive energy. You were not alone."

"I've never felt more alone in my life," I said.

"Well, you weren't. We were all with you."

"But you said my name was familiar. You mean to tell me you even knew my name?" I was incredulous.

"Oh yes. We knew all about it. It's all we talked about when we got together. We were really glad when you sold your house and got away from them."

Oh my god, maybe it really did happen after all. But it's spooky to think that people can know so much about you when you don't even know they exist. That applies to "white witches" as well as "black witches".

Fast-forward a few years. A lot more water over the dam . . . under the bridge . . . whatever.

In 2001, when I moved to Reno I made an appointment with Lorraine Schenk, an amazing massage therapist. When it was time for my appointment I arrived at her door. She seemed surprised.

"I was sure you weren't coming," she told me.

"Why?"

"I felt strong resistance. I thought it was from you. But maybe it came from somewhere else." She asked me about witches, "the dark side", and the like. She asked if I knew of anything like that in my past. When I told her about living in Manitou Springs, she said, "That's it. They've still got their hooks in you. They're still using their evil powers on you. Let me ask you this: Have a lot of bad things happened to you since you left Manitou Springs?"

"Oh yeah. Lots."

"I thought so. They're still messing with you, I don't know why. But you're not to worry about it. I'm going to take care of it for you. You just forget about it and let me handle it."

There it was again. Yet another psychic in my life. And yet another "verification" of the wicked witches of Manitou Springs and their evil campaign.

I had to wonder, *If they're still chasing me around after all this time, still poking their broomsticks in my bicycle spokes, will it ever end?*

I honestly don't know, to this day, if it really happened. And, if it did, has Lorraine "handled" it? My life seems to have smoothed out some. I want to believe it's over – *if* it existed in the first place.

I am grateful for the caring counsel of Jo, Evelyn, Jim, the carpet cleaner guy, and Lorraine, and for the prayers and positive energy of the spiritual community of Colorado Springs and Manitou Springs.

Alex Is Okay

The call every parent fears came in the middle of the night. At 1:30 a.m. the phone jarred me awake and shifted my heart into overdrive. It was John, my first husband, my kids' father.

"First of all, Alex is okay," he began urgently. "But he's in the hospital. He's been stabbed. But he's stable -- at Boston Medical Center. That's all I know right now."

Judith's husband Bill Morris drove me to Denver International Airport and, after the plane was de-iced, I flew off to Boston. On my way out the door I snatched a small book from the hall table -- *A Book of Angels,* by Sophy Burnham. A gift from a woman in my Women's Self-Empowerment class, back in Santa Rosa, it had arrived in my mailbox that very day. The note with it said simply, "This reminded me of you." I slipped it in my bag, thinking it might keep my mind occupied while en route to New England.

But my mind was way too busy and the book remained unopened. When I got to Alex's bedside John was already there. We began to hear the story, which came in bits and pieces over a very long time. Neither of us got the whole story for a number of years.

On the morning of January 18, 1991, Alex went skiing and broke his big toe. After a visit to the E.R. he went to work as Chef in the fine dining restaurant at the Copley Plaza Hotel.

He cooked a $1000-a-plate dinner for Republican big-wigs that night. Just after the start of the Persian Gulf War, they were all revved up by the war news. On his feet all day, by quitting time he was limping. Kevin, his buddy and *Sous Chef,* would drive him home to Watertown.

They changed from their black and white checked pants and white chef jackets into soft, faded-to-perfection Levi's and started off down St. James Ave, turning onto Clarendon Street. Kevin, a 6′4″ hulk of a kid, and Alex, a skinny, limping 5′10″, loped along, joking and laughing. They didn't pay much attention when two black guys in red jackets and black baseball caps on backwards approached, separating to go around them. The one nearest Kevin alerted him to danger by brushing the big guy's shoulder with a fist.

Kevin said, "Let's get the hell outa here," and took off running, thinking Alex followed.

But he wasn't. The two black guys had picked him, the smaller of the two, the gimpy one, for their victim. With Kevin out of the way they could concentrate on Alex. They were quickly joined by two others, similarly dressed, who emerged from a dark doorway.

After multiple stabs on the chest, head and legs, when Alex was down on the sidewalk, they kicked him and kicked him.

"We're gonna kill you!" they threatened.

In an effort to save himself, Alex took his wallet from his Levi's pocket, extending it toward them. To his shock and amazement they turned and ran, leaving it in his hand.

By the time Kevin realized Alex wasn't with him he was at the next corner. He looked back. When he saw what was happening he gathered a couple of volunteers. "Hey, my buddy's gettin' killed back there! We gotta help him!" They ran back down the street. Alex's attackers must have seen them coming and taken off.

But Alex was unaware of his would-be rescuers. He struggled to his feet and staggered off in the opposite direction toward the nearest busy street, where he tried to flag a taxi. A couple of cabs slowed, but he was gushing blood, so they sped up and drove on. The third one stopped.

Alex got in. "You gotta get me outa here," he gasped, settling in the back seat.

The cabbie said, "It's okay. I think yuh been stabbed. I'm an EMT, I'll getcha t' a hospital." He questioned Alex to keep him talking. "What's yuh name?"

"Yuh live around heah?" "Wheah do yuh wohk?" "What d' yuh do?" *Et cetera. Et cetera.* He radioed his dispatcher to call the hospital so they'd be expected. "I'm takin' yuh t' Boston Med. It's the closest ...... and it's got the best trauma team in the city."

When Alex could no longer speak, the cab driver said, "Yuh gotta stay awake. If yuh pass out, yuhr'a dead man. Clap yuh hands. Keep clappin' yuhr hands."

Alex clapped slowly and deliberately, though weakly. It was the best he could do. By the time they pulled up to the entrance to the E.R., he was barely conscious. The cabbie ran around to open his door. "I'm takin' yuh in," he said, reaching into the backseat to pick him up.

"Nah," said Alex, a.k.a. John Wayne. "I'm goin' in under my own power." He made it in all right, with the driver holding the door for him, but felt very woozy.

The cabbie ran to the doors of the E.R.'s inner sanctum, shouting for them to come quick. Then to Alex he said, "Yuhr about t' pass out. Yuh bettah lay down befoah yuh fall down."

As Alex lay on the black and white floor tiles, his driver smiled down at him. That's the last thing he remembered.

Boston Medical Center's crack trauma team, led by "Dr. N.", a pretty young Surgery Resident, took over. Alex's heart had stopped. He was dead. His rib cage was full of blood. If they used paddles to jolt his heart alive it would explode. Instead, they shot adrenalin directly in to restart it. It worked. Thank God!

He came to just as an O.R. nurse was about to take scissors to his jeans. "Don't!" he shouted. "Don't cut my jeans! This is my best pair!" They grinned and nodded -- and cut his jeans off.

Over the next couple of hours they stitched up his stab wounds -- repaired a punctured lung -- straightened his broken nose, inserted a tube between his ribs to drain blood from his thoracic cavity into a plastic box, and hooked him up to IVs to hydrate him and alleviate the pain.

In the meantime, Kevin was frantic. He called the police station. He started calling hospitals and eventually located the one where Alex had been admitted. Upon arrival at Boston Med he learned his buddy had made it.

In the kitchen of the Copley Plaza's Oak Room the next day, he told their co-workers the terrible story.

Alex had a steady stream of visitors. Although he'd lived in Boston only a few months, a lot of friends and co-workers cared about him. When I arrived in his hospital ward, one of his waiters, an older gentleman, sat weeping by his bed, stroking the back of his hand.

At this time, neither John nor I knew of Alex's "near-death experience". We only knew he'd been mugged, had multiple stab wounds, and was stable. No one told us he'd actually died that frightful night. He didn't want to upset us. But everyone else knew.

Boston Medical Center, in Roxbury, one of Boston's roughest neighborhoods, was like a fortress, with armed policemen walking the halls, two-by-two. At its outside doors, including the E.R., stood armed guards.

Alex was in a large ward in which other patients were visited by guys dressed like his attackers -- in gang colors. It was learned, at some point, that his attack was part of a gang initiation. To become members, his attackers were to kill somebody that night. It didn't matter who. Policemen came into the ward to question him about his attackers. Surely word got around the open ward that he was accusing their fellow gang members.

Arrangements were made to move him to another hospital in a more peaceful part of the city. At first he didn't want to go. Smitten with Dr. N, the pretty young E.R. surgeon who saved his life, he wanted to hang around. But he changed his mind in a hurry when members of the gang that attacked him came over to his bed and stood, reading his chart. He was moved across town. Perhaps that saved his life a third time.

When John and I learned about the cabbie who saved our son's life the night of the attack we wanted to thank him, but didn't know who he was. Before Alex was moved across town, we went down to the Emergency Room and asked the uniformed, armed guard who'd been on duty when Alex came in, "Do you know the identity of the man who brought our son in on the night of January 18?"

"Huh? What're yuh talking about?"

"The cab driver who brought Alex Purroy in, around midnight?"

"There wasn't nobody with him. He came in on his own."

"Wait a minute. Are you saying the cab driver wasn't with him?"

"Yeah, that's right," the guard insisted. "He walked in all by himself."

After further questioning, we went back to Alex's ward scratching our heads. How could that be? Is it possible that he had a Guardian Angel visible only to him?

Once Alex was out of danger, John flew back to California. I stayed on to be there when Alex went home -- to cook for him, change his bandages, *et cetera.*

Eager to connect with Dr. N. again, he suggested that we make cookies for the nurses *and doctor* at Boston Med -- as a thank you. I remembered the recipe for Russian Tea Cakes, Alex's favorite, having made them a few weeks earlier at Christmas. Alex mixed up a batch of his other favorite, Rice Krispy Treats. We boxed them up and drove to the hospital. The nurses were thrilled. At that hospital, in that part of town, no one had ever brought them anything . . . . or even said Thank you.

Alex was disappointed that his doctor was off-duty. The nurses said they'd tell her who the cookies were from, and that they were for her, too.

His friends teased him about his crush on his doctor. One said, "Yeah, he was just *dying* to meet her!"

Alex and Dr. N. ended up having a 2-year romance. Then Alex had to return to California, and N. had to finish her residency in Massachusetts, so they went their separate ways. Although both are now happily married to others, they stay in touch.

After ten days in Boston, I flew back to Colorado. On the return flight I read every word of *A Book of Angels,* becoming more convinced with every page that Alex did indeed have a guardian angel in the guise of a cab driver.

To this day, he pooh-poohs it, but that's my story and I'm stickin' to it.

"Hey Guys"

I t was midnight, mid-winter, in mid-Colorado, and I was almost out of gas. I planned to stop somewhere on the way home. However, driving down Highway 25 from Denver toward Colorado Springs, not a single gas station was open. By the time I reached the town of Monument -- 17 miles from the northern rim of Colorado Springs -- my gas gauge was below Empty, the *Get Gas* light glowed. Certain the mega-station at Monument would be open, I pulled off the freeway. A sinking feeling enveloped me as I drove up to the dark, deserted station.

I couldn't stop there. I'd freeze to death by morning. But if I pressed on, I'd be out in the middle of nowhere if the car sputtered to a stop, and still be dead by morning. All too aware I should have a down comforter, food and water in the car at all times in Colorado, especially in winter, I said, "No sense crying over what I don't have. What do I do now?"

My stomach jittered. Panic rushed through my body as my heart raced and fire burned in my chest. I decided to keep going, hoping for the best. My foot quivered pushing the gas pedal as I got back on Highway 25 South. There's *zilch* between Monument and Colorado Springs. And I was still 27 miles from my house in Manitou Springs.

Recalling the stories of miraculous angel rescues in the book I carried to Boston and read on the way back, and remembering Alex's "guardian angel", I thought, *It can't hurt to ask. The worst thing that can happen is nothing. I'll be no worse off than I'd be if I did nothing.*

Taking a deep breath to gain courage, though feeling a little foolish, and realizing I had no idea how to speak to spirit entities, I said, out loud, with passion and urgency, "Hey guys, I really need your help. If you could see your way clear to give me enough gas to get home, I'd really appreciate it. I'm thanking you in advance – thank you, thank you, thank you. I really appreciate it."

To my surprised eyes, within a split-second the *Get Gas* light went out and the needle on the gas gauge rose slightly. I kid you not. It'd be enough to get me home. "Thank you, thank you, thank you!" I shouted, stepped on the gas, and drove on confidently.

I know this is hard to believe. I hardly believe it myself. But I swear, it's exactly what happened.

As I got to Manitou Springs and started up the mountain from Manitou Avenue, the *Get Gas* light was back on and the needle on the gas gauge was again below Empty. It dawned on me that they – whoever *they* were – had given me what I asked for. *Exactly* what I asked for – enough gas to get home. But I didn't ask for enough. Once I pulled into my driveway, turned off the engine and set the parking brake, I probably wouldn't be able to restart the car. I'd have no fuel to get to the gas station.

Back to the drawing board.

"Hey guys, I really appreciate what you did for me back there. But I have another small favor to ask. Could you please give me enough gas to get down to the gas station tomorrow morning? Please. I'm thanking you in advance – thank you, thank you, thank you!"

Again, to my absolute amazement, the needle rose the tiniest bit. The *Get Gas* light stayed on, but I knew I'd make it.

If you scoff at this story, read on. The next one is even more incredible, but equally true.

Ask and Ye Shall Receive

onths later, in a huge rush to get to an appointment in downtown Denver, I raced along, rehearsing what I'd say and do once I got there. I couldn't be late.

My gas tank was full. I wouldn't make that mistake again. I'd left home in plenty of time and was dressed properly for my ultra-important appointment. Highway 25 was just normally busy for that mid-day drive time, so I sped along at my usual fast pace, slowing for the known speed traps.

About halfway there, with 35 miles to go, my little beige Champ hatchback shuddered and lost power, slowing to 25 mph. No matter what I did, I couldn't get it to go any faster – or stop shaking. Minimum highway speed was 35 mph, so I pulled off into the emergency lane. I continued on, snail-crawling and shimmying down the road.

I didn't want to think about the fact that my 12-year-old Champ, which Wayne always called a "puddle jumper" or "throw-away car", might be about to give up the ghost. I wouldn't be ready to buy a new car for some time. Choosing to concentrate on my more immediate problem, I obsessed about being late for this crucial appointment. "Oh my god, oh my god, I can't be late."

Plummeting into panic mode, I remembered my late-night plea to "my guys" and the astonishing results. Again, reasoning it couldn't hurt to ask, I repeated my fervent plea to my angel(s) – or whatever he, she, it, or they were. "Hey guys, I need your help. I *really* need it. See, I have this appointment that I have to get to, and my car isn't cooperating. If you could smooth it out and power it up, I'd really appreciate it. I'm thanking you in advance. Thank you, thank you, thank you!"

Nothing happened. The Champ shook, poking along at a measly 25 mph in the emergency lane.

"Oh well, it was worth a try. No harm done. Nothing ventured, *et cetera*. ………….. Thanks anyway." A full 60 - 90 seconds later, the car stopped chattering and sped up. It was as if nothing had been wrong. Normality was restored.

I stepped on the gas and drove 85-90 mph the rest of the way, careened into a parking space and ran inside, right on time.

Wow! This was amazing. Another miracle.

Over the next year or so, this miracle was repeated several times. The car would lose power and shake like the paint mixer at Kelly-Moore. I would ask for help out loud – always out loud -- and within 90 seconds I'd get it. Several times I waited quite awhile to see if it would stop by itself. It wouldn't. If I didn't ask I didn't receive. Help always came 60 - 90 seconds after my plea.

A couple of times, it happened when someone was in the passenger seat to witness and validate it. One time, it was my sister Pat, a card-carrying skeptic. On our way to Cripple Creek, my little car had a spas-attack. Pat's eyes widened; her knuckles whitened.

I said, "No problem. I have to talk to my guys. Maybe angels. They'll fix it for me."

She gave me her best big-sister *Yeah, right!*-look, which she's been practicing since I was born.

"I'm not kidding. You'll see. I have to talk to them. And it only works if I do it out loud." I went into my "Hey guys" routine. When finished, I told her, "We have to wait about 90 seconds."

Again, with the *Yeah, right!*-look. But after 1–1¹/₂ minutes, when the car started running smoothly and picked up speed, she became a little less skeptical.

With my guys' help I got another year's service out of that car. Since I sold it I've never again asked them for help, but it's nice to know they're there for me if I really need them. It's not that nothing terrible has happened since then, it's just that I didn't go into panic mode. I could handle it myself. Or maybe it's only for "Carma".

As for the oh-so-important appointment I couldn't be late for, I don't even remember what it was.

Gotta Dance! Gotta Dance!

A man wearing an emerald sport coat entered the second floor lounge at the Broadmoor. I sat at a window table overlooking the lake while a guy in a cut-away tuxedo played dreamy tunes on the grand piano. I watched everyone who came through the door.

The green sport coat and the man wearing it matched the description given over the phone. In the center of the room, near the piano, he came to a stop and glanced around the room, looking for someone.

That must be him. I approached somewhat tentatively. "You must be 'Lucky.'"

Giving me the once-over, the old head-to-toe-to-head perusal, he nodded, exhaled, and, with a lopsided grin, said, "I damn sure must be!"

The headline of Personals ad in the Colorado Springs Gazette read: "Dance Partner." That's all. Just somebody to dance with. No romance was promised. No entanglement. No commitment. No future. Just dancing.

I'd always loved to dance but had never had a good dance partner. On impulse I answered the ad. Thus began one of the pleasantest interludes of my life. Lawrence Green, Air Force Lt. Colonel Ret., a.k.a. "Lucky", was a dancin' fool. How that man loved to dance!

Colorado Springs has one of the best dance venues in the country. At the Broadmoor, a Five-Star destination resort hotel, excellent small dance bands played in the first floor lounge every night of the week. No cover charge; just buy a drink or two and dance all evening. Lucky and I became regulars, dancing at the Broadmoor three or four nights a week.

One of its two bands assigned a special song to each of the regulars. Mine was "Pretty Woman". Every time I went dancing at the Broadmoor, when they struck up the band with my special song the leader acknowledged me with a nod or a wave.

Lucky and I became good friends. He once said, "I just wanted a lady to dance with. I didn't expect to like you." But he did. And I liked him too. He often told me, "I'm in 'great-like' with you -- great-like." We were intimates -- as in close friends.

Over the next few years, we learned just about everything there was to know about each other and were totally comfortable with one another. We knew each other's family and friends; each other's history. And each other's jokes and stories. From the first, we looked like a long-time couple. Once, a man on the dance floor challenged us when we said we'd just met -- "It's our second 'date.'" Which it was.

"Oh, come on. You two have been married 30 years, haven't you?"

Without missing a beat, Lucky said, 'Yes we have. But not to each other." True. We'd both been married twice, each for a total of 30+ years.

He was a raconteur -- a storyteller, a fun person to hang out with. He never forgot a joke and had an impressive repertoire on every topic. We spent a lot of time together. We often dined together, went on outings, and even traveled together a few times. (Photo - page 355.)

And we danced.

Then he moved away to Rèno to be near his son and grandsons. Before he left we went dancing at the Broadmoor one last time. Soon after we walked in, the band played my song -- "Pretty Woman".

As we came off the dance floor, a man seated at its edge reached out and touched Lucky on the arm. We stopped. The man -- "Daniel" -- asked, "Would you mind if I danced with your lady?"

"No. But you'll have to ask her."

When he did I said I'd be happy to.

I danced first with one and then the other. Both were terrific dancers. I barely caught my breath all evening.

Daniel lived in New York but traveled a lot on business. Thus started a new phase of my life. Several times a year over the next six years, he sent me a ticket to an assignation -- a tryst. It was mostly about dancing, but we came to care about one another. Never in love, but caring.

To this day, Daniel says I was his best dance partner ever. We danced divinely. "You make me look good," he'd say. "I don't know how you do it, but you seem to know what I'm going to do before I do."

Once, in San Diego, we found a large dance hall atop a large hotel. But when we went back the second night it was reserved for a private party. Daniel said, "I'll go make some phone calls and see what else I can find." As he passed through the first-floor lobby, wonderful music wafted from behind a closed door. He went to investigate. What he found was a big band -- 18-strong -- playing to an empty ballroom. A dance in that ballroom, part of a Shriner's convention, had been left out of the program. No one knew about it.

But they had been paid to play so they were playing, whether or not anyone was there to hear them. Daniel asked if we could come in and dance. They were happy to have us.

Like Fred Astaire and Ginger Rogers, we covered every inch of that huge floor, dancing every style of dance. The music was just for us. The night was ours. My god, it was marvelous!

Another time, we sailed the Caribbean for two weeks. A couple of nights we anchored offshore and tied up the dinghy at a fancy resort: The Bitter End on Virgin Gorda, British Virgin Islands. We danced the night away, showing off a bit, as usual.

Hey, when you're good you're good! Don't hide your light under a bushel.

When the time came to leave we skipped, laughing giddily, out to the dock. As we untied the dinghy, a woman ran after us. "Oh, I'm glad I caught you. I just had to tell you, I don't know when I've enjoyed watching someone dance as I did you. You're fantastic!"

Remembering moments like these warms my heart and makes me glow. I wouldn't trade my dancing "career" for anything, and wouldn't have missed it for the world.

California Here I Come

ight back where I started from.
As I drove the U-Haul truck past the "Welcome to California" sign on
Highway 80, I cried out, "I'm home, I'm home!" To my surprise,
I choked up, croaking the final, "I'm home".

Colorado Springs is in one of the most beautiful places on earth. A great
place to live. Except .... some years earlier, about the same time I moved
there, in the interest of securing a non-polluting tax base the city invited fun-
damentalist evangelical Christian organizations to move their headquarters to
The Springs. *Be careful what you wish for.*

Those groups, their administrators and employees packed up and moved
to Colorado Springs. With them came their ideologies, which changed the com-
plexion of the area. They put stealth candidates[32] in races for seats on the City
Council, every school board in the area, El Paso County, and state offices. Once
in office, they sought to quash homosexuals' rights, women's rights, and science,
i.e., evolution. They preached -- and lived -- the politics of hate, intolerance, and
judgement (to my way of thinking).

In my opinion, they, along with the witches of Manitou, created a toxic,
oppressive atmosphere in and around Colorado Springs. But I didn't realize how
oppressed I felt until I returned to live in California, especially San Francisco.
From my first day there, I felt as if a huge weight had lifted. Why this should be
I don't know. But, in retrospect, the atmosphere in Colorado Springs seemed
dense and heavy. (Maybe I still did have some ability to feel a place's energy,
after all, for I certainly felt its absence in San Francisco.)

---

10. Candidates with a hidden agenda, i.e., the Born Again Christian agenda.

I moved to San Francisco to start a publishing company in partnership with "Ben," who knew the ropes and had a sure-fire business plan. I checked him out with the police department: his only record was a DUI and a warrant for telephone harassment, which, according to the policeman on duty, wasn't worth arresting him for. "He'd be out before we started the paperwork."

His documents for business contacts seemed authentic.

In addition to our main products -- annual industry-specific publications, just in the planning and funding stage -- we put out a monthly newsmagazine for seniors. Ben was the business manager. We hired an ad sales staff, which he trained and supervised.

My job was to produce the magazine, 28 pages (11 X 17"), the equivalent of 56 letter-sized (8.5 X 11") pages, small print, every month. I interviewed people and wrote articles, including an extensive cover story on an interesting Bay Area person every month. I scoured the community for feature articles, which I wrote. I wrote stories of every description under multiple pseudonyms -- my favorite: "Sue Denim". I did restaurant reviews under "Claire van Zant", travel articles using "Jeann Ohmurr", and human interest features by "Sarah Silverstein". I wrote small regular features, such as, "Where Did That Come From?", the origin and meaning of commonly used words and phrases. And I created some ads.

We did have a few other contributors. I started a feature called "In Your Own Write", which ran stories and essays by readers. One reader's submission was "Silent Vigil", a story by Bruce Allen. His accompanying brief biography so intrigued me that I wanted to meet him. We had a lot in common. After meeting at a funky little café on Grove Street, we became close friends. I ended up printing one of his stories in each edition.

I did the typesetting, design and layout for the monthly mag. Except for the cover photo, I did all the photography. I was the editor. And I delivered the magazines all over the Bay Area.

Oh, I also funded it, having sold my real estate holdings to do so.

Cutting to the chase, to paraphrase Tony Bennett's signature ballad, *I lost my ass in San Francisco.*

A "smooth-talkin' cowboy", Ben was a pro at gaining people's confidence, then reeling them in for the kill. The fleecing operation, accompanied by verbal abuse, began.[33]

Abandoned multiple times by his unwed mother and abused in foster homes, he aimed to abuse and destroy women, all of whom represent his mother (in my opinion). I was 14-15 years older than he, the perfect mother-figure on which to vent his wrath. When I had so much money in the business that I couldn't cut and run, he turned into a monster, screaming insults at me all day every day and railing against me to our employees: "She f✻✱ked it up again!" and other such pleasantries.

Before long, my money was gone, and then some. I laid out my case to San Francisco's District Attorney who told me I had the evidence to (probably) put Ben in prison. But it was only a "white collar crime" and he'd be released in six months, or less. I was certain that when Ben got out he'd come after me and I'd be featured on the obituary page.

I didn't file charges. I had too much to live for.

I was not Ben's first victim, nor his last.[33] I feel some guilt; I let him get away with it, as had others before me, so he was free to scam others. He once said, "I only go after very intelligent people. 'Proves I'm smarter than they are.'"

To my amazement, four of my friends offered to put out a contract on my erstwhile business partner. I had no idea anyone I was acquainted with had those kinds of connections. I declined. The Law of Karma will take care of it. I don't have to do a thing, I'm certain he'll get his just desserts, one way or another, sooner or later, if not in this life, then surely in the afterlife.

In spite of everything, I'm prouder of that magazine than anything else I've ever done, except raising my children. It was applauded over and over and acknowledged as "…the best thing out there." I busted my *derriere,* working practically 24/7, but I did it. And no, I didn't "f✻✱k it up". It wasn't perfect, but it was good, if I do say so myself.

I hated to shut it down, and a great many people begged me to hang on. But after a few more months I had no choice.

---

33. In my opinion.

Remains To Be Seen

I invite readers to use this for inspiration
or in any way you wish.

(Printed in my S.F. senior newsmagazine and sent to my sons in 1995.)

This is to inform you, my children, of my wishes regarding the disposition of my remains, and related subjects. As I write this I am only 60 years old and have no intention of popping off anytime soon. But, as we all know, life is uncertain, and it occurs to me that I should get this in writing and into your hands in the event of the unexpected.

First of all, if you have anything to say about it, do not let me, under any conditions, be placed on life support systems or have "heroic measures" taken to keep me alive. I do not fear death, nor do I wish for the prolongation of life. Life is to be lived, not just endured. I have no desire to continue on, merely breathing in and out. Please just let me go and be grateful for it. Let me return to spirit gracefully and with dignity. It will be a blessing for all concerned.

When I have breathed my last breath, you, my children (and your families) may view my remains, if you wish . . . . just to make sure I'm really dead. I do not believe in reverence for dead bodies, so under no circumstances are my remains to be seen by anyone else. My body is an *it*. It is not *me*.

If any bits and pieces of this old body can be used by anyone, donate them, and God bless.

For whatever's left, I request cremation (the cheapest, easiest, quickest), and the disposition of the ashes someplace where it won't cost much, if anything. You can dump them in the ocean, flush them down the toilet, blast them into outer space, or anything in between. I don't care. I will have departed. Their outcome is irrelevant. Do not place them in a cemetery or mausoleum. Space on this planet does not need to be taken up by my hermetically sealed remains. You have my permission to give my body to a medical school for use as a cadaver, if that's your choice, and if you can get them to take it.

If there is to be some kind of service, I want it to have lively music, jokes, laughter, singing, storytelling. I want my passing to elicit a celebration of life -- each person's life, not just mine -- a reminder that life is for living and forgiving, for enjoying and laughing and dancing and singing and learning and growing and adventuring and loving. Especially loving.

And please, no "Amazing Grace". Play "When the Saints Go Marching In", "What a Wonderful World", "That's Life", for example.

Hey, how about a Rodgers & Hammerstein Sing-along? Do you remember, I used to sing "Oh What a Beautiful Morning" to wake you up and get you out of bed?

As I write this, I'm not sure you know how much I love you . . . . always have and always will. You, my children, are my most important life purpose. I am grateful to have been your mother and participated in your lives. I loved you and gave you the best infancy and childhood possible. If I've hurt or disappointed you, I beg your forgiveness. If there are issues, resentments or anger you harbor against me, please, while there's still time, let's talk and get them aired and resolved. Life is too short not to live in love and harmony.

I am aware that each of you came into this life with your own agenda, your own character, your own personality (evident from day-one), your own abilities and interests, to work out your own issues. I may be just a small part of that, perhaps only the vessel through which you passed to get onto this planet at this time. You are here to be the best *you* you can be, not an extension or reflection of me or your father, spouse, grandparents, children, teachers, employers, *et cetera*.

My greatest wish is that we have all gotten from one another, and will continue to do so for as long as we live, what is needed and desired in this life, and that when we meet in spirit, we will rejoice and celebrate a job well done.

The Lottery Ticket

The payoff for that week's California Lottery was the biggest in history -- $126 million! I don't often buy lottery tickets, but this one was so huge I couldn't help fantasizing. What I couldn't do with $126 million!

At the last minute I couldn't not do it. I raced the six or seven miles to St. Francis Shopping Center in Santa Rosa. A lot of other people had the same idea. At Safeway, I waited in the long line and forked over five bucks for five tickets, printed on a single slip of paper. I went back to the home in Oakmont where I was house- and dog-sitting: two adorable, frenetic Schnauzers, "Ruff" and "Tuff".

I was doing a lot of house and/or pet sitting at that time. I'd do just about anything to get away from the 10 X 12' room where I lived, in someone else's house. And it *was* her house. When she was home, I had to stay in my room and keep quiet. If I was cooking when she got home, I had to stop immediately and turn her kitchen over to her. If I talked on the phone or played my TV, she complained because it disturbed her quietude. My friends couldn't come to the door to pick me up; I had to meet them at the corner.

It was a roof over my head, though, and I was grateful for it. But I stayed away as much as I could.

When I got back from Safeway, I carefully placed my glasses on the Lotto ticket at the center of the coffee table and turned on the TV. I'd be ready at 8 o'clock, in just a couple of minutes, when the winning number was announced. I wouldn't have to spend time looking for my glasses or the ticket. I turned away, probably to visit the bathroom, and got back just in time.

As the first numbered Lotto ball burst from the pack, bouncing a couple of times before coming to rest, I sat on the edge of my seat and reached for my glasses without taking my eyes off the TV. My hand came up empty. They weren't there. Frantically, I looked for the lottery ticket. It was gone too.

The dogs must have jumped onto the coffee table and snatched 'em.

I searched like a maniac. The glasses, chewed askew, I found under the couch. The third numbered ball was selected. I'd missed #2. I continued hunting. Ball #4 jumped out. I put on my mangled glasses and tore the living room apart looking for the ticket. Cushions flew off the couch. The dogs thought I was playing and got into the spirit, leaping and pouncing, treating them like toys. Ball #5 separated itself from the pack. And finally, #6.

The complete array of six numbers showed on the screen. I grabbed a pencil off the kitchen counter and scribbled them on a scrap of paper, just in case.

I scoured the house but never did find that lottery ticket. It had simply disappeared. The only place it could be was in the gullet of one of the dogs.

What if I won the biggest lottery in California's history, but my ticket is inside a dog?!

Should I take the little darlings to the vet? I couldn't know which dog had swallowed it, so they'd both have to be opened up. But they weren't my dogs. Did I have that right?

For $126 million, who cares? I'd buy them new dogs.

I'd wait. If the winning ticket was purchased at Safeway in St. Francis Shopping Center, and if no one claimed the prize, I'd take them to the vet. But, by then, would the numbers be readable? Or would the ticket be digested?

Oh, how I hated those little Schnauzers!

On the 11 o'clock news, the store that sold the winning ticket was announced. It wasn't St. Francis' Safeway. I could relax. I could stop hating the dogs. And I could go to bed, my dismal financial situation unchanged.

Rats!

Do I Look That Stupid?

The embodiment of Tall, Dark & Handsome, the young man emerged from the back room of Canovanas' Office of Civil Defense and walked toward me.

"You need a guide?" he asked.

"Yeah."

"C'mon. Let's go." Taking my arm, he waltzed me out the door and onto the parking lot. "Which car is yours?"

That was the entire job interview. I'd just hired my local guide. I was about to start my career as a FEMA Field Inspector. On September 21, 1998, *Hurricán Georges* had ravaged Puerto Rico. I was assigned to Canovanas, just south and east of San Juan. Since I'd be working in largely unmapped rural areas and was not fluent in Spanish, I needed a guide. Lewis Lopez and I hooked up on September 24, and would be constant companions for the next 3 months.

"It's not Luís?" I inquired.

"No. Lewis. Like Jerry."

He started every morning with a booming, "Are you ready to rumble?" and off we went. "Who's our next customer?" he asked as we finished one inspection and returned to the car to search out the next applicant.

After a couple of weeks in Canovanas I was reassigned to Yabucoa, an hour-and-a-half drive farther south, then west. My friends and fellow disaster relief workers, Leo and Jeannie, and I were assigned to the same area and rented a house on a sea cliff, on Highway 53, toward Maunabo. I told Lewis I'd have to let him go and hire a new guide in my new territory.

"No, that's okay," he said. "I went to high school in Yabucoa. I know it. And I have family there."

"But you live in Canovanas. Are you willing to drive all the way to Yabucoa and back every day?" I asked.

"Sure. No problem."

And, bless his heart, he did. Seven days a week he showed up in our driveway. "Are you ready to rumble?"

That's not to say our relationship was always smooth. It wasn't. But we both have well-developed senses of humor, so we got through our difficulties. We had a lot of laughs. And we talked a lot, about all manner of things. But spending ten-to-thirteen hours a day together, seven days a week, we sometimes rubbed each other the wrong way. Such as the day he brought a huge bag of unshelled sunflower seeds. All day long he cracked them with his teeth and spat them out the window. By the end of the day I wanted to strangle him.

And there were misunderstandings -- cultural misinterpretations.

One afternoon, approaching an inspection, we climbed down a steep hill toward a Pepto Bismol-pink house. Walking ahead of me, Lewis turned, offering his hand. I brushed it aside. "I can make it."

The next few days he pouted. He sulked. He wouldn't look at me. He showed up for work every day, but he wasn't happy. Finally I said, "Lewis, we gotta talk. What's the problem?"

"Remember the other day, when we were going down the hill to the pink house?"

"Yeah."

"And you pushed my hand away?"

"Yeah? What's the matter?"

Petulantly, he stated, "You don't want people to think I'm your lover."

Mind you, he was a 29-year-old hunk and I was a 63-year-old bag.

Dumbstruck, I replied, "It never occurred to me that anyone would think you were my lover. I just didn't want you to treat me like an old lady."

Different realities: A *Macho Latino vs.* An Aging *Americana.*

Lewis' family often fed us. FEMA inspectors are always on a dead run, and often don't eat. When we were starving and near one of their houses, we stopped by for thirty seconds and grabbed a snack. Puerto Ricans, generally, are among the most loving and generous people on earth. In my four months there I visited close to 1100 homes and did that many inspections. I felt loved and appreciated in virtually every one of them. And many of the "Apps" (applicants) shared their meals with Lewis and me.

Most Puerto Ricans are as honest as the millennium is long. However, a few attempted fraudulent claims. One woman claimed her treadle sewing machine was damaged by the hurricane's driving rain.

"What's wrong with it?" I asked.

"It doesn't work."

She didn't know I'd learned to sew on a Singer treadle like hers. I pulled up a chair, set my feet on the treadle, gave the turning wheel a push with my right hand, and started to operate it. It worked fine.

"Oh," she said sheepishly.

Then there was the time a woman took us into her dining room and, with a tear in her eye, mourned, "My dining room set was ruined."

"Where is it?" I asked.

She took us out to a rubbish heap and pointed to a strip of veneer that had peeled off of wall paneling. "That's all that's left of it," she said sadly.

I made some notations in my hand-held computer. As we headed for the car, Lewis demanded, "You're not going to give it to her, are you?"

"Do I look that stupid?"

From that time on, whenever an applicant tried to put something over on us, on our way back to the car Lewis would look at me and say, "Do I look that stupid?" We'd laugh.

At Christmas I got some white tee shirts and iron-on letters. On the fronts I put FEMA (small letters over the heart), and on the backs, in larger letters:

DO I LOOK
THAT STUPID?!

Two of them were for Leo and Jeanie, and one for me. We wore them to our company Christmas party, and took extras for the boss and the gift exchange. They were a huge hit. Of course, they were gags; we couldn't wear them on the job.

Another time, when Lewis was mad at me (probably with good reason), we had an assigned inspection out in the boonies, way up a mountain. The owner said we'd never find it without his help, so we arranged to meet him in town. We followed his Jeep through town, over a winding mountain road that narrowed to one lane of choppy pavement, then to dirt, and finally to mere wheel-ruts separated by tall grass, before petering out. Eventually, his Jeep came to a stop and we pulled up behind him, thinking we were there. We weren't. He led us on foot another half-mile through the jungle. I was scared.

This would be a great place for a murder, I thought. *I bet this guy and Lewis are in cahoots. They've got it all planned. They're going to kill me and leave my body here. It'll never be found. My kids will never know what happened to their mom.*

To my relief, there really was a house at the end of the trek. I did the inspection and we made our way back to civilization.

A week or so later we had a similar situation, without anyone to lead us. Distant neighbors gave us directions to the old man's house. We parked the car, climbed up a hill and down a valley, around and over, on a barely discernible path. This place was jungley too, but Lewis wasn't mad at me that day, so I was light-hearted. When we were deep in the jungle, he said, "This would be a great place for a murder. No one would ever find the body."

I never told him I'd had that same thought at that other place.

The old guy we visited was flabbergasted to see us. He had no phone, no electricity, no plumbing. His house was a shack. He had applied to FEMA after every hurricane, but no one had ever showed up.

There *are* FEMA inspectors who only do the easy ones. Not me. I did 'em all. It was the tough ones that were the most fun, and the most memorable.

One day, en route to an inspection, we got stuck in the mud on an unpaved trail crossing a field. I went back to the main road to get help while Lewis stayed behind, trying to free the car. I was picked up by a man whose house I'd inspected weeks earlier. After trying unsuccessfully to find someone with a Jeep, he took me to the highway where he flagged down a large truck with big-treaded tires and a *motor muy fuerte.* The two guys in the truck drove me several miles back to the car and spent an hour or more pulling it out. A second truck stopped and its driver assisted as well. They waved off my efforts to pay them, saying, "We're family."

Lewis agreed. "Everyone in Puerto Rico is related. We all help each other."

What a wonderful place.

Sometimes Lewis drove me nuts -- and vice versa, but by and large we did okay. Leo and Jeannie had trouble keeping guides. A guide would work a couple of days and never show up again. (Jeannie finally got a reliable, devoted guide who stayed with her to the end, though.) Although Lewis had to drive three hours a day, there and back, he was faithful and dutiful. Even when he was mad at me he came to work. A few weeks before Christmas, though, he quit.

In his "other life" he was a DeeJay, and Christmas was his busy time. I had to find other guides -- plural -- which made me appreciate him all the more.

Throughout the time I worked with Lewis, he continually warned me about dogs, especially big mean-looking guard dogs -- doberman pincers, rottweilers, pit-bulls -- which everyone seemed to have. "Get back! He's gonna bite you!"

"He's not going to bite me," I replied derisively. "I've never been bitten by a dog in my life. Dogs love me."

I petted dogs that Lewis backed away from. They just wagged their tails and licked my hand.

On my very last day as a FEMA inspector on that deployment in Puerto Rico, Lewis worked with me again. I'd gone to his family's "Three Kings Day" party on January 6, at which I told him, "You were with me my first day on the job, and you should be with me on my last." He agreed. On the very last inspection on that last day's schedule, the applicant wasn't home, so I stuck a note in the screen door. Their little bitty chihuahua must have thought I was burgling the house or attacking her pups. As I strode back to the car, she snarled and growled, then attacked my calf, drawing blood.

"Oooooh!" I screamed, stunned and furious. "You little bitch!"

Lewis nearly died laughing. "Yeah, dogs love you! Hahahaha!" He was bent over, holding his sides. "Dogs love you! Hahahaha!"

Yabucoa, surrounded by fields of sugar cane, is known as *La Ciudad de los Azúcar* -- The City of Sugar. This area is full of sugar cane fields and abloom with flowers of every size and shape in the most glorious colors imaginable. It's incredibly lush and fertile. Along the roads, fence posts stuck in the ground take root and grow. When I arrived in Puerto Rico, *Hurricán Georges* had ripped all the leaves off the trees, leaving entire forests naked. But in a very short time, new leaves sprouted and the island's vegetation returned to normal.

Before leaving Puerto Rico, after our job was finished, my housemates and I did some sightseeing and relaxing on the beach. We visited *El Yunque* National Park, the Arecibo Observatory (Outer Space Listening), and explored the 400+-year-old *El Morro Fortaleza* in San Juan. We swam in the river, catching fresh-water lobsters for our dinner.

On our last night, we threw a party and Lewis bought his DeeJay equipment. We danced into the night before saying sorrowful goodbyes to our friends and beautiful Puerto Rico.

Over the next seven years I worked as a FEMA Field Inspector in 16 states, plus Washington D.C., Guam, and Puerto Rico again. Only in Puerto Rico did I have a guide, though, which quadrupled the fun.

As a Disaster Relief Worker, I had a great many heartwarming moments, as well as a few scary ones, and numerous that were devastatingly heart-wrenching.

Despite the serious nature of the job -- dealing with tragedy and loss -- it was the best I've ever had. It allowed me to be out running around the countryside and meeting wonderful people; be my own boss; help people in need -- and get paid for it.

It's very hard work, requiring tremendous stamina and drive, good people skills, compassion, a good sense of direction, and an abundance of common sense.

I loved *almost* every minute of it.

Reno, Nevada

I moved to Reno right after "9/11".

I'd just finished six month's work for FEMA and had money in my jeans. I could finally get out of that miserable 10 X 12' room.

My old friend, Lucky, who had moved to Reno and bought a house with a view, was moving to San Diego. He planned to rent out his Reno house. When I visited him, I asked how he'd feel about renting to me. He answered, "It never occurred to me. I couldn't be more delighted."

Before returning to Santa Rosa, I drove a couple of hours north to Greenville, CA, to visit my close friend, Carol McConkie.

The next morning, around 7 o'clock, she came into my room looking undone. "Lizzie[34] just called. Something terrible has happened. C'mon, get up, I've got it on TV."

We were stunned to learn that an airliner had flown into one of the Twin Towers of the World Trade Center in New York City. Its upper floors were on fire and thousands of people were trying to escape. Unable to sit down, we stood in our peejays and slippers, coffee mugs in hand, watching in horror as a second plane crashed into the second tower, and later, as the Twin Towers tumbled down, crumbling like sand castles. The site came to be known as "Ground Zero".

Carol's other daughter, Catherine, had arrived in New York City just the night before. My friend was a nervous wreck until Catherine called to say she was safe. She and her friends were across town, watching the nightmare from the roof.

It was September 11, 2001, which came to be known as "9/11". The country

---

34. Her daughter.

was in shock. All airplanes were on "No-Flight status" over the U.S. Everything ground to a halt. As individuals and as a nation, we struggled to regain our equilibrium.

Two-and-a-half weeks later, I moved to Reno. My belongings had been stored in friends' barns and garages all over Sonoma County. The day before the move, I drove my rented U-Haul truck around the county collecting them. The last of which (except my grandfather clock, which was entrusted to Martin) was in a barn in Petaluma, on the country estate of my friend, Bruce. He had graciously and generously offered to drive the moving van to Reno so I could drive my car up.

On September 28th, I left from Santa Rosa while he started in Petaluma. The only place Bruce knew how to find in Reno was his brother Ron's office building, so we arranged to rendezvous there. He'd stay to visit with his brother for a couple of days before flying back to the Bay Area.

While still in Reno, Bruce and Ron came by for a glass of wine on my deck which overlooked Reno. A widower, Ron was an interesting, nice guy.

A few weeks later, Ron and I hiked up Peavine Mountain. Feeling patriotic, like so many in the wake of "9/11", he grabbed his cordless Mikita drill from the back of his pick-up and bore a hole in a tree stump. With a bit of ceremony, he stuck the pole of a small American Flag in the stump. We left it there for others to enjoy, and maybe salute, as they hiked Peavine.

We climbed higher and higher. I puffed and panted, stopping every few steps to get my breath. *Must be the altitude,* I pretended.

Although patient and kind, I'm sure Ron wondered what on earth he was doing on that mountaintop with this wretched creature who threatened with every step to collapse. He wasn't even breathing hard.

I was certain I'd never hear from him again.

To my great relief, I did.

My Best Christmas

This has always been my favorite part of Christmas, at least, as a grown-up. The candles on the tree and elsewhere in the house had burnt out, carols had been sung, drinks had been drunk, food had been eaten, the guests had gone, and my family were all in bed. Except for tiny electric lights on the tree, which I lit just for myself, the house was dark. And still.

I sat, glowing with love and joy, the spirit of Christmas cascading over and through me.

On Christmas Eve, 2001, that feeling was amplified exponentially. I could never remember feeling that happy, that contented, that much love. Tears of happiness flowed as I sat alone in my living room.

Once again, my three sons and granddaughter were under my roof. That moment was soul-stirring. I loved them all so much. We'd had our difficulties, but tonight we were together again in my home, loving one another. With *9/11* fresh in our minds, I think we felt closer because of it.

In addition, I was once again surrounded by my own things, which had been in storage for four interminable years. And just that day, Martin brought my grandfather clock home to me. The final piece was in place.

Earlier that day, Steve walked into my new home, looked around, and exclaimed, "My god! It's a 'Carol Purroy Museum.'"

It occurs to me that all our homes are our museums, filled as they are with the treasures we've gathered over a lifetime, some valuable, some valueless, but all precious to us.

Family photos hung on my walls once again, pieces of furniture my kids grew up with -- and some newer ones -- were in my house, the table was set with the china, sterling, and linens we'd always used on special occasions. Old Christmas ornaments, including my sons' grade school creations, hung from the tree, and our traditional Christmas items decorated the house. The *Bowlem Schüssel,* our Christmas gift in Jugenheim so many years ago, was once again in its place of honor on my old pine sideboard. From it we served hot spiced cider, as we had in years past.

This truly *was* my museum.

Since my "treasures" had been out of sight, scattered far and wide, for such a long time, Steve's outburst was understandable.

Now, years later, if someone asked, "What was the happiest moment of your life?" the one that would come to mind is that wonderful Christmas Eve night when everything came together again -- my house filled with love and peace and harmony, my family at rest, and I, awake in the stillness, basking in the glow of love.

No More Surprises

Ron's birthday was coming up in late February (2003), and Luciano Pavarotti was coming to town a week or so later on his "Farewell Concert Tour". Concert tickets would be the perfect birthday present.

Ron loves Pavarotti -- plays his CDs over and over and is transported by the magnificence of his voice backed by a superb orchestra. Every time he plays them he remarks about Pavarotti's crystal clear High C, which was known to move people to tears.

Tickets were expensive, but it would be worth it. I put it on my American Express card to be paid off over time and bubbled with excitement over my fantastic surprise. I knew nothing would please him more.

The weekend before Valentine's Day, Garrison Keeler, on "Prairie Home Companion" (National Public Radio), admonished, "Don't give flowers or candy for Valentine's Day. That's uninspired. Humdrum. Write your sweetheart a poem." (Paraphrased.)

I took it to heart and wrote a poem I call "Late Life Love". (Page 327.)

For Valentine's Day we went to San Francisco to see a play, and that night I presented him with the poem tied up with a red ribbon. I'd intended to read it to him, but chickened out. As he read it my heart pounded, my insides trembled. I clenched and unclenched my hands while trying to breathe normally. It seemed as if he took forever to read it. I had laid my heart on the line. Was it too much? Sure that it was, I wished I'd stuck to humdrum.

Much later he told me, "It's the nicest thing anyone's ever done for me."

And his Valentine gift for me? Tickets to Pavarotti's Concert!

"But that's what I'm giving you that for your birthday! I got the tickets weeks ago."

After laughing about it we promised, "No more surprises. From now on we'll check with each other before buying any tickets." We gave the extra set to Ron's daughter, Barbara, and her husband, Dylan. We'd make it a big night out. The four of us would get as gussied as we could muster and dine at an upscale restaurant before the concert. Barb and Dylan were as excited about it as we were.

The weekend before the big concert, Ron and I went to Surprise Valley, a resort 200+ miles north of Reno, for a romantic get-away. After settling in, we went for a walk, hot-tubbed in our private hot spring pool, and drove to Cedarville for dinner, then lounged on our patio under the stars, bundled up against the cold night air. It was ever-so romantic and we were loving every minute of it.

Then, in the middle of the night, Ron had a heart attack. Not wanting to wake me, he meditated through his pain and anxiety the rest of the night. I hit the ceiling when I found out, but it was too late to do anything except check out of the resort and find a hospital. The desk clerk warned, "Whatever you do, don't go to a local doctor. Get back to Reno."

If there's ever a next time we'll call for a med-evac helicopter, but we thought they wouldn't come that far. I packed up our stuff, including the keyboard Ron had snuck in behind my back. His plan was to wake me in the morning playing a happy little tune. But when morning came he played a very different tune.

While Ron meditated to calm himself I drove as fast as I dared back to Reno and the E.R. By that time he had stabilized, so, although the heart attack was confirmed, there was no hurry to do anything about it except keep him comfortable. Over the next couple of days, every time an angioplasty was scheduled, someone in worse shape than he came in to the E.R., so Ron got bumped. He even had another small attack, but restabilized, and wasn't considered "critical".

Finally, on the evening of the Pavarotti concert, he went in for the angioplasty. Ron begged Barb, Dylan and me to go to the concert without him. "There's nothing you can do here." We declined. I offered our two tickets to a friend who rushed right over to get them. On such short notice, Barb couldn't find anyone to take hers.

Stents were imbedded in Ron's coronary artery and recovery was quick.

We've never been back to Surprise Valley.

No more surprises!

Late Life Love

I come to you, not young and innocent,
   not fresh and untouched.
My body bears the scars of living,
   of childbirth-giving,
     of years taking their toll.

I come to you, not young and innocent,
   not fresh and untouched.
My psyche wears the wounds
   of inside-out love,
     an upside-down life.

Part of me wishes you were my first love,
   but alas, that cannot be so,
     for truth-be-told,
   down to brass tacks,
     this ain't my first rodeo.

I come to you late,
   shaped by life's loves and losses,
     by lessons so hard-won.
I'm fearful, hopeful . . .
   scared to love, more scared not to.

When you look at me,
   touch me, make love to me,
I'm young and fresh again,
   a frolicking nymph,
     carefree, childlike, joyful!

When you speak to me and hold me,
   and show me that you care,
     my wounds are healed.
You make me whole,
   you restoreth my soul.

Part of me wishes you were my first love,
    but if that were so,
        I'd not appreciate you as I do,
    or recognize you for the
        treasure that you are.

Experience is the best teacher;
    the harshest judge;
        its own reward.
I'm thankful for the lessons learnt.
    the trials endured and overcome.

Part of me wishes you were my first love,
    wishes I could
        give myself to you
    unscathed . . .
        pristine.

But destiny had other
    things in store,
It gave us others
    first, to love . . .
        and learn from.

In our Golden Years,
    fate brought us together,
in friendship, companionship,
    affection, passion,
        intimacy.

It's all so unexpected,
    so not-even-dreamt-of
        at this late date.
I'm overwhelmed with
    gratitude and love.

Cool Bike!

Who would ever have imagined that a bicycle would change our lives? We're practically addicted. Any day we don't get to ride feels incomplete; we feel cheated. The red tandem Cruiser bike was a gift from Ron's kids, Pete and Barb, and their families.

And what a gift it is!

It's given us so much pleasure and enjoyment – and it gives enjoyment to others, too. People of all ages and types can't help smiling seeing a "mature" couple on a bicycle built-for-two. A lot of young people have never seen one in motion – many have never even heard of one. It elicits interaction. We get a lot of whoops and shouts, like, "I want one of those!" Kids call out, "Cool!" or "Great bike!" Once, when we passed a couple of young guys on bikes, one of them said, "Look at them go. They're haulin' ass!" As we ride the streets and bike trails, clever guys -- it's always guys -- often yell out something like, "She's not pedaling!"

The bike fits neatly into Ron's Honda Odyssey. We load it up and drive down to the bike path along the Truckee River. We have a system: it takes 30 seconds to load or unload it, and off we go. The bike trail follows the river, from the beautifully landscaped industrial park west of Reno, through parks, open spaces and downtown, past kayak runs, fishermen/women, to the lovely industrial park and beyond, east of Sparks.

In the summertime, downtown Reno is glorious, especially in July when its month-long arts festival, ARTOWN, is in full sway. It's abloom with flowers, and music fills the air. From noon on, Wingfield Park usually has entertainment, from ethnic music (Cajun, So. African, Cuban, etc.), to Hip Hop, to classical by the Reno Philharmonic.

One recent summer evening, as we rode through town, we stopped to listen to Celtic music in Wingfield Park. At the basketball courts across the way, a rock band played between "testimonies for Jesus" at a Youth for Christ rally. We continued on. A guitarist played for a wedding beside the river at Virginia Street, and blues rhythms came from the courtyard of the Wild River Grill. On our way back through town, gospel music emanated from a paint-splashed piano[35] on the street corner, played by a virtually toothless man. Then, as we rode down Riverside Drive, a trumpeter and a saxophonist, playing for their own enjoyment on a park bench, swung into *But you'll look sweet upon the seat of a bicycle built for two.*

We gave them a wave and pedaled on down the path, laughing.

The bike path goes to the far eastern edge of Sparks. Sometimes we ride that direction. It's the fragrances that get our attention there. Wild roses line large sections of the river. In early summer, as we ride by, we inhale deeply of their scent. Sagebrush along the way releases its herbal aroma. But best of all is the Ralston company, which makes breakfast cereals. Some days the scent is cinnamony, others it's chocolatey, and sometimes brown sugary or mapley, but it's always yummy. If the wind isn't blowing the right direction we'll circle the whole plant to get a whiff.

Bicycle-built-for-twoing a togetherness thing. On one bike, we're close enough to talk, joke, laugh, and sing.

It motivates us to stay active and enjoy the outdoors. It's splendid to ride with the wind in our hair and a song in our hearts. In good weather we go every single day if we can. And we're committed to riding at least once in every month of the year.

The day after getting the bike, three years ago, Ron had open-heart surgery (the bike was an act of faith on his kids' part), and has since had a hip replacement. During his recuperation we didn't ride, of course. But as soon as he was able, we did. I'm convinced it aided his recovery.

I never thought that at this age I'd be a biker chick, but hey, I'm always open to new adventures. And I'm so glad Ron and I have shared this one.

---

35. As part of ARTOWN-2010, old, whimsically decorated pianos were placed around town to be discovered and played by anyone passing by.

All Things Come

Ill things come to her who waits. As George Eliot wrote, "It's never too late to be what you might have been."

I finally have the relationship I've yearned for all my life. Ron is often introduced as "the nicest man in town." And it's true. That's exactly who he is. He doesn't have an angry cell in his body or mean thought in his head. He uses humor -- the kind kind -- to deal with difficulties.

We remain independent, although committed. It was his idea initially. At first, I felt rejected and unloved, and said so to my women friends.

The married ones said, "Are you **nuts**? When you get pissed off at him or just need some space, you can say, '*Adios, Muchacho*. See ya later!' and traipse off to your house or send him home to his. Sounds perfect to me."

And my single friends said, "Are you **nuts**? You've got someone you care about to go to concerts with, go out to dinner with, travel with, *et cetera*. But he's not underfoot all the time. Sounds perfect to me!"

Okay, they convinced me. I've got the best of both worlds. So, leave it alone, girl. We see each other every day and most nights. We truly enjoy the time we spend together – and our time apart, secure in the knowledge that we have each other.

We bike-ride. We swim in the Truckee River. We read and sometimes write together. We produce TV shows. He reads poetry to me. We enjoy plays and concerts, take fabulous trips, and have wonderful times. We take care of each other when it's needed. And, as my friends say, when we need some space we go to our respective homes. *"Adios, Muchacho!"*

It's possible, I suppose, that everything is for a purpose. My San Francisco debacle -- the worst thing that ever happened to me -- led indirectly to the best thing, via Ron's brother, Bruce. Maybe there is a grand design, after all -- a splendid choreography that gets us to the right place at the right time. We just have to dance the dance.

My family -- my sons and granddaughter -- and I are copacetic. Living apart as we do, we don't do the Sunday dinner at Grandma's thing very often. But when we do get together, we're happy. My sister Pat is well. She and Stan are happily retired in Sonoma County, surrounded by their offspring. We get together when we can.

Since coming to Reno I wrote and published *Your Life Oughta Be A Book; Write the stories of your life.* I've taught Memoir Writing and Creative Writing (and other subjects) at Truckee Meadows Community College and senior centers. I wrote and published *Miss Rogers Stinks,* a historical novel inspired by an event in my 5th grade year, and now this one -- *That's Life.* More are in the works.

I lead women's writing retreats, and produce and host TV shows, including *Author! Author!* I co-founded Nevada Storytellers Network and produced a storytelling festival as part of ARTOWN - 2006. I founded Writers of the Purple Sage Publishing Consortium. I do public speaking. And just this year I was named "Woman of the Year (2010) in Publishing" by the National Association of Professional Women.

What a wonderful life! What a wonderful world!

People often exclaim, "But you're 74 years old! How do you do all those things?" Sometimes it's *"Why* do you do all those things?"

This mystifies me. "What has 74 got to do with it?! I'm just being who I am and doing what I do. Maybe I'm a late bloomer. All I know is, I have finally gotten to be "what I might have been".

I'm going to have to live a very long time and stay busy. I've got places to go, people to meet, things to do. And, aside from when my children were young, I've never been happier.

I'm particularly fond of this Hunter S. Thompson quote:

Life is not a journey to the grave with the intention of arriving safely in a pretty and well-preserved body, but rather to skid in broadside thoroughly used up, totally worn out, and loudly proclaiming 'Wow! What a ride!!!'

That's Life

My 75th birthday is just around the corner, and, as I wrote at 60, I have no intention of popping off any time soon, but it occurs to me that I should get this -- my many mini memoirs --in writing.[36] It seems that every 15 years or so I get an unreasonable urge to write something meaningful. The last one was "Remains To Be Seen." (Page 311.) Who knows what I'll write at 90?

All in all, I've had a wonderful life. Very little turned out as I expected, but maybe that's the lesson. I believe we're on earth to learn and grow. If everything turned out in a planned, predictable fashion, that probably wouldn't happen.

I learned early-on that life holds no guarantees: it may be too short or too long. At times it may be difficult; at times it may be unjust. It will hold trauma and tragedy. It will treat you unfairly. You may lose what you love most and keep what matters little. Not everyone will like you or wish you well. You'll encounter people who misuse and abuse you.

That's life.

Life will also, at times, be fabulous. People will come into your life who enhance it immeasurably, who love and appreciate you just because you're

---

36. This memoir may seem disjointed. It may seem more like a crazy quilt than a tapestry. You may have felt frustrated that in the middle of the difficult times I jumped to neutral or happy times. I apologize. But that's life. Bad things happen, you get through them, life goes on. You straighten your spine and stiffen your lip, hoping things will improve, and get back to normal life. Then, when the bad stuff comes back around, you deal with it again. *That's life.*

you. Miraculous things will happen, restoring faith in yourself, the human race, and destiny. You'll experience people, places and things that fill you up with joy and mirth, excitement and thrills, peace and tranquility, awe and wonder.

That's life too.

My first "defining moment" was the early loss of my parents. The knowledge that life can end anytime has given me the courage to live it fully. It made me aware that life is for living, not for preparing to live.

Helen Keller said, "Life is a grand adventure or it is nothing at all."

Mine has been a grand adventure. Living a life that is "nothing at all" has never appealed to me. It's up to me to make it a grand adventure. I can invite others to join me on my journey, but it's my journey -- my grand adventure. They're busy having theirs, which, although right alongside mine, are exclusively theirs.

"Now is the hour." The present moment is one's only certainty, so it doesn't do to wait for the "perfect time" to take action. There's no such thing as the "perfect time". I now know that every time I have waited for the "perfect time", it was out of cowardice. And when I finally pushed through it (whatever it was), although uncomfortable or terrified, I was empowered.

A life without risk is not possible. Being alive means taking risks. "Avoiding danger is no safer in the long run than exposure." (Helen Keller again.) As the Nike slogan says, "Just do it."

And it doesn't do to waste one second wishing I were somewhere else, someone else, in some other time. As Ram Dass (Richard Alpert) wrote, "Be here now." I've learned to be in the present moment. It's all I've got.

I've learned that the best lessons come not from easy success and good times. I've learned the most from my mistakes, failures, tragedies, difficulties, heartbreaks.

I've learned that love is subject to interpretation. What is love? A question for the ages, and the topic for another book.

The real question may be, What is marriage? Yet another book.

I've often said, "All I ever wanted was a man who would be kind to me." As was true the first time I spoke to my angel-guys, I got exactly what I asked for. Ron treats me with love, respect and kindness, but isn't at all interested in a second marriage.

And that, it turns out, is a blessing. I've got what I need. I thought I wanted "the whole enchilada", but that may be subject to interpretation. I thought it had to mean marriage and the happily-ever-after Cinderella-thing. By insisting that we remain separate and independent, he has given me the most precious gift of all -- the freedom to be me.

My experience with husbands is limited -- only two. But neither of them had a clue who I was, nor did they care to. They thought they loved me, but, in my opinion, what they loved was an idealized image of what their wife was *supposed* to be. Whereas John wanted me to be introverted and as modest and devoted to cleaning house as an Amish housewife, Wayne wanted me to be an extroverted, powerful career woman, dedicating my life to creating copious wealth. Neither idealized image had anything to do with me.

Trying to be a good wife, I leaned toward what they wanted, but in the end couldn't be what I wasn't. But I wasn't free to be who I was, either.[37] I spent a huge number of years in limbo. No matter what I did, I wasn't what or who I was *supposed* to be.

Ron, my last love, is supportive without controlling. He encourages but doesn't pressure. There are few expectations, requirements or demands on either side. Unmarried, we don't take each other for granted. Nor do we feel we have the right to try to change each other. "What you see is what you get." (Flip Wilson) Perhaps that's the result of maturity -- and of having learned from previous relationships. In any case, it's pretty wonderful and I feel so lucky.

I thought I wanted "the whole enchilada", but have much more. (Is that a rationalization? Perhaps.) I treasure Ron and our every moment together.

It's possible that my life up to this point was readying me for the present. Many believe we come into life with "contracts" with certain people; that we made agreements on the soul level to "work together". Through our relationships with them we're given opportunities to learn and grow in the ways needed for our spiritual growth.[38]

If that's the case, I am indebted to all those (some of whom are profiled herein) who taught me life's hard lessons. I only hope I got from those painful experiences what I needed in order to evolve *soulfully*. And that they got what they needed as well.

37. According to the Myers-Briggs Personality Assessment, I'm 50% Introvert and 50% Extrovert.

38. I've taught workshops on this topic and am working on a book.

I've learned that when someone mistreats, judges or disrespects me, it's more about them than me. Although it's difficult not to take it personally, there's probably little in it that's personal.

More importantly, I've learned I don't have to put up with it. I cannot change others or their behavior, but I can change me and mine. I don't have to stick around. To quote Charles Swindoll:

> The remarkable thing is we have a choice every day regarding the attitude we will embrace for that day. We cannot change our past ... we cannot change the fact that people will act in a certain way. We cannot change the inevitable. The only thing we can do is play on the one string we have, and that is our attitude...
> I am convinced that life is 10% what happens to me and 90% how I react to it.

Best among my many blessings were my parents. Although I didn't have them long, I was lucky to have the parents I did. I always knew they loved me -- which gave me the sense of security and confidence that has gotten me through the tough times. I inherited their sense of humor, which has made life infinitely easier than it might have been. (Both of my ex-husbands told friends, who told me, that the thing they missed most about me was the laughter. That's not such a bad thing from an ex-husband.)

I'm blessed to have three wonderful sons who grew up to be fine, responsible, caring, moral, ethical, hilarious, hardworking, handsome, loving, intelligent men.

The wonderful women in my life, the all-important sisterhood, are blessings too: my incredible mother, Zelpha ("Pat"), my sister Pat, my aunts -- Margaret and Billie, my grandmothers, Elsa Marie and Kittie, and my cousins, Kitty, Virginia, Leta, Dottie, Linda and Susie, my precious granddaughter, Hannah, and daughters-in-law, Jill Lowenstein and Jackie Nakayama Purroy.

The other women in my life are a blessing beyond measure too --all the fantastic women throughout my life who gave me friendship and support. They've nurtured me and enriched my life. I'm so thankful for each of them.

I'm grateful that I've lived long enough to get old, 'though I feel young. I'm blessed with excellent health, which allows me to feel a lot like my teen-aged self.

This statement by an unknown author that has circulated via email echoes my feelings:

> ...I am so blessed to have lived long enough to have my hair turning gray, and to have my youthful laughs be forever etched into deep grooves on my face.
> So many have never laughed, and so many have died before their hair could turn silver.
> As you get older, it's easier to be positive. You care less about what other people think. I don't question myself anymore. I've even earned the right to be wrong.
> I like being old. It has set me free. I like the person I have become.

Life turned out a lot different than I expected. Looking forward to my life from the vantage point of my high school graduation or wedding day, I thought that at this point I'd be married to the same man I married in 1954, I'd have earned a college degree and maybe held a job or two, taken a few nice trips; we'd be surrounded by children and grandchildren in a house we'd lived in many years, watching the garden, as well as our children, grow to maturity.

I never could have imagined I would:

- be divorced, not once, but twice. As you may have figured out, I take marriage very seriously.
- live at a distance from my children and grandchild(ren).
- enter old age a tough single broad.
- moved from house to house and state to state.
- be an unwed wife.
- be called a "Type-A personality".
- be called a "perfectionist".
- be called a "guru".
- be a psychotherapist and clinical hypnotherapist.
- be a past-life therapist. (I'd never even heard of that.)
- have a working relationship with angels and spirit guides.
- be a world traveler.
- be a mentor to many in various areas of life.
- be a disaster relief worker.
- produce and host TV shows.
- be an acclaimed, award-winning publisher.

and a whole host of other things.

The difference between my expectations and my reality clearly demonstrates significant changes not only in me, but also in the culture of the U.S. and the world. The era in which I've lived is the most amazing in history.

In my lifetime, western women have gone from being suppressed, repressed and oppressed -- excluded from well-paying jobs and jobs in authority -- to being corporate CEOs, senators and congresswomen, Supreme Court justices, and even presidential candidates. I'm hoping to see a woman president in my lifetime.

Telephones have gone from crude attached-to-the-wall party lines to Go-everywhere/Do-everything marvels.

Communication has progressed from slow surface mail to instantaneous email, texting, and social networking. Phone calls, written communiques, and photographs zip around the world and back in the fraction of a second.

Toilets have gone from outhouses to self-flushing. Some even have heated cushioned seats and lids that raise and lower automatically.

When I was a child, the family car was liable to overheat, needed frequent repairs, and required cranking to get the engine running. It had no heater or air conditioner, no radio. Cars today talk to us, have climate control, TV screens and GPS; automatic windows and seats; even a remote voice to give us directions and call road service.

Air travel has gone from slow propeller planes to jets, space travel, moon walks, robots on Mars, and inter-galactic photographic explorations.

Nearly every household, at least in industrialized countries, has one or more computers with instant world-wide-web internet access providing unlimited information at our fingertips. And everyone who wants to can have his/her own website and be an entrepreneur.

Whereas we used to read only bound books with paper pages, we can now read books on computers and even phones.

African Americans have gone from being discriminated against, persecuted, and even lynched, to being president and first lady on the U.S. I never imagined that would happen in my lifetime. I've met both Michelle and Barack Obama, up close and personal, and am thrilled they're in the White House.

Other minorities now have opportunities and privileges unimaginable when I was young. Thank God.

Advances in medicine are mind-boggling: micro-surgeries, organ transplants, artificial organs and joints, miracle medicines, DNA, *et cetera*. Life expectancy is longer than ever.

Whereas people with disabilities were once confined to their homes or an institution, now we have motorized wheelchairs and scooters; sidewalks and public buildings are "handicapped accessible". Electronic prostheses mimic natural limbs. Many businesses are proud to hire the handicapped.

I could go on, but there's no need. I've truly lived in the Golden Age. Life is more comfortable now than at any time in history. Opportunities have expanded and the world has shrunk.

I can't begin to imagine what new inventions and innovations will come along in my remaining years, to say nothing of my children's lives and beyond.

Even at my advanced age I don't understand humans' need to fight and kill each other. Why can't we all just get along?

What is there about the human psyche that makes us, by and large, want to believe the scurrilous, rather than the good, about others?

Why do so many of us love to hate, and allow ourselves to get all riled up by hate- and fear-mongers? And why do hate- and fear-mongers do what they do to rile people up?

But I admit to some fears myself:

I fear our descendants' lives will be less healthy, shorter, less filled with opportunity than my generation's.

I fear for my country. I *hate* politics, and fear that our corrupt politicians (a redundancy) will destroy it. They may have already.

I fear the planet will be devastated by humans' stupidity and greed.

I've lived in the Golden Age. And I take my share of blame for using, as an American, more than my share of the earth's resources, ignorant or disdainful of the consequences.

I pray we'll begin to live with heightened awareness and consciousness.

In spite of everything, I'm still an optimist.

Appendix

- My Grandparents
- Photo Album

My Paternal Grandparents

Jens Christian Petersen   Elsa Marie Seewaldsen
b. Jutland, Denmark   b. Haderslev, Denmark
d. Fresno, California - Age 86   d. Fresno, California - Age 79
9/30/1855 - 4/13/41   3/15/1861 - 12/16/1940

The following is the translation of the letter in which my paternal grandfather, Jens Christian Petersen, proposed marriage to Elsa Marie Seewaldsen, my grandmother. He was from Jutland, in northern Denmark; she lived on a farm near Haderslev, in Schleswig-Holstein, Denmark. In 1881, at the age of 25, Jens journeyed south for the summer to work on his aunt and uncle's -- Elsa Marie's parents'-- farm. She was 20. This letter came at the end of that summer.

. . . .

Maltbæk Mill, September 5, 1881

My dear little cousin,

At this late hour of the evening, after returning to my home, I will immediately take my pen and write you a letter to let you know how my journey went, but to tell the truth, there is something in my heart worth more than all the treasures and gold in the world, and this is what I am going to write down in these lines at this late hour. But I beg you so deeply, little cousin, do not be angry with your cousin for my boldness or chaff me with it, but dear Marie, give me a sincere answer to what I am writing, because what I am writing is laid up to a proposal.

On my eastern journey I fell in love with a little girl and here you could maybe give me a bit of information, if I could ever expect you to reciprocate my love. Now you are going to ask me, who is that girl I speak about, her name is Marie Seewaldsen.

Now give me a sincere answer, do you like me as I do like you? Then I am going to ask for your parents' permission. Then we are going to the provincial town to announce our engagement in public. If you are going to come here we will travel to Varde, or I can come to Haderslev. But please observe, my girl, if you do not like me, do not let yourself in for it.

If I, in the next letter from my dear cousin, could expect just that little word, Yes, I love you, then I am the happiest man on earth.

Concerning your parents, I will write them if you like. In case you do not love me, I will never write anything about it, little cousin. Give me a sincere answer, but most of all, do not be angry with me. You may not want a man with a broad forehead from Jutland. Please write me as soon as possible because whatever the answer will be, take a journey down here anyway. I will do everything to entertain you. We could go on a trip to the west coast to see my brother Hans, but please write to me eight days before you arrive. You are going to take the day carriage Saturday morning; you will know at what time you will arrive in Haderslev. The train will leave at 11 o'clock from Haderslev, and then you will be with me at 4 o'clock. The ticket to Vamdrup costs 1 mark and 56 pfennig. From Vamdrup to Vejen 60 oere, in coins they take German as well as Danish.

When you arrive I will pick you up in Lunderskov because the train stops for two hours and that is a little boring. Write to me and tell me the date you are coming.

Yes, my return journey went very well, and why not? Because I had a small conversation and I think that the whole group was amused, but my thoughts were not exactly within the carriage, they landed beside my little cousin, but no one thought about that. I enjoyed myself very much at your parents'. It was the most wonderful days in my entire life. I will write them as soon as I have received a letter from you.

Dear Marie, please write to me as soon as possible. I am longing very much for a letter. I do hope that you will give me an answer to what I have written.

Please send me your portrait, one of those you have.

Your mother mentioned that she wanted a number in the lottery. If she can choose one, please let me know, and then I will take care of the rest.

In the hope that you will write to me immediately, I will post these lines to my little cousin.

With love from your cousin,

Jens Christian Petersen
Miller
Maltbæk Mill, 6 September 1881

Enjoy life!

They were married in Haderslev, Denmark, probably in 1882. What I think I know is that Grandpa left for America soon after and established a home and dairy farm south of Fresno, California, then sent for his bride. All their children were born in that farmhouse. They had four children: Caroline, Signe, a boy (name unknown) who died in infancy, and my father, Arthur.

Some time later, Grandma's mother, Caroline Seewaldsen née Knudsen, immigrated, and lived the rest of her life with them.

Elsa Marie was an only child.

Jens was the second of the eight children of Ole and Margarethe Petersen.

They had good life. They were founding members of the Danish Brotherhood in Fresno, and the Danish Creamery, a dairy cooperative. They were quite social and fun-loving.

As is indicated in the above letter, Grandpa had a sense of humor -- typical of Danes -- and enjoyed entertaining others, which was passed on to my dad, who, I'm told, had a terrific sense of humor.

I'm so grateful Grandma saved his letter of proposal and wish Grandpa had kept her reply.

Jens Christian & Elsa Marie Seewaldsen Petersen

Wedding portrait - 1882   1940

My Maternal Grandparents

William Henry Bartlett	Kittie Trower
b. Lincoln County, Missouri	b. Pike County, Missouri
d. Fresno, California	d. Fresno, California
3/22/1868 - 6/26/1957	2/24/1870 - 5/19/1951
Age 89	Age 81

Married October 4, 1899

. . . .

Grandma: daughter of Henry Anderson and Margaret Butler Trower.

The Trowers descended from the kings of England, and before that, the kings of France. My 70th great-grandfather in that lineage was a Roman nobleman: Marcus Antonius Tirumvir, a.k.a. Marc Antony (of Marc Antony & Cleopatra fame), via his first wife, Octavia the Younger.

Grandpa: William Henry Bartlett, was also English. The son of William Henry and Erlinda Whiteside Bartlett.

Having arrived on this continent early-on, the ancestors of both Grandma and Grandpa were colonists who fought in the Revolutionary War. They stayed in New England a few generations, then headed southwest. The Butlers and the Trowers, as well as the Whitesides and the Bartletts, all settled in Kentucky awhile (Daniel Boone was Grandma's grandfather's first cousin), then continued on to Missouri, where both Kittie and William were born.

. . . .

"Hank" and "Kitt" got married when Kittie was an "old maid" of nearly 30. By then, everyone in town (Middleton, MO) must have concluded that Miss Kittie Trower was doomed to a life of spinsterhood.

Grandma believed she was then so old that they'd be unable to have children. But a year and a week into their marriage, a daughter, Freda Margaret (Margaret), was born. Sixteen months later, a second daughter was born. By now, Grandma was an old lady of 32. They despaired of ever having a son, so they'd better name this daughter after her daddy, William. Willie Katherine (Billie) it was. Shortly thereafter, sons Harry Clayton (Harry) and Henry Lindell (Hank or Lindell) arrived on the scene. And, finally, my mother, Zelpha Louella (Pat). About her name, Mom said, "It could have been worse. I was named after two aunts, but I had two other aunts named Beulah and Cordelia."

At some point, Grandma got "saved", which she took very seriously. She was a God-fearing, God-loving, good Christian woman. She read the Bible every day, and quoted from the scriptures. She and her husband and children went to church two or three times a week.

I have to believe that she got pleasure from *knowing* she was living the right life, guiding her children along the right path, and doing her Christian duty. I hope she found joy in praying, singing hymns and praising her Lord. Her brand of born-againism was of the Pentacostal/Holy Roller variety, which apparently didn't allow for much joy, except in the practice of religion.

Nor did it leave any room for doubt. Her world was one of absolutes, blacks and whites, with no gray areas whatsoever. She *knew* God, up close and personal. She *knew* what God liked and did not like, what God wanted and did not want. She *knew* what every biblical passage meant.

Grandpa indulged her. After all, he was born and raised in the Bible-belt, too, where being "born-again" was customary -- required. It was the rite of passage that allowed one to participate fully in that society. But Grandpa did not share Grandma's fervor. He could take it or leave it, putting God and religion into perspective.

Grandma *knew* about sin. Just about anything that was modern or fun was a sin. Gambling was a sin. Dancing was a sin. Drinking was a sin. The use of tobacco was a sin -- for women. Sex outside marriage was a *mega*-sin. Wearing lipstick and nail polish was a sin. Exposing skin, other than face and hands was a sin -- for women. Divorce was a sin. Frequenting places where there was dancing, smoking, drinking or gambling was a sin. Watching stage shows or movies was a sin.

And the Catholic church was the anti Christ.

When my cousin Virginia married a Catholic, someone drove Grandma and Grandpa to the church. Grandma kept giving the driver incorrect and confusing directions so that they arrived too late for the ceremony. By the time they got there, guests were already leaving. So Grandma didn't have to set foot inside a Catholic church, which would surely have been a sin. (By the time I married in the Catholic church, Grandma had gone on to her heavenly reward.)

Grandma had never seen a movie, nor did she want to. But her namesake and favorite grandchild, Kitty (O'Malley), wanted to take her to see "Joan of Arc," starring Ingrid Bergman. Grandma resisted mightily, but finally gave in and let her granddaughter drag her into that magnificent palace of sin, a movie theater. To make a long story short, she loved the movie, reluctantly allowing that maybe not *all* movies were sinful. She was enthralled with its heroine, but declared with absolute certainty, "Joan of Arc was *not* a Catholic. She couldn't have been."

It goes without saying that Grandma didn't dance. So, of course, neither did Grandpa. But even as an old man, he walked with a graceful lilt, stepping jauntily as he walked down the street. So I doubt that he'd have been averse to it. All the Bartlett descendants love to dance and are naturally good dancers. That had to have come from *somewhere*. I'll attribute it to Grandpa.

Grandma often said, "Idle hands are the devil's workshop." She made exquisite quilts, with tiny, perfectly even stitches, and lovely, colorful "Granny afghans". And, using a large wooden crochet hook, she made rag-rugs out of old clothes she'd rip up. Grandma could always "make do" with what she had, and never had much. She often pointed out that whatever she had was "better 'n' nuthin'", which became her nickname.

As the old saying goes, "Man's work goes from sun to sun but woman's work is never done." Grandpa was a hard-working man who bore the burden of supporting his family. Then, he saw no problem with playing *Solitaire* for hours at a time, trying to "beat the Chinaman", or playing *Rummy* or *Sorry* with one of us children.

Grandma's sense of humor was dry and subtle. Quite English, you know. Her humor was very tongue-in-cheek, so that you were not sure if she was making a joke or not. If you caught on you'd get a congratulatory smile from Grandma. It was as if she was checking to see if you were quick enough to "get it".

Kitty tells of Grandma's deathbed scene. Kitty was called to her bedside, because her old grandmother was holding onto life until she (Grandma's favorite) got there. (The rest of us had already said our good-byes, but Kitty had to come from out of town.) Whoever was sitting with Grandma saw Kitty drive up out front and announced her arrival. When Kitty walked into Grandma's bedroom, she noticed that the old woman was holding a book, as if she were reading . . . only it was upside down.

Kitty said, "Hey, 'Better'n'nuthin'! You're not fooling me, pretending to read. Your book's upside down!"

Grandma gave her the smile that said, "You got my joke." (That, within an hour of her death.)

Grandpa's humor, on the other hand, was more jocular. He was quick to smile and laugh and joke and tease. He had a twinkle in his eye that let you know he was a lot of fun.

Grandma was a stern disciplinarian who followed the biblical admonition: ". . . spare the rod and spoil the child". Grandma would not have a spoiled child.

When the family moved to California from Missouri in the 1920's, my older cousins all lived -- together with their mothers and my mom -- in Grandma and Grandpa's house. My cousins well-remember what a loving family it was. They were poor -- the kids slept 3 or 4 to a bed -- but there was tremendous love and fun in that household.

Grandma was the matriarch. She ruled the family with a firm hand. My cousins remember getting hit by Grandma -- random smacks or actual spank-ings, sometimes with a switch. And, of course, our parents got lickin's aplenty as they were growing up, for their own good, of course.

Grandpa, who was pretty easy-going, flinched whenever Grandma hit one of the kids. And the story goes like this: When Grandma would whack one of the kids on the head, Grandpa would rebuke her. "Don't hit the children on the head, Kittie. They've little enough sense as it is!"

There was one time, however, when Grandpa hit one of his kids. Billie -- who was never one to back down when she knew she was right -- was accused of something by her mother. Grandma insisted Billie had done it, while Billie argued that she hadn't.

Grandpa demanded, "Are you calling your mother a liar?"

Billie answered, "If she says I did it, then she is one!"

Grandpa hauled off and whomped his daughter a good one! There were some things even Grandpa would not tolerate.

I don't ever remember seeing Grandma play with a baby or a child. She was a no-nonsense kind of a person. There was no doubt that she loved us fiercely, but her love was of a sterner nature. She did her duty by her family, she took extraordinary care of the children and grandchildren, but it was dutiful rather than playful.

Grandpa, however, played with us kids and taught us games, and we loved being around him. When we were little we used to pester him to make "trumpety" music through his mustache, and he always obliged.

Grandma was fond of saying, "If a thing is worth doing, it's worth doing well." Fastidious and meticulous, she demanded perfection of herself as well as others.

She believed that cleanliness was next to godliness, and cleaned and polished her house and her children to a fare-thee-well. Grandma would not let her kids sit on their beds because they'd soil or mess up the bedspreads.

I'm sure Grandpa was proud of his wife's housekeeping. . . . but Grandpa chewed tobacco. He had a coffee can spittoon in every room. which I bet drove Grandma crazy.

Grandma carried on a prodigious correspondence with her family and friends back in Missouri. Always, on her desk at her right hand, was a dictionary, which she used constantly. I once asked her about it. Her answer was, "I'd rather die than send a letter out with a mistake in it."

And she was very particular about grammar. In her family, proper English was spoken. Any grammatical errors were corrected on the spot. Neither she or Grandpa went beyond the 5th grade in school, but they were not uneducated. They took pride in speaking and writing correctly. Both loved to read. Grandma's reading was mostly confined to the Bible or religious books, and letters from "back home". Grandpa's interests were broader. When I was about 12, he gave me a novel he'd enjoyed; *The Egg & I*, by Betty MacDonald.

Grandma and Grandpa were in agreement about the importance of good manners, but, of course, it was up to Grandma to enforce them.

Grandma was an expert seamstress and demanded perfection in that area, too. My cousin Leta told of the time when she was in junior high school, and her best friend had made matching plaid skirts for the two of them. Leta was so tickled. But when she proudly showed Grandma her new skirt, Grandma took it from her and ripped it apart because the plaids didn't line up perfectly. She remade it so that they did. No granddaughter of hers was going to wear a garment so poorly made. (Another of her sayings was, "If you want something done right, do it yourself.")

Grandma's stern religiosity forbade gambling of any kind. And Grandpa loved to gamble. That is, he loved to play cards, which was more fun if a small wager was involved. And he loved to win. And he saw to it that he did win, so to his way of thinking he wasn't gambling. He was betting on a sure thing.

He managed to sneak downtown to the poker parlors to have a little fun every now and again. He was known to say, with a twinkle in his eye, "When I get to the point where I can't cheat without gettin' caught, I'll have to give up playing cards." But he kept going off to poker parlors until he was in his mid-eighties. Then one day, the inevitable happened. He got caught, and was escorted out of the establishment and told never to darken its doors again.

In Grandma's house, the radio was mostly for spiritual inspiration. Aside from her weekday soap operas, *Ma Perkins* and *The Guiding Light,* her radio was tuned to evangelists all day long. And all day long, they'd plead for donations so their missionaries in far-off places could go on saving souls for Christ. And, although in their later years Grandma and Grandpa were getting by on their meager income from Social Security, Grandma religiously sent the evangelists money ". . . to do the Lord's work." She put a couple of dollars in an envelope for each of them, then gave the envelopes to Grandpa to mail.

Grandpa walked down the street to the corner mailbox, where he dropped in a couple. "That's enough for the Lord. The rest is for me." He opened the other envelopes and took out the dollar bills, which he put in his pocket.

Grandma's strictness and restrictiveness in the Lord's name practically guaranteed that her children would find a different path. Of the five, only Margaret continued as a regular church-goer. The other girls, Billie and Zelpha, hedged their bets by sending their children to Sunday School, but did not attend themselves. And her two sons were not religious.

Uncle Lindell (a.k.a. Hank) was a really good man, sweet and kind, Clark Gable-handsome, and charming. He was the one you'd go to when you had a problem, knowing he'd understand and help if he could. But he wasn't religious in the least.

And Harry? The less said about him the better. Definitely not religious.

So far as I know, Grandpa was never known to utter a swearword. Grandma would go through the day heaving great sighs, followed by, "Lordamercy", or "'LanticOcean". I didn't figure out until I was grown up that "Lordamercy" was "Lord have mercy", and " 'LanticOcean", was "Land o' Goshen." That was as close to cussing as she'd have liked to have you believe her capable of. But, in fact, this fine upstanding Christian woman was often heard to mutter, "Oh shit!" or "Shit shit shit a mile a minute." We all laughed behind our hands, delighted with this more human side of Grandma.

In some ways, the Bartlett kids took after Grandpa more than Grandma. But in at least one way we took after Grandma. And it's come down to the next generation, and the next. We've all adopted her favorite cussword and enjoy using it.

As different as they were, if William and Kittie Bartlett had been born 50 years later, their marriage might not have survived. But they weren't. They grew up and got married in the latter part of the 19th Century, when one's understanding of marriage and its commitment truly was " 'Til death do us part."

They were married 51 years, until parted by Grandma's death. It never occurred to them not to be. And no one can imagine it any other way.

When I tried to write about just one of them, I couldn't. The story of one without the other is impossible. They complemented one another. They filled in each other's gaps and compensated for one another's shortcomings. So, different as they were, maybe they had a perfect marriage, after all.

Grandma and Grandpa's union, comprised of two contrasting, opposite halves, like the Yin-Yang, was one that worked.

William, Zelpha & Kittie Bartlett - 1916(?)

Grandma & Grandpa Bartlett
Carol & Pat - Easter 1941

Carol's Photo Album

Carol 18 mos

Zelpha, Patty & Art Petersen

Pat & Carol on the farm
1941

Carol Pat Barbara

7th Grade

High School Graduation

Mom, Carol, Pat, Tracey
1945

Pat & Mom
1952

Carol & John
1953

Cathie & Carol

June 12, 1954

November 1955

Steve - 1957

1959

Martin

1960

1963

Alex

Graduation Day - SSC
1973

Teotihuacán Pyramid

In Tai Shan China
1980

Carol, Fred, Frances
Singapore 1986

Carol, Ibu Gedong,
Wayne on Bali

Hannah - 1987

1988

1989

Wayne & Carol
1989

1997

Carol & Lucky

Jackie, Carol, Alex
1995

Maui   1996

Hannah & Carol
2000

Ron

2002

TMCC
2005

Kauai
2008

Women's
Retreat

Author! Author!

Hannah, Steve, Carol

Cool Bike!

Carol & Ron

Ziplining in Juneau, AK
2010

The end? Not hardly!

LaVergne, TN USA
06 November 2010
203833LV00006B/1/P